Cosmopolitan Archaeologies

MATERIAL WORLDS *A series edited by Lynn Meskell*

Lynn Meskell, editor

❊ COSMOPOLITAN ARCHAEOLOGIES

Duke University Press   Durham and London   2009

© 2009 Duke University Press
All rights reserved
Printed in the United States of America on acid-free paper ∞
Designed by C. H. Westmoreland
Typeset in Carter & Cone Galliard by Achorn International, Inc.
Library of Congress Cataloging-in-Publication data appear on the
last printed page of this book.

CONTENTS

Lynn Meskell

✳ INTRODUCTION

Cosmopolitan Heritage Ethics

Cosmopolitan Archaeologies asks pointed questions about the politics of
contemporary archaeological practice. Specifically, it reveals a new suite
of roles and responsibilities for archaeology and its practitioners and it
suggests that these newly forged relationships are inherently cosmopolitan in nature and ethos. Cosmopolitanism describes a wide variety
of important positions in moral and sociopolitical philosophy brought
together by the belief that we are all citizens of the world who have
responsibilities to others, regardless of political affiliation. This ethical
commitment is the thread that connects cosmopolitan thought from
the classical tradition to contemporary philosophy. Similarly, it is this
ethical concern that has energized the debate in anthropology (e.g.,
Breckenridge et al. 2002; Kahn 2003; Rapport and Stade 2007; Werbner
2008) and has prompted archaeology to rethink the scope of its commitments at home and abroad. The subject of this volume, archaeological heritage and practice, is increasingly entwined within global
networks, prompting scholars gradually to accept that our research and
fieldwork carries ethical responsibilities to the living communities with
whom we work. But more than simply adhering to ethical codes developed for our own discipline (Meskell and Pels 2005), a cosmopolitan
approach both extends our obligations to these communities and steps
up to acknowledge our role as participants in national and international
organizations and developments. Honoring these obligations might
take many forms and is dependent upon context, which means that
we cannot expect to formulate a set of prescribed solutions that can be
applied internationally. As the following chapters illustrate, our obligations may entail addressing the political and economic depredations
of past regimes, enhancing local livelihoods, publicizing the effects
of war, or tackling head on the incursions of transnational companies
and institutions. Archaeologists are increasingly being called upon to
straddle these multiple scales, in large part because of the nature of our
fieldwork but also, more importantly, because heritage now occupies a

new position in the global movements of development, conservation, post-conflict restoration, and indigenous rights.

Cosmopolitanism may not provide a stock set of solutions, but I would argue that it offers a useful lens through which archaeologists might consider this new set of multi-scalar engagements. On the one hand, it encompasses the overarching framework of global politics and, on the other, it directs our attention to the concerns of the individual and the community. In this introduction I attempt to chart some of the propositions put forward in recent cosmopolitan writing that are particularly relevant to heritage ethics. While there are different inflections to cosmopolitan thought in contemporary philosophy, economics, and politics—and in historic cosmopolitanisms from Greek, Roman, and Enlightenment writings—I focus here on what is often described as "rooted cosmopolitanism" and draw largely from discussions in anthropology and philosophy. A brief historical outline then follows, charting archaeology's development of a political and ethical awareness. Here I also consider new developments such as the growing interconnections between archaeology and anthropology, specifically in the heritage sphere, as well as the blending of ethnographic and archaeological methodologies in a new generation's field projects. Finally, cosmopolitan heritage ethics are outlined for the individual chapters in the volume, particularly as they connect to local specificities and international processes. As we will see, many heritage practitioners are now willing to go beyond merely describing our negotiations and are attempting to redress historic injustice, social inequality, and the legacies of colonialism, exploitation, and violence.

Cosmopolitan Propositions

One of the key figures of contemporary cosmopolitan theory, Anthony Appiah, observes that cosmopolitans "take seriously the value not just of human life but of particular human lives, which means taking an interest in the practices and beliefs that lend them significance. People are different, the cosmopolitan knows, and there is much to learn from our differences. Because there are so many human possibilities worth exploring, we neither expect nor desire that every person or every society should converge on a single model of life. Whatever our obligations are to others (or theirs to us) they often have the right to go their own way" (2006a: xv). In terms of managing the past, this means that our archaeological responsibilities cannot be limited to beneficence or salvage; they must include respect for cultural difference—even if that sometimes means relinquishing our own research imperatives. Archaeologists no longer have the license to "tell" people their pasts or adjudicate upon the "correct" ways of protecting or using heritage. As Appiah rightly reminds us, "there will be times when these two ideals—universal concern and respect for legitimate difference—clash" (2006a: xv). Appiah has been at the center of just such a clash himself, caught between his universal concerns for access to heritage versus respect for indigenous heritage practices (see Engmann 2008; chapter by González-Ruibal, this volume). Specifically, he maintains an elitist stance on cultural heritage in his native Ghana by suggesting that claims to global patrimony might trump local community control. As in the Ghanaian case, the chapters that follow underline the complexities archaeologists now face as they are being subject to the force of world conventions, international codes, sponsors, and other global projects, while respecting and often protecting local, communal, or indigenous understandings of the past, of heritage practices, and ways of being.

Certainly, the ideals of cosmopolitanism are not new. They stretch back to the Cynics and Stoics, and forward to Kant, Mill, Habermas, Gilroy, Žižek, and Appiah. Yet there has been a strong resurgence in cosmopolitan theory and ethics since the 1990s. Reasons for this new recasting of cosmopolitanism are manifold and must surely include recent military adventures in the Middle East, proliferating sites of genocide, and crises in humanitarian intervention, as well as global indigenous movements, environmental concerns, desires for world heritage, and the subsequent calls for return of cultural properties to source nations. Thus anthropologists have argued that the late twentieth century forces of nationalism, multiculturalism, and globalization have fostered a historical context for reconsidering concepts of cosmopolitanism (Pollock et al. 2002: 7). Given the effects of resurgent nationalism on the one hand and the ever increasing claims of culture on the other, many scholars advocate a cosmopolitanism that is very much rooted in place. While synonymous with Appiah's writing, "rooted cosmopolitanism" was first coined by Cohen (1992: 480, 483), when he called for "the fashioning of a dialectical concept of rooted cosmopolitanism, which accepts a multiplicity of roots and branches and that rests on the legitimacy of plural loyalties, of standing in many circles, but with common ground." Rooted cosmopolitanism acknowledges attachments to place and the particular social networks, resources, and cultural experiences that inhabit that space. As various authors in the book illustrate, archaeologists are increasingly wary of strong nationalisms that may in fact mask the rights of disempowered minorities, often unacknowledged within the confines of nation. This is particularly salient in the realm of heritage, where individual and community attachments to place are often sacrificed in the abstract framing of world heritage, transacted solely by and among nation states.

Cosmopolitans take cultural difference seriously, because they take the choices individual people make seriously. What John Stuart Mill said more than a century ago in *On Liberty* about difference within a society serves just as well today: "If it were only that people have diversities of taste, that is reason enough for not attempting to shape them all after one model. But different persons also require different conditions for their spiritual development; and can no more exist healthily in the same moral, than all the variety of plants can exist in the same physical, atmosphere and climate. The same things which are helps to one person towards the cultivation of his higher nature, are hindrances to another" (Mill 1985: 133). Cosmopolitans, by Appiah's account (2006a), want to preserve a wide range of human conditions because such a range allows free people the best chance to constitute their own lives, yet this does not entail enforcing diversity by trapping people within differences they long to escape. This means that a cosmopolitan archaeology will not always be preservationist in ethos, nor would it attempt to congeal people within some preserved ancient authenticity. This is why many have called for a rooted cosmopolitanism that emanates from, and pays heed to, local settings and practices (see chapters by Lydon and Lilley, this volume).

Cosmopolitanism might look suspiciously like another version of multiculturalism. However, in this book we suggest that theories of multiculturalism differ from cosmopolitanism since multiculturalism seeks to extend equitable status or treatment to different cultural or religious groups within the bounds of a unified society (see Benhabib 2002, 2004). While the ideals of multiculturalism are admirable, many cosmopolitans find this position problematic since it can deprivilege certain forms of cultural difference and subsequently disempower indigenous and minority communities who already have less visibility and representation under the state (Ivison 2006a). Many of the authors here speak to, if not explicitly name, the inherent problems of multicultural states such as Australia or the United States, which have diverse populations and manifold tensions over the claims of culture, economic opportunity, and indigenous rights. Charles Taylor (1994: 61–64) argues that multiculturalism results in the imposition of some cultures upon others with a tacit assumption of superiority. Western liberal societies are supremely guilty in this regard. In relating this to heritage, archaeology is increasingly employed in land claims and other forms of restitution for indigenous groups. A multiculturalist position might challenge indigenous privilege in the management and control of sacred places or objects for the democratic ideals of free and equal access for all. Conversely, a cosmopolitan stance might go beyond this recognition of equal value and access by considering whether cultural survival and indigenous practice should be considered legitimate legal goals within a specific society. Today, many archaeologists would consider the claims of connected communities primary and, in many contexts, give them greater weight than other stakeholders. But archaeologists must also be aware that while some groups may opt for cultural "preservation" and distinctiveness, other groups may prefer cultural integration and sometimes even "destruction" of the material past (see chapters by Lydon, González-Ruibal, and Colwell-Chanthaphonh, this volume). These developments represent a marked departure from the archaeology practiced in previous decades, which was satisfied with an ethos of minimum intervention or aspired to a "do no harm" model of coexistence.

The political ramifications of heritage have been an object of archaeological research and writing for some time. However, the scale and interconnectedness of archaeology's materials, research, and field practices within larger global interventions and organizations represent a much newer arena for reflection. From this perspective we find ourselves closest to the discussions raised in anthropology around the ethics of cultural cosmopolitanism, yet the large-scale and collaborative nature of archaeological field practices provides an additional, complementary dimension. Cosmopolitan approaches to an archaeological past, such as those in this volume, posit a new challenge to the impositions of Euro-American heritage discourse by destabilizing the presumed cultural "goods" of world heritage, global patrimony, and other universalisms. These studies, with their particular materialities and histories, also demonstrate that "cosmopolitanism is not a circle created by culture diffused from a center, but instead, that centers are everywhere and circumferences nowhere. This ultimately suggests that we already are and have always been cosmopolitan, though we may not always have known it" (Pollock et al. 2002: 12). Not surprisingly, the anthropological academy has been charged with being much less cosmopolitan than some of the seemingly "remote" communities within which we work (see essays in Werbner 2008).

In the forgoing I have suggested that the ethical responsibilities surrounding heritage sites and practices now inhabit ever wider cosmopolitan circuits. In addition, the basis of archaeology is itself inherently cosmopolitan through its disciplinary tactics and spatiotemporal practices. At every level our work is both multi-scalar and contextual, making archaeology rather different from her sister disciplines of history and anthropology. Cosmopolitanism is thus inescapable for archaeologists who deal with uncovering human histories that transcend modern national borders and Western understandings of cultural affiliation, and when the results of our research have serious ramifications for living peoples, many of whom live in non-urban contexts, depend on local livelihoods, and have emotive connections to place (see chapters by Breglia and Benavides, this volume). Cosmopolitan archaeology acknowledges its responsibilities to the wider world yet embraces the cultural differences that are premised upon particular histories, places, practices, and sentiments. In the heritage domain we must wrestle with the tensions of universalism and particularism and constantly negotiate some middle ground. But as discussions of human rights demonstrate, according to Chakrabarty (2002: 82), universalistic assumptions are not easily given up, and the tension between universalism and historical difference is not easily dismissed. In his view cosmopolitanism is a particular strategy formulated in the course of this very struggle. Access to one's own cultural heritage as a fundamental human right represents a new challenge that is fast appearing on our disciplinary horizon. Rights to heritage and heritage rights are gradually emerging within archaeological discourse (O'Keefe 2000; Prott 2002; see also chapters by Lydon and Hodder, this volume) whereas researchers were previously ill-prepared to enter debates that traversed international, national, and indigenous platforms.

How might cosmopolitan heritage discourse prepare us for these emergent struggles in which archaeological pasts are drawn into contemporary struggles for recognition and self-determination? Cosmopolitans tend to be strong proponents for the survival of cultural diversity. They value the inherent differences between societies and support the maintenance of those differences. But as a cautionary note, we cannot assume that striving for cultural diversity is a necessary good for everyone in the arena of heritage and identity politics. Surely it is problematic to privilege *diversity* for its own sake, and rather more important to recognize the situations in which individuals and groups actually choose to retain their distinctive traditions and relationships to the material past. There is a danger that we might force indigenous and minority groups to succumb to oppressive legal frameworks in order to gain recognition or to even claim their heritage through the language of international rights. We should not presume that the maintenance of cultural diversity is an a priori desire for all people in all places. Moreover, the tenets underpinning diversity, biodiversity, and natural heritage cannot easily be sutured to a model of cultural heritage (see chapter 4 by Meskell, this volume). As these struggles emerge, we might instead consider another cosmopolitan commitment, namely the equal worth and dignity of different cultures, instead of falling back upon the trope of diversity. Such perspectives find wide resonance with the concerns of political and postcolonial liberalism (Ivison 2002, 2006b; Rawls 1993), specifically as they pertain to issues of indigenous heritage, recognition ethics, and social justice.

As archaeologists and ethnographers writing together and supporting a strong contextualism, we trace outward the relational webs that result from our engagements both in the field and beyond. As many of us have already noted, researchers will have to partake in wider social and political conversations, with the caveat that archaeologists are not the primary stakeholders or arbiters of culture and that we cannot always mandate mutually reconcilable outcomes around heritage issues. Cosmopolitans suppose, however, that all cultures have enough overlap in their vocabulary of values to begin a conversation. Yet counter to some universalists, they do not presume that they can craft a consensus (Appiah 2006a: 57). As many of the chapters imply, archaeologists should expect to spend more of our time in conversation and negotiation with various constituencies and be prepared to increasingly relinquish some of our archaeological goals.

Developing Cosmopolitan Heritages

Cosmopolitan theory is being redefined differently by scholars across disciplines as diverse as geography, anthropology, political and social theory, law, international relations, and even business management

(Beck and Sznaider 2006: 1). As stated above, our closest dialogue understandably remains with our colleagues in anthropology, specifically in regard to issues of internationalism, migration, identity politics, indigenous movements, postcolonialism, and ethics. Archaeology has been a relative latecomer to the discussion and our current contribution stems from the discipline's gradual acknowledgment that the past is always present and that we are indeed responsible for the sociopolitical interventions and repercussions of the archaeological project.

Archaeology's engagement with politics and its larger framing within global developments are direct outgrowths of a specific disciplinary trajectory that has only recently incorporated social theory, politics, philosophy, feminism, and indigenous scholarship. During the 1980s and 1990s many archaeologists deepened their awareness and application of social theory, whereas the 1990s and the decade 2000–2009 were marked by our recognition of the field's sociopolitical embedding. This volume is also a product of that acknowledgment. In recent years practitioners have become increasingly concerned with the ethical implications of their research and, more importantly, the politics of fieldwork, and with collaborations with local people, descendants, indigenous groups, and other communities of connection (e.g., Hall 2005; Hodder 1998; Joyce 2005; Lilley and Williams 2005; Meskell 2005a, 2005b; Smith 2004; Watkins 2004; Zimmerman et al. 2003). Ethics has become the subject of numerous volumes (e.g., Lynott and Wylie 2000; Meskell and Pels 2005; Messenger 1999; Vitelli and Colwell-Chanthaphonh 2006), as had politics and nationalism before that. Importantly, these were not simply Euro-American trends but were more often driven by archaeologists from Latin America, Australasia, Africa, and the Middle East (see Abdi 2001; Funari 2004; Ndoro 2001; Politis 2001; Scham and Yahya 2003; Shepherd 2002). Indigenous issues and potential collaborations are slowly becoming mainstream in archaeological discussions and, while there is much that still needs redressing, I would argue that the language of restitution, repatriation, and reconciliation has gradually gained ground. Organizations like the World Archaeology Congress acknowledge the discipline's colonial history and present, and they have a public mandate of social justice that seeks not only to instantiate a model of best practice but to go beyond in terms of reparations and enhanced livelihoods, to make a positive, felt impact for the communities within which archaeologists work (Meskell 2007b). These are all vital disciplinary developments that have irrevocably changed how we undertake our research.

It is not simply our situated contexts that have been exposed and challenged: our methodologies have also recently been expanded and reimagined. Given the current climate of research briefly outlined here, and the types of transnational ethical and political work undertaken, a new generation of archaeologists has pursued a broader suite of techniques and multi-sited field methods. Blurring the conventional disciplinary divides, archaeologists have increasingly conducted ethnographic work around the construction of heritage, excavated the archives, investigated media-based productions of knowledge, and worked creatively in conjunction with living communities. Sometimes this work is focused on the materiality of the past, but more commonly such research enjoys a strong contemporary emphasis and is concerned with deciphering the micro-politics of archaeological practice, the effects of heritage on an international scale, and the entwined global networks of tourism, development, and heritage agencies, nongovernmental organizations, and so on. Additionally, there is a burgeoning literature by anthropologists on archaeological and heritage projects (Abu el-Haj 2001; Benavides and Breglia chapters in this volume; Castañeda 1996; Clifford 2004; Fontein 2005; Handler 2003). Crossover or hybrid projects such as archaeological ethnography (Meskell 2007a) bring a new set of connections and conversations to the fore, as well as disciplinary alliances, as we hope this volume demonstrates. Yet where this work diverges from mainstream ethnography is with the foregrounding of the past's materiality, specifically those traces of the past that have residual afterlives in living communities, traces that are often considered spiritually significant, and that often invite a kind of governmental monitoring and control that many indigenous communities and archaeologists increasingly find problematic. Moreover, archaeological ethnography often entails collaborating with, rather than studying, the people with whom we work in the heritage sphere, as the following chapters demonstrate.

I would argue that the new millennium also brought with it a new set of concerns for archaeologists and heritage practitioners. It was no longer possible to take refuge in the past or in the comfort that the subjects of our research were dead and buried. Rather than operating within a circumscribed set of practices, archaeologists now find themselves ever broadening out to embrace the discourses and effects of environmentalism, protectionism, and international law, or to confront the modalities of war and conflict. This expansion underlines a cosmopolitan commitment that follows from the discipline's first forays into sociopolitics during the 1980s and stretches ever more widely into the larger, international political arenas in which we are all enmeshed. It is timely and appropriate that the first volume in this series, *Material Worlds*, should address these interdisciplinary concerns, which have become the hallmark of an engaged archaeology. As argued above, archaeology has always been cosmopolitan by the very nature of its subject matter and field practices. However, these chapters go much further by examining the changing nature of multi-sited fieldwork, exploring hybrid modes of research, and tackling the implications of transnational or global heritage. In the main this is not a collection devoted to traditional accounts of ancient societies, but rather to our contemporary commitments, heritage ethics, and sociopolitical linkages between residual pasts and projected futures.

Contributors in this volume focus largely on the "past in the present," rather than the traditional "past in the past" analyses that tend to be synonymous with the discipline of archaeology. The past matters a great deal in the present and its material residues are increasingly crucial for imagining possible futures, particularly for developing beneficial trajectories based on the economic, political, and social potentials embedded within valued archaeological sites and objects. The chapters deal with forms of "heritage ethics"—the fusing of contemporary concerns for ethical collaborations, the politics of recognition, and redress around sites and objects in the heritage landscape. Much of this work connects to indigenous communities and their rights to culture, but not in every case, since there are other minorities, descendants, diasporic communities, and communities of connection with whom archaeologists and ethnographers collectively work. However, the chapters extend out even further from these networked relationships, to the worldwide organizations and entanglements with which we are inexorably bound: these too form critical loci for engagement with heritage ethics.

Cosmopolitan Heritage Ethics in Practice

To illustrate the complex cosmopolitan arrangements in which archaeologists and their objects of study are increasingly embroiled, the contributors to this volume describe various forms of cosmopolitanism and take different paths to documenting or reconciling social differences and understandings across local, national, and multinational scales.

One salient thread running through many chapters is the politics of something I call heritage protectionism, and by this I mean the desire and means to preserve certain valued sites for the global benefit of humanity. Traditionally such moves have been mobilized from a Euro-American platform based on the presumed universalism of something called "world heritage"—the logic of which has widespread effects in both international and localized settings. It has been argued that the ideal of universal salvage often betrays a "hypocritical neutrality, behind which the domination by another conception of the good (precisely the secular ethos of equality) is merely taking refuge" (Habermas 2003b: 24). The construction of world heritage, a supposed cosmopolitan good, is often used to culturally demonize certain polities with which the West has irreconcilable differences. Recently we have seen the language of sanctions being used to combat the scale of looting in Iraq, although we know that the largest market for illegal antiquities remains the United States (Eck and Gerstenblith 2003). The imperatives for heritage protectionism are tightly wed to the familiar global processes of development, neoliberalism, and governmentality, with their attendant array of concerns. Though often filled with promise, many of these internationally deployed strategies also produce heritage victims, as Alfredo González-Ruibal documents in his chapter in this volume.

Instigated in the name of humanitarianism and development, the forced relocations of communities in Ethiopia and Brazil rely on decisions underwritten by narratives of underdevelopment bolstered by the work of archaeologists, who have placed people such as the Awá and Gumuz at the far end of modernity's spectrum. Framing such events in terms of an archaeology of failure, González-Ruibal goes further by suggesting that even some seemingly charitable community-based projects, based on the neoliberal rhetoric of development, only instantiate the inequities they purport to alleviate. Those who ultimately benefit are generally state authorities that can showcase pristine archaeology, the transnational companies whose business is tourism, and those who might gain employment in the process. Many more have something to lose in these new reconfigurations of heritage and tourism, namely the immediate residents and stakeholders who happen to live amid the ruins. Using archaeology and ethnography in tandem, González-Ruibal's cosmopolitan project takes him from Spain to Brazil and Ethiopia, tracking the effects of development, globalization, and universalistic policies. This project includes uncovering the interventions of USAID, the World Bank, the European Union, and Italian, Dutch, and former Soviet organizations. His work is an example of the move toward an "archaeology of the present" or an archaeological ethnography, working with living peoples, their object worlds, and the remains of their contemporary past.

Generally, González-Ruibal is suspicious of archaeological lip service to multiculturalism and multivocality that draws attention to "local communities" but constructs their concerns and agendas as secondary to academic research ambitions. Heritage humanitarianism has become its own fetish, immersed in philanthropy and aid that generally serves to buttress paternalism and cultural superiority. He rightly asserts that archaeologists have willingly accepted funding and participated in heritage development projects, following the path of international agencies, sometimes without the consent of those most affected. In doing so they are simply papering over the cracks of global disorder. He argues for a vernacular or marginal cosmopolitanism that aligns itself with the victims of progress and does not presuppose a transcendent human universal. Finally, he calls for an archaeology that excavates the devastation of modernism, which is accompanied by the betrayal, and often annihilation, of the communities within which we work.

Jane Lydon's chapter guides us through the pitfalls of multicultural discourse in Australia today and critiques the kinds of elision and attenuation of diverse cultures through globalized heritage discourses. In the Australian case, indigenous accounts are most vulnerable to the hollow multiculturalism that would purvey a singular narrative of nation. Multiculturalist, not cosmopolitan, discourse underlies many of the claims of powerful nations to appropriate, house, and manage the cultural riches of others, whether on their own territory or on foreign soil. Multiculturalism is mobilized within nations both to embrace and curtail certain diverse groups that challenge the dominant fabric of nation. John Howard (2006), the former Australian prime minister, used the rhetoric of multiculturalism to flatten diversity, particularly Aboriginal claims for primacy, and celebrate the "great and enduring heritage of Western civilisation, those nations that became the major tributaries of European settlement and in turn a sense of the original ways in which Australians from diverse backgrounds have created our own distinct history" in his call for "One People, One Destiny." We might well ask whose pasts and properties are privileged or marginalized in those claims for multiculturalism? The seemingly positive equation of democratic inclusion and equality effectively trumps the preservation of cultural distinctiveness (Benhabib 2002: x), yet it assumes that legal democracy was already forged with cultural diversity in mind—a situation we know is historically untrue. Furthermore, "reparations for past injustices by the state, law and morality can become entangled in contradictions, even if both are governed by the principle of equal respect for all. This is because law is a recursively closed medium that can only reflectively react to its own past decisions, but it is insensitive to episodes that pre-date the legal system" (Habermas 2003b: 24). Proponents of strong multiculturalism would be willing to sideline the cultural and political understandings of law for nations with minorities or indigenous groups, for example, disavowing the possibilities for states within states. Lydon's chapter explains that even the Australian referendum of 1967, while ushering in significant changes, did not entail full citizenship rights for Aboriginal people. Thus it cannot be presumed that they have an inherent allegiance to a nationalist framework, nor can it be assumed, conversely, that the dominant white culture necessarily embraces indigenous places and objects as sacred or even meaningful. International heritage discourse exacerbates the dual tension between valuing diversity and difference and propounding universalism. Lydon underscores the specific link between heritage discourses and those of human rights, using UNESCO's program of world heritage as the linchpin and organizational node for a global cultural commons. On the one hand, UNESCO's documents purport to support group rights, minorities, and traditional lifestyles; on the other hand, its expressed allegiance to the Universal Declaration of Human Rights accords those rights to individuals, not groups (see the chapter by Hodder, this volume).

In Australia, Lydon contends that a cosmopolitan ethos of openness to cultural difference is effectively countered by the commitment to universal heritage values, themselves bolstered by transnational heritage practices and organizations, and other sets of professional and disciplinary alliances. Archaeologists and heritage workers are situated in this uncomfortable impasse. Increasingly, indigenous peoples seek to forge international connections, often in preference to national ones, constituting yet another site of emergent cosmopolitanism (see the chapters by Breglia and Benavides, this volume). In 1998 Aboriginal people petitioned UNESCO to stave off the incursions of the Jabiluka uranium mine, which threatened the Mirarr Aboriginal community and its lifeways. At a UNESCO bureau meeting in Paris, compelling presentations by Aboriginal leaders led to a situation where the site was placed on the world heritage "in danger" list without the permission of the host country. Juxtaposing the fractious internal heritage politics of Australia and its indigenous past, Lydon then documents the recent movement to project the nation's heritage beyond the boundaries of the nation-state with the historic site of Gallipoli, Turkey. Now famed as a pilgrimage site, the Gallipoli Peninsula Peace Park marks the conflict of 1915 during which thousands of young men from Australia and New Zealand lost their lives to the Turks over eight months of bitter fighting. Claiming heritage in a foreign conflict zone has clearly proven more palatable to the Australian government than addressing its own internal repressions and seeking equitable restitution for segments of its citizenry. As this chapter evinces, debates over multiculturalism, indigenous rights, and the possibilities of transnational or cosmopolitan justice bring to the fore twofold tensions, namely between states and their minorities (or majorities), as well as states and the international community as defined by particular ruling bodies. The thorny relationships between national sovereignty and international intervention, surrounding heritage and social justice, are thus bound to resurface continually.

Although echoing Lydon's assertion of Australia's shameful history with its indigenous minority, Ian Lilley resists the pessimism of scholars such as Peter Thorley who express skepticism about successfully translating indigenous archaeology into practice. Within Australian heritage debates Thorley has claimed that indigenous and Western values cannot be bridged since even the notion of "indigenous archaeology" is the product of an external and powerful settler society. Taking a more positive stance, Lilley imputes that Australian archaeology has developed closer relations with indigenous peoples than that of other nations such as the United States (see also Lilley 2000b). Using the example of the influential Burra Charter, he argues that Australia has effectively led the way in bringing indigenous and archaeological interests together as a matter of conventional professional practice at a national scale. Moreover, the charter has been inspirational for a host of other countries from China to South Africa. One reason for this positive move within Australian archaeology, Lilley posits, was the profession's recognition in the early 1980s that decolonization raised profound questions about archaeology's relationships and responsibilities to descendent communities. A second was the pragmatism of the discipline's response and its development of creative solutions to these newfound working collaborations.

Lilley's other fieldwork in New Caledonia provides an alternative national context and a site of potential conflict where Kanak interpretations and those of traditional archaeology are fundamentally oppositional. Understandably, Kanaks remain unconvinced of the virtue of archaeological accounts and find themselves glossed in disciplinary discourse as simply one group in a long series of "migrants" and "invaders." Such tensions are played out in many heritage locales and find resonance in the following chapters on South Africa, Turkey, and Brazil. From the communities' vantage, archaeologists should pay less attention to historicizing the past and more to historically bolstering indigenous rights. Negotiating different disciplinary and political aims is crucial and, as Lilley rightly recognizes, takes time, trust, and transparency. His chapter recalls that archaeologists have long performed the role of dangerous interloper, and despite long-term intense cross-cultural interaction researchers frequently find themselves entangled in encounters of profound difference. He suggests that a crucial way to lessen the divide is through language, specifically by practitioners adopting local languages and lingua francas, which he suggests are themselves forms of hybridized or vernacular cosmopolitanism.

A further contribution Lilley makes is methodological. He and an Aboriginal colleague have begun a collaborative project that attempts to see and experience the Australian landscape from indigenous perspectives. Linked to the new moves in collaborative archaeologies, the project takes seriously the animate spiritual quality that inheres in certain features and places and combines these with ancestral knowledge and storytelling. The work is part of a growing corpus of field practice in Australia and the Pacific, coupled with developments in Native American indigenous archaeology (for example, Colwell-Chanthaphonh 2003a; Colwell-Chanthaphonh and Ferguson 2004; Ferguson and Colwell-Chanthaphonh 2006; Stoffle et al. 2001). As the second Daes Report, commissioned by the United Nations, attests (1999): "Indigenous peoples have explained that, because of the profound relationship that [they] have to their lands, territories and resources, there is a need for a different conceptual framework to understand this relationship and a need for recognition of the cultural differences that exist. Indigenous peoples have urged the world community to attach positive value to this distinct relationship." As the first Daes Report made clear in 1997, each indigenous community must retain permanent control over its own heritage, but reserve the right to determine how that shared knowledge is used. This is tantamount to a *lex loci*, or the law of the place (Brown 2003: 210, 225).

The instantiation of an indigenous conceptual framework that embraces cultural difference is exemplified in Chip Colwell-Chanthaphonh's chapter addressing the North American context. Here he employs ethnographic archaeologies from contemporary Zuni, Hopi, and Navajo communities to underscore our obligations to embrace indigenous practices and worldviews, rather than retreating into a narrow view of protectionism. He concludes that there is no "universal" preservation ethic, since preservation itself is a cultural construct, yet international bodies like UNESCO insist that we universalize just such an ethic. Instead, our only recourse as practitioners is to a cosmopolitan heritage ethic. He calls for a "complex stewardship" modeled on rooted cosmopolitanism that acknowledges that preservation is both locally enacted and universally sought. For Colwell-Chanthaphonh this translates into maximizing "the integrity of heritage objects for the good of the greatest number of people, but not absolutely." His views have strong resonance with the tenets of postcolonial liberalism, which assert that "cultural difference is real, especially in the case of clashes between liberal institutions and indigenous societies, but it does not follow from this that the differences are therefore radically incommensurable" (Ivison 2002: 36). Negotiation and discussion is key as Colwell-Chanthaphonh himself has demonstrated. Heritage practitioners are increasingly learning that *process* is everything and their commitment to inclusion, participation, and ongoing discussions with affected groups is paramount. Importantly, cosmopolitanism entails openness to divergent cultural experiences (Hannerz 2006), which has inevitably become the hallmark of recent writing in interpretive, contextual, collaborative, and indigenous archaeologies (see Colwell-Chanthaphonh and Ferguson 2007).

Heritage negotiations, however, cannot simply be interpolated into blanket multiculturalism, since they pivot around the issue of individual versus group rights, as Ian Hodder spells out in his chapter. He advocates that rather than imposing a priori strictures (group or individual rights, for example), archaeologists should embark upon a process of deliberation and negotiation. Throughout such a process Hodder argues that it will often be necessary to empower local groups or individual voices through complex cosmopolitan alliances that cut across individual, local group, regional and national group, and global scales. Drawing on three contemporary examples from Turkey, Hodder demonstrates that complex cosmopolitan interactions highlight the need for wider legal framings around cultural heritage rights in relation to human rights. The first case he puts forward involves the silencing of a local Turkish woman in a public heritage display in Istanbul: Mavili plays an integral role in the archaeological project of Çatalhöyük, which Hodder directs. The elision of a local voice, literally and meta-phorically, haunts any attempt to present an ethical or comprehensive picture of the project and illustrates the internal national tensions that would be rendered mute under any banner of multiculturalism. The Turkish state is strongly nationalist and republican, in the tradition of its founder, Kemal Atatürk, and promotes national unity over cultural diversity as Hodder's next example lays bare. This second case involves an issue of reburial, specifically secularist-Islamist tensions over sixty-four graves excavated at the site: in the summer of 2007 the first C14 dates came back as thirteenth to fifteenth centuries AD, which could indicate early Islamic burials. The third case recounts relations with a local university in Konya, whose students participate on the project, specifically detailing how the university is caught between the state's desire for secularism and individual expression of religious rights. As Hodder's work demonstrates, cosmopolitanism has come to embrace a wider and more nuanced analytical reach than the traditional bifur-cations of global and local. Certainly, community can be envisioned variously, and while several authors focus upon political institutions, Hodder focuses on moral norms, relationships, and forms of cultural expression. As he notes, the fabric of the nation-state is being eroded by claims to and about heritage, some operating at the international level, others instigated by intranational minorities. Others provoca-tively ask why states are perceived to possess legitimate and exclusive sovereignty over all their territories (see Ivison 2006a). Why presume that state institutions and processes dealing with distributive justice are legitimate? Going further, one might even question the carving up of the global into something called states in the first instance. These heuristics allow us to see the state strictures, not to mention international mandates, that have been naturalized at the intranational level. Transnational governance represents a new and proliferating mode of global politics.

At present, a decentralized political system is operative where global allegiance around heritage ethics is thin and populated largely by intellectuals and activists. Ultimately for transnational agencies to be modified, progress must occur in cooperation with and through nation-states, and in the nation-state's role in those negotiations reside the same potentials for emancipation as for domination. The present aporia recognizes that nationalism, even in its most oppressive times, cannot be easily transcended by cosmopolitan solidarity (Cheah 1998: 312). The international public sphere is typically represented by nation-states—the United Nations is the obvious case in point and exemplifies the uneven nature of member representation. For Hodder, it is a matter of negotiating or balancing these supra- and infra-politics of engagement at Çatalhöyük, from the international funders, including the U.S. State Department, Boeing, Yapı Kredi Bank, and Shell, to the local support and labor of villagers like Mavili and her family. He is candid that the whole project of local engagement in Çatalhöyük is borne out of his own interventionist agenda, while neoliberal market economies have also played their role in the shaping of a heritage landscape. Ultimately he steers us away from multiculturalist discourse to focus instead on human rights to counter inequalities and injustices. In doing so he describes the difficulties in some universal privileging of individual heritage rights as opposed to the group or community (see the chapter by Lydon, this volume). In the process he does not fetishize the "local" but insists that national and international entities be brought into the frame to ensure full participation at various levels.

Other chapters deal more pointedly with the discourse of heritage conservation and its linkages to natural heritage and ecology movements. For archaeologists, cultural heritage discourse has historically borrowed much from the tenets of nature conservation and increasingly from the global desire for biodiversity, as the chapters by Byrne and Meskell respectively demonstrate. Conservation at these scales is already prefigured as a cosmopolitan value and legacy, yet a more political cosmopolitanism lies behind our efforts to draw attention to those who happen to dwell in or near protected areas and whose own heritage is marginalized for the sake of some greater, global good. For Denis Byrne, these individuals join the ranks of the "conservation refugees," the victims of fortress conservation that, in his words, is clearly incompatible with a cosmopolitan respect for plurality. Thai practice provides the context from which Byrne explores popular culture and religion, the "magical supernatural" that imbues objects and places and is respected by Thais across the social spectrum. Archaeological sites themselves become the receptacles of empowerment, though foreign practitioners have difficulty in integrating indigenous religion into their own field practice and subsequently elide the most interesting contemporary dimensions of their research. Moreover, they grapple with the Thais' abilities to incorporate state-sponsored, nationalistic accounts of their past while simultaneously venerating archaeological objects as supernaturally endowed, as in the case of the iconic heritage site of Sukhotai. Byrne sees Thai cosmopolitanism as sharply contrastive with the strict taxonomies that heritage practitioners and archaeologists regularly enforce. And as a result local people and popular religion are decoupled from heritage management, leaving both parties somewhat bereft. Paralleling the development of archaeology, the rise of the nation-state in Southeast Asia also encouraged the jettisoning of certain uses and experiences of the past that were deemed uncivilized or premodern. Acknowledging those *felt* perspectives and cultural differences toward materiality, however, might lead to more tolerant and less polarized decision-making processes regarding heritage, preservation, conservation, and use. As Byrne reminds us, popular religious practice does not require our consent, but rather it is the students of heritage who stand to gain by taking a cosmopolitan approach.

Just as Byrne and González-Ruibal have shown the negative intersection of the politics of natural and cultural protectionism in Thailand, Brazil, and Ethiopia, my own chapter documents the dangerous narratives of *terra nullius* or "empty lands" in South Africa and the communities that are forced to pay the price of global conservation and biodiversity. My own archaeological ethnography asks how different black communities living on the edge of a celebrated national park envision the global. Like Lydon's case of Jabiluka, the communities bordering Kruger National Park draw upon the networks of indigenous rights, international law, and expert international researchers to craft a particular identity and stake in the reclaiming of the natural commons. And even so-called national parks are *ipso facto* transnational bodies composed of American funders, European aid agencies, NGOs, government officials, impoverished park workers, and foreign research scientists. Identifying competing conceptions of the common good, and the practices by which new and emergent social realities come into being, is very much at issue in this chapter and others throughout this volume. Multicultural discourse cannot hope to explain or encompass these processes, since they are not confined to a notion of pluralism, but to cosmopolitan openness, self-constitution, and transformation. Philosophers such as Benhabib (2002: ix–x) adopt an academic stance by opposing social movements that maintain the distinctiveness of cultures, finding them fundamentally irreconcilable with democratic considerations. Her position finds little purchase with those individuals and communities around Kruger and elsewhere who currently struggle for recognition and restitution from the state. What is troubling with bourgeois theories of justice is the propensity to detemporalize or decontextualize, presenting themselves as fixed and unchanging standards (Ruiters 2002: 120). Such abstractions fail to account for real institutions and relations in practice. How would such a theoretical position account for the situation in South Africa, where the majority is not synonymous with colonizer and the minority with indigenous community per se, where indigeneity is multiply claimed across many ethnic categories, and where ethnicity and religion are complexly cross-cutting and even fractious?

Discourses of biodiversity form the backdrop to this chapter, specifically its global success and ability to outstrip cultural heritage on national and international agendas. These discourses privilege nature over culture and typically sacrifice historic recognition and restitution for the "greater good" of conservation. Irrespective of leadership or regime change in South African national parks, state power continues to devalue the archaeological past and its human histories. Narratives of *terra nullius* have resurfaced in dangerous and familiar ways. The now discredited discourse erases indigenous histories and is perilously hitched to the celebratory discourses of conservation and biodiversity, since both espouse global desires for pristine wilderness, minimal human intensification, the erasure of anthropogenic landscapes, the primacy of non-human species, sustainability, and so on. There is a denial of indigenous presence, irrespective of the documented rock art, pre-historic sites, and Iron Age remains that number well over one thousand within Kruger's borders. Without recognition of the complex and continued human history in Kruger's landscapes there is little chance of historical justice and restitution for indigenous South Africans in these regions. Archaeologists have played no small part in this erasure, certainly during the apartheid years, and their racialized narratives, and even their silences, have had tremendous residual force to this day for black South Africans. Cultural heritage is seen as divisive and particular, whereas natural heritage is global and encompassing, entreating us all to subscribe to its world-making project.

A consistent concern throughout the chapters is the fallout for local communities and other stakeholders who inhabit heritage landscapes and inadvertently bear the brunt of our archaeological fieldwork and findings. Sandra Arnold Scham's chapter reveals that even our current crises in the Middle East are not free from archaeology's disciplinary misadventures. She asserts that archaeologists have narrativized the East as more religious, irrational, ritualistic, and oppressive. And the premises and practices we enjoy are often directly fed back into popular conceptions of the Middle East, or perhaps worse, U.S. foreign policy discussions. Archaeologists working in the region, in Scham's view, continually stress sacred or ritualized material culture, thereby capitulating to an image of the East as being more religious and less secular by the very nature of our research. Our taxonomies are mutually exclusive rather than permeable, she imputes, and the resultant picture constructs religion in a wholly Western guise that is all pervasive, extremist, and impractical, existing as a force external to culture and society.

Taking this squarely into the realm of heritage ethics, Scham interrogates the Archaeological Institute of America's *Open Declaration on Cultural Heritage at Risk*, which was circulated to the U.S. government before the invasion of Iraq. Surely, she muses, human life is not secondary to cultural property? But scholars of the Middle East have inevitably couched their preoccupations with invasion and conflict "in terms of preserving things rather than people." Instead of focusing on these preoccupations she extends the cosmopolitan idea of hospitality, inspired by Derrida and Habermas, and tempered by her own excavation experiences, as a set of obligations on the part of hosts and guests, which is becoming so crucial for our continued fieldwork in the archaeological present. Critical of those who fail to honor obligations to those with whom we work, she suggests that these decisions are sometimes premised upon derogatory views of Middle Eastern culture, and that even our oft-critiqued "Orientalist" forebears assessed the situation with greater savvy by employing local workers rather than wealthy Western students. Her work poignantly demonstrates who wins and loses in our disciplinary and personal refusals to engage, whether at the local or international scale. While the Middle East is always positioned as the most extreme or volatile heritage scape, the attitudes and fallouts she exposes occur globally, as other chapters in this volume detail.

Lisa Breglia's chapter critically examines the consequences of achieving world heritage status for those who live and work in the shadows of global patrimony. Her ethnographic study reveals how a celebrated Mayan heritage has ultimately failed its immediate stakeholders and what remains is a shrinking horizon of possibility for social, economic, and cultural uplift. Despite Chichén Itzá's cosmopolitan underpinnings and the promise of neoliberal development, the inequities of labor regimes, land use, tenure, and ownership remain intransigent. Moreover, she draws a distinction between the attitudes and experiences of Yucatec Maya and other Mexican citizens around the site as they are polarized within a disjointed nationalism, itself a reminder of the fractious nature of the local. In the context of Mexican heritage, nationalism is an artifice that is exposed and effaced through an archaeological past and thus the nation-state falls short. Ethnographic interviews with Chichén Itzá's heritage workers reveal that their attitudes extend beyond indigenous appeals toward a cosmopolitan discourse on global culture, internationalism, and supranational constructions of rights and duties connected to citizenship (see the chapter by Lydon, this volume). Tensions between Mexicans and indigenous Maya site custodians abound: the former flagrantly resist site rules and restrictions, damage the monuments, and litter the site, according to the latter. Breglia asserts that site workers are implementing their own "cosmopolitan, postnational politics of location that highlights the tenuousness of the modern apparatus that grafts together archaeology, heritage, tourism, and nationalism, hiding the diverse interests of each in order to create the illusion of a supposedly transparent site of Mexicanness." As with Hodder's contribution, archaeologists cannot simply tack between community and state entities, as the nation-state so often fails its minorities, sometimes silencing or erasing their pasts and presents. Breglia further argues that while heritage scapes are tacitly cosmopolitan due to their global connectedness and tourist markets, the social relations between workers, local residents, landowners, managers, archaeologists, bureaucrats, and tourists reflect an even greater quotidian cosmopolitanism.

In such heritage settings, cosmopolitans would consider that though indigenous individuals and connected communities have certain rights and claims to culture, they are not trapped by ancient identities and necessarily expected to perform them in the present. However, identity politics may be a necessary avenue to pursue in order to gain adequate restitution for the past in the present. Hugo Benavides's ethnographic work in Ecuador lays bare the fiction of cultural authenticity within a nationalizing project, as the latter abuts the "progressive" neoliberal entities of sustainable development, eco-tourism, and indigenous human rights that are invested in reproducing global difference. He asks how the archaeological remains of a pre-Hispanic past become a tool for hegemonic reproduction against a backdrop of transnational cultural diversity. In his account, Indian and black diasporic communities are reified as the national "other" despite claims to a grounded national identity based on geographical legitimization that is equal to or greater than the white elite. Referencing three archaeological sites, Benavides describes the contemporary fashioning of a politically expedient "Indianness" through heritage, the narratives of continuity, and the fallbacks to hardened categories of race and pristine culture, all of which are influenced by the machinations of global capital and struggles for political recognition. However, with the palpable disinterest in excavating black maroon sites, an Afro-Ecuadorian archaeological research legacy is left languishing. Those of us working in the interstices of cultures and histories have held deep expectations on how indigenous groups are meant to behave or supposed to perform their historical connections. Archaeologists must be more embracing of cultural difference in the present, in our own contact zones and our own clashes of cultures. There are myriad ways in which past inheritance can be embodied, felt, narrated, mobilized, and experienced: there is no single path to cultural legitimacy.

Like those of many other authors in this book, Benavides's findings impel practitioners to consider the interventions of multinational bodies, international legal framings, and rights movements that go beyond cultural heritage imperatives, because they are frequently interpolated into broader development schemes, the involvement of NGOs, corporations, and the workings of global capital. In his words, "Ecuador as a whole cannot be a competitive player in today's global market without a coherent story of a pre-Hispanic historical narrative." And archaeologists proffer the means of legitimating political struggles and thus enable hegemonic entry into the contested domain of transnational market imperatives. This is by no means a celebratory cosmopolitanism, but rather a fraught cosmopolitics, emphasizing the "need to introduce order and accountability into this newly dynamic space of gushingly unrestrained sentiments, pieties and urgencies for which no adequately discriminating lexicon has had time to develop" (Robbins 1998: 9). As the chapters in this volume elucidate, an attention to cosmopolitanism is a recognition of our obligations and responsibilities, historically and presently: it is neither a theoretical gloss nor a political trend scholars could hope to bypass or one day overcome. It is the position we as archaeologists find ourselves in today, much as social anthropologists and others have previously acknowledged (Breckenridge et al. 2002; Cheah and Robbins 1998; Hannerz 2006; Latour 2004; Mignolo 2002). Stimulated by the discipline's political and ethical engagements and bolstered by a new incursion into ethnographic and hybrid field practices, archaeologists and heritage workers are already caught up in cosmopolitics. With such a legacy from the past and set of responsibilities for the present and future, archaeologists should accept that there will be troubling terrain ahead. The challenge may require us to relinquish some of our own goals and set those within a wider international arena, as well as redress the hierarchical relationships of power in which we are all enmeshed.

Implications for the Archaeological Present

The subject of our research, the archaeological past and present, is situated firmly within a suite of cosmopolitan dispositions and practices: extensive mobility and travel; consuming places and environments; curiosity about people, places, and cultures; experiencing risks in encountering others; mapping various cultures and societies; semiotic skills in interpreting others; openness to different languages and cultures

(Szerszynski and Urry 2006: 114–15). *Cosmopolitan Archaeologies* recognizes that particular "locals," "communities," and "national" bodies have complex interactions with various international sponsors and universities, conservation agencies, development organizations, and NGOs, thus challenging simplistic notions of globalization or homogenization. The shorthand of local and global, caricatured by imputed cultural designations of traditional versus capitalist, falls short of the current complexities we all necessarily face on the ground. The utility of the term *globalization*, once descriptive of the macroeconomic turn, is further restricted by the fact that it now stands for everything and nothing simultaneously. What is appealing about cosmopolitanism is that while the processes of globalization lay claim to an overarching homogeneity of the planet in economic, political, and cultural spheres, the term *cosmopolitanism* might be employed as a counter to globalization from below. It also effectively overturns any notion that the local, situated contexts in which we work as archaeologists or ethnographers are isolated, traditional, disengaged, or disconnected from larger processes, institutions, organizations, consumer networks, and knowledges. While globalization is seen as something happening "out there," cosmopolitanism happens from within (Beck and Sznaider 2006: 9). As archaeologists and anthropologists, we are primed to be attentive to specific local contexts and histories that plan and project global designs and understandings in particular modalities (Mignolo 2002: 157). Studies of the archaeological present have lately evinced this local dimension, placing local communities and understandings at the forefront of our research agendas.

The chapters in this book are testament to a range of diverse cosmopolitanisms around the broad topic of heritage ethics. Through sustained case studies we examine the ways in which local and national heritage politics are made and unmade through international discourses and regulations; how transnational bodies and organizations such as UNESCO, the World Bank, and conservation and funding agencies are curiously brought into play in local arenas. Balancing appeals to universalism with that of cultural difference remains a critical tension that underlines much of the existing literature on heritage and our engagements as practitioners. These strange proximities and multiplicities are experienced in particular regions and locales in distinct ways, even though the organizational directives might aspire to a presumed universality and neutrality. We have also explored the politics of salvage, with its incentives of the common good that are based on promises, driven by the future, and depend upon networks of participation, discipline, and sacrifice that discursively create desirable heritage citizens (see Hayden 2003). In an Orwellian tone, interventionist policies that control the past also serve to predict future outcomes, promising sustainable development, betterment, and socioeconomic uplift. What must be sublated in the present will be recouped in the future by coming generations, while international elites and the adequately resourced will be able to enjoy the spoils of heritage and conservation in the present in the form of cultural and ecological tourism and research. Such promissory strategies tend to deprivilege indigenous and minority communities, often disempowered constituencies whose land, livelihoods, and legacies are threatened.

Collectively we take seriously the intellectual foundations and political economies of heritage—the legal, political, and ethical strata that underlie implicit tensions over access, preservation, and control of the material past in an unstable present. We question the translatability of heritage terms and practices across a wide array of sites and locations. Through the lens of cosmopolitanism we consider the discursive production, consumption, and governing of other people's pasts through examination of the participants, organizations, stakeholders, beneficiaries, and victims. In the future, a cosmopolitan archaeology is likely to fuel lines of inquiry into emergent experiences, commitments, and relationships, as well as critique its opposites and adversaries in debate (Hannerz 2006: 84). Taken with our obligation to reflexivity and alongside further theoretical and methodological developments, those of us working within heritage ethics will continue to reexamine and recast our own commitments and identifications in true cosmopolitan spirit.

Note

Versions of this chapter were given at the Cultures of Contact Conference at Stanford University, the plenary panel of the Thirty-ninth Annual Chacmool Conference held in Calgary entitled "Decolonizing Archaeology: Archaeology and the Post-Colonial Critique," and the "Identités, Mémoires et Culture: Une Vision Transnationale du Patrimonie" workshop at the Collège de France, Paris. I am grateful for comments and suggestions by those participating.

Emma Blake, Denis Byrne, Ian Hodder, and Carolyn Nakamura read and commented on earlier drafts. Lindsay Weiss has also offered intellectual directions and key references for this work over the years that have proven invaluable. Finally, I want to thank Ken Wissoker, who patiently offered his invaluable direction and insight throughout the writing process.

Jane Lydon

1 ✳ YOUNG AND FREE

The Australian Past in a Global Future

Australians all let us rejoice
For we are young and free
We've golden soil and wealth for toil,
Our home is girt by sea:
Our land abounds in nature's gifts
Of beauty rich and rare,
In history's page let every stage
Advance Australia fair,
In joyful strains then let us sing
Advance Australia fair.
—"Advance Australia Fair"

The Australian national anthem continues to resonate with a popular sense of the country's relatively recent origin, unfettered by a grim European past—Australians feel "young and free," with a history still to write, no choice but to advance. This identity is of course defined in relation to an international community, as indeed it has always been—but in an age of increasing global interconnectedness, the importance of the nation as a framework for understanding the Australian past (and therefore its present and future), has in some respects only strengthened. However, against this powerful narrative, a well-established critique of Australian heritage has identified problems with this national framework, and especially the suppression of indigenous experience entailed in creating a solid national foundation. Calls for transnational histories that re-site the nation within more global accounts of migration and exchange (for example, Curthoys and Lake 2005) potentially de-emphasize the state and reaffirm the status of "first" peoples within longer-term trajectories of human endeavor. Heritage is now a global discourse and can also be seen as a discourse of globalization that enfolds diverse cultures and attitudes toward the past into a single narrative. Internal tension between an openness to cultural difference and simultaneously a commitment to universal values remains unresolved, yet new forms of significance that are emerging within international heritage praxis, as people become enmeshed within transnational alliances, reveal new modes of political community. Processes such as the participation of indigenous peoples in international institutions in preference to national ones do not merely challenge the legitimacy of the states' claim to exclusive jurisdiction over territory, but in fact constitute an "emergent cosmopolitanism" (Ivison 2006a) that is compatible with universal notions of justice and yet is also rooted in particular, local ways of life.

Cosmopolitanism and Heritage

Many theories of global interconnectedness focus on the tension between different conceptions of human subjectivity and difference, often expressed as an opposition between universalism and relativism, and linked to notions of individual versus collective rights, and concomitant conceptions of culture as either fluid and contingent, or as bounded and local. International heritage discourse is similarly structured by this dual commitment—to global peace and prosperity grounded in universal human rights, but also to cultural diversity.

As formative analyses of the complexity and flux of globalization suggested (for example, Hannerz 1992; Featherstone 1990), diffusionist models (sometimes caricatured as *coca colonization*) are inadequate to explain processes of global interconnectedness, which are characterized not merely by homogenization and integration but also by the proliferation of diversity. The dissolution of some boundaries—most clearly, through mediatization and capital flow, travel and migration—has simultaneously acted to strengthen others and, most notably, a sense of local distinctiveness. Despite the persistence or even intensification of some normative orders within global processes, a sense of difference is constructed in relation to others in an enhanced awareness of plurality. Although cultural forms may be global, their interpretation and use are shaped by local values.

Visions of the ethical, emancipatory potential of an interconnected world, such as Kantian conceptions of cosmopolitanism, are characterized by a commitment to the equal worth and dignity of all human beings, linked to standards of justice that are intended to be applicable to all while at the same time retaining an openness to local different ways of life (Appiah 2006a). As an intellectual ethos this stance transcends the particularistic and contingent ties of kin and country, constituting "an institutionally grounded global political consciousness" (Cheah 2006: 491). The tension between the principles of universalism and local difference is central to current analysis of global networks, linked to concepts of universal human rights and local values. As I explore further, this apparent conceptual paradox is identified as a dilemma within both human rights and heritage discourse as well as theories of political community such as cosmopolitanism; it is a problem not merely of articulation between different orders of practice, but of how to conceive human subjectivity and difference.

It is often argued that the proliferation of international human rights law over recent decades has rendered it "one of the most globalized political values of our times" (Wilson 1997: 1), giving rise to "feasible global forms of political consciousness" that may regulate the excesses of capitalist globalization (Cheah 2006: 491). One of the central issues in this area has often been expressed as a contradiction between universal human rights with their emphasis on individual equality, and local culture and group rights—sometimes termed the "universalism versus relativism" debate. Relativist critique of universalism identifies the socially and historically contingent nature of human rights discourse, which emerged in its current form in Europe in the aftermath of World War II (with the Universal Declaration of Human Rights of 1948) within a Western ideology of liberalism and the bourgeois categories of possessive individualism. Such critique points to the global diversity of legal systems and especially indigenous peoples' claims to communal rights to land ownership or self-determination. The relativist critique relies upon a conception of culture as an *entity*—static, internally uniform, and historically bounded, rather than a contested and emergent *process*. In practical terms, the concept of "unity in diversity" becomes problematic when "culture" violates "universal rights"—or conversely, when minority cultures are objectified and penalized for changing.

The tension between universalism and cultural relativism is also apparent within international heritage discourse. Like human rights, heritage now constitutes a world network of organizations, policies, and practices, represented at a global level by the United Nations Educational, Scientific and Cultural Organization (UNESCO), which aims "to build peace in the minds of men" and to promote prosperity around the globe. Many have noted that in its promotion of Western notions of heritage—as material and authentic, for example—heritage can also be seen as a discourse *of* globalization (Ireland and Lydon 2005: 20). One of its key programs is the preservation of "culture," deployed largely through the framework of "world heritage" and the "world heritage list," conceived as universally owned. As UNESCO's website declares, "What makes the concept of World Heritage exceptional is its universal application. World Heritage sites belong to all the peoples of the world, irrespective of the territory on which they are located," in a vision of a global cultural commons. To be listed, places must be "considered to be of outstanding value to humanity" (UNESCO 1972), yet this notion of universal value is predicated upon an understanding of humankind as irreducibly diverse.

It is also linked to a commitment to a universal right *to* culture, as human rights discourse is increasingly drawn upon by the international heritage movement. First articulated by UNESCO during the 1960s, in a climate of postwar decolonization, demands by the indigenous included the right to "enjoy their own culture."[1] By the 1990s the perceived effects of globalization in homogenizing local cultures prompted the protection of diversity as a major theme of UNESCO's activity. The World Commission on Culture and Development's statement of 1995 regarding culture in the contemporary world—*Our Creative Diversity*—articulated a new ethic of diversity that reached its fullest expression in the *Universal Declaration of Cultural Diversity 2001*: here for the first time cultural diversity was termed "the common heritage of humanity," the defense of which was deemed to be an ethical and practical imperative, "inseparable from respect for human dignity" (UNESCO 2001: 20). But as Thomas Eriksen's discussion (2001) of *Our Creative Diversity* points out, UNESCO's insistence upon cultural difference contradicts its promotion of a universalist view of ethics. Placing an exoticist emphasis on culture as *difference*—focusing on those symbolic acts that demarcate boundaries between groups, and the traditions associated with a single set of people and their heritage or "roots"—is linked to the anthropological paradigms of cultural relativism and structuralism. Yet the report simultaneously deploys a more fluid conception of culture as globalization, creolization, and "impulses"—a view linked to poststructuralist deconstructionist approaches. Hence the report simultaneously defends "group rights," "the protection of minorities," and the identification of claimants as living "traditional lifestyles" while also expressing a commitment to the Universal Declaration of

Human Rights, which accords rights to individuals, not groups. As I have noted, the dilemma in this dual position is the inevitable conflict between collective minority rights and individual rights.

Too often, the reification of culture has trapped minority groups between the identification of claimants (as leading "traditional lifestyles") and their own need to change and engage with global processes to survive. By detaching heritage from the local context that gave it meaning, heritage may disenfranchise communities. For example, Kirshenblatt-Gimblett (2006: 2, original emphasis) argues that through its metacultural application of museological methods to living people and culture, an asymmetry is produced between "the *diversity* of those who produce cultural assets in the first place and the *humanity* to which those assets come to belong as world heritage." Others suggest that in practice local concepts of value may be incorporated into Western heritage methodology, for example through heritage tools such as Australia's Burra Charter (Sullivan 2005).

Recent moves toward broadening the concept of culture to include intangible cultural heritage make these problems more explicit. As practices, representations, expressions, knowledge, and skills "embodied in people rather than in inanimate objects," such heritage highlights its vulnerability to repressive cultural practices that contravene human rights—such as in Myanmar, where the use of forced labor for monumental restoration is argued to fall within the traditional Buddhist practice of merit-making. William Logan (2008; and see the chapter by Hodder, this volume) argues for the use of human rights instruments to regulate heritage practice and the development of a hierarchy of human rights forms, with rights to cultural heritage giving precedence to rights to freedom from slavery or torture.

Notwithstanding the recurrent framing of the relationship between universalism and cultural relativism as a dilemma, it seems more productive to avoid opposing these tendencies in any absolute fashion. Dichotomization of universal and local values overlooks the effects of globalization and transnational juridical processes: many indigenous peoples, for example, are adopting human rights doctrine, and referring to themselves as "indigenous"—that is, choosing to identify with a pan-global category. Such phenomena undermine bounded, static conceptions of culture as "values," expressing rather a dynamic, fluid conception of culture that is not necessarily at odds with human rights (for example, Merry 2003). To understand the "social life of rights" we need to attend to the actions and intentions of social actors, within the wider constraints of institutional power; ethnography of a network considers "the way people are drawn into a more globalised existence and become enmeshed in transnational linkages" (Wilson 1997: 13). Universality becomes a matter of context. Such analysis reveals the sets of conjunctural relationships that constitute local meanings and identities (e.g., Breckenridge et al. 2002), at the same time as transnational practices and categories are resisted and appropriated according to context; meaning does not reside within culturally bounded and set values but flows through global interconnections at local, national, and global levels.

Universal or Elite Value? Reinscribing the Nation

Recent critique of the notion of "outstanding universal value," a key concept for the World Heritage Convention, has pointed out that despite the centrality of liberal values and particularly participatory democracy to international heritage discourse, in practice such discourse reproduces elitist Western methodologies and ideals; through implementation at the level of the state, national myths continue to feature the heroic male, excluding other groups and notably women (Labadi 2005, 2006). Heritage management frameworks have overemphasized a bounded national past and underplayed the nation's involvement in transnational histories—for example of migration and empire.

Certainly, the nation has not lost its salience as the dominant framework for understanding the Australian past—it seems that an enhanced awareness of a global context has only increased this sense of distinctiveness, as nationalist legends are retold as a way of asserting membership in an international community. As the website of the federal Department of the Environment and Heritage (2007a) declares under the banner of "Australian Heritage," "By knowing our heritage—our past, our places and the source of our values—we can better understand our special place in the world."

A substantial body of critique has demonstrated (e.g., Byrne 1996; L. Smith 2000; Ireland 2002) that from its inception during the 1960s Australian heritage was used to tell a unique national story that masked internal complexity while marginalizing the nation's broader entanglement within transnational historical processes such as the spread of humans across the Pacific, indigenous settlement, and migration. As a form of historical consciousness, a focus of social memory and shared narratives, heritage has become the primary way in which the past is invoked by cultural institutions such as museums, enfolding conflict within a consensual national past (Ireland and Lydon 2005; Young 1999: 12–13). Heritage representations, grounded in archaeological and historical narratives, continue to reinscribe the national stories of colonial discovery and settlement, "pioneer" achievement, and freedom won through heroism at war. Such stories are linked to the values of "mateship," decency, courage, and egalitarianism that continue to structure current political arguments about issues such as immigration restriction, border defense, and the treatment of Aboriginal people. Postcolonial critique of the celebratory version of white settlement over the last two decades has shifted mainstream perceptions of the nation's origins, as indigenous experience and injustice have challenged or been integrated into public memory. Yet while such reappraisal is hotly contested (e.g., Macintyre and Clark 2003), the centrality of the nation endures.

Changes to the Australian national heritage regime in 2005 marked a tension between new modes of practice that acknowledge shifting public interests in the past—such as "intangible cultural heritage" and an emphasis on social value—and the heritage inventory as a tool for producing a seemingly apolitical and unambiguous national story. The new National Heritage List, where places are protected by stronger commonwealth powers, has further reified the concept of "national significance" within legislation, heightening the existing tendency for a national "high culture" to be promoted and policed by the state's normative cultural institutions. One issue here is that this method of assessing places according to their degree of national importance— whether they reach a particular "threshold" of significance—is clearly at odds with the way that Aboriginal people have valued their places, which has been inclusive rather than comparative. For Aboriginal people, representing hundreds of small linguistic and cultural entities across the continent, and excluded from citizenship until 1967, no allegiance to a national framework can be assumed. By the same token, the places held dear to these groups may not be considered important enough to qualify for listing at this level, omitting what many would consider to be a key aspect of Australian culture (Lydon and Ireland 2005).

Gallipoli: Hills, Ridges, and Gullies

Within an expanded international context, key national stories have been reanimated, as an enhanced global interconnectedness has simultaneously acted to strengthen a sense of distinctive Australian identity. The site of Gallipoli, in Turkey, has long held a sacred dimension for many Australians as the "birthplace of the nation" and as a symbol of shared core values. It marks the landing on April 25, 1915 of the seventeen thousand troops of the Australian and New Zealand Army Corps (ANZACs) in support of the British in a campaign that aimed to capture Constantinople and remove Turkey from the war. After a protracted and ruinous eight-month siege, the allies were forced to withdraw with heavy losses. But the "ANZAC spirit"—courage, endurance, initiative, discipline, and the mateship born of egalitarianism and hardship—continues to be invoked by Australians. In popular parlance, the ANZAC "digger" "rejected unnecessary restrictions, possessed a sardonic sense of humour, was contemptuous of danger, and proved himself the equal of anyone on the battlefield" (Australian War Memorial 2007).

Over recent years there has been an astonishing rise in the popularity of the ANZAC legend, evident in growing attendance at ANZAC Day ceremonies around Australia, in an explosion of books, films, and museums on the subject, and especially in the emergence of a well-trodden tourist pilgrimage to "the Peninsula," made possible by mass global travel. In 1998, two hundred people attended the Dawn Service at Anzac Cove on April 25, and this increased to ten thousand in 2000, and eighteen thousand in 2004, while organizers anticipate at least twenty thousand visitors for the one hundredth anniversary in 2015 (Parliament of Australia 2005: 27). On one level, this intensification of sentiment is testament to the privileged role of war in the national psyche. The surge in Gallipoli commemoration also coincides with the passing of the last "diggers," suggesting that we are witnessing a process of valorization as the campaign slips out of lived experience, and bereavement turns to nostalgia. This process also seems to have changed popular assessments of the campaign's military impact, for example, with one observer claiming: "I think it's important that we're now no longer saying . . . that in the First World War Australians fought other people's wars and died in vain, which I think was historically wrong, but also a dreadful commentary on the suffering of the fallen. I think what political leaders . . . are now saying is that the men and women who went there did a noble thing, and essentially the cause for which they fought was a noble cause" (Kirk 2000). Hence the ANZAC Day address of John Howard, the former prime minister of Australia, expressed the prevalent attitude in declaring that "today's generations thank you for making this a free society. We thank you for the way of life that we all enjoy" (Howard 2005).

Celebration of the legend reached a climax of sorts in late 2003 when Howard pledged that "the Anzac site at Gallipoli should represent the first nomination for inclusion on the [new] National Heritage List." But one year later it was revealed that the Turkish government had rejected this suggestion because it had concerns that the listing would compromise its sovereignty; instead the governments agreed to seek "some symbolic recognition" (Griffiths 2005). This rebuff followed a long history of commemoration and protection of the ANZAC territory: in 1923 the Treaty of Lausanne had provided for granting the land "in which are situated the graves, cemeteries, ossuaries or memorials of their soldiers and sailors" to host governments; in 1973 the Gallipoli Peninsula National Historic Park was listed in the UN's List of National Parks and Protected Areas; in 1996 the Gallipoli Peninsula Peace Park was established, expanding the area's extent to thirty-three thousand hectares (Cameron and Donlon 2005: 133). The Australian government's attempt to list the peninsula reveals the enduring link between identity and bounded territory; its decision—astonishing to some—to inaugurate a category of national icons by recognizing a place on the other side of the world expresses an impossible impulse to transcend time and space by incorporating this sacred site into the national body.

The physical terrain and bodily experience of visiting the peninsula has also become an increasingly important part of the legend, as pilgrimage to the site, especially by young backpackers, combines a spiritual quest, a search for family, a post-Vietnam revival of patriotic fervor, and a desire to witness a defining moment in the national past (Scates 2002, 2003, 2006). Crucially, the expatriate's need to reassert a unique national identity has led to the incorporation of the site into an international tourist itinerary, commemorating the importance of home for those so far away from it, and providing a sense of shared history: as one young visitor explained, the experience "gives you something to tie yourself to while you are travelling overseas" (quoted in Scates

2002: 12). For the global traveler, the Gallipoli pilgrimage provides the juxtaposition of a key moment in recent Australian history with the ancient, exotic world of the guidebook, enfolding them into a coherent, satisfying journey into the past.

Commemorative ceremonies such as the prime minister's ANZAC Day speeches also celebrate the harsh terrain, a dramatic landscape that evokes the hardship and futility of the campaign. Howard (2005) said, "Ninety years ago, as dawn began to break, the first sons of a young nation assailed these shores. These young Australians, with their New Zealand comrades, had come to do their bit in a maelstrom not of their making. Over eight impossible months, they forged a legend whose grip on us grows tighter with each passing year. In the hills, ridges and gullies above us the Anzacs fought, died, dug in and hung on. Here they won a compelling place in the Australian story." For this reason tremendous controversy surrounded roadworks carried out in 2005 in preparation for the ninetieth anniversary, causing damage to the landscape and exposing the remains of soldiers killed without burial in the conflict (Cameron and Donlon 2005). Following this scandal, further archaeological assessment of the landscape has been commissioned by the Australian government, but the scope of this proposal has been broadened to encompass the ancient archaeological remains of the peninsula, distancing the government from the recent controversy by downplaying the most recent episode of the place's significance in heritage terms, and contextualizing it within a much longer history of conflict and reconstruction.

Gallipoli: "Victories for Our Common Humanity"

The shifting significance of Gallipoli in the Australian imagination reveals how the configurations of meaning, memory, and identity that define national heritage are reinscribed on an international stage. The legend's importance has been enhanced by an increased popular awareness of its international context. One important aspect of this development is the perception of places such as Anzac Cove as symbols of reconciliation and international fraternity in the present (Howard 2005). These sentiments echo those of the diggers themselves, such as Harold Edwards, who in 2000 thanked the Turkish people for the friendship shown to those who invaded their land and stated, "We feel there's a collaboration of spirit which is going to be helpful to mankind, and if only we could all be friendly to each other, live and let live, free to do anything we like, provided it doesn't limit or interfere with other people's freedom or rights" (Kirk 2000).

The Turkish people also view the naval battle of Canakkale and the land battle of Gallipoli as founding national events, albeit for different reasons. The conflict at Gallipoli was Turkey's sole victory in five campaigns of the First World War, and it is seen as the last great victory of the Ottoman Empire. More particularly, it flagged the military capability of the Turkish leader Mustafa Kemal Atatürk and the beginning of his role in Turkey's transition to a secular republic. Atatürk still welcomes Australians who visit Turkey and invites them to remember their lost soldiers through a monument at Anzac Cove that reads:

> Those heroes that shed their blood and lost their lives . . .
> You are now lying in the soil of a friendly country . . .
> You, the mothers,
> Who sent their sons from faraway countries,
> wipe away your tears; your sons are now lying in our bosom
>   and are in peace.
> After having lost their lives on this land they have become
>   our sons as well.
> Atatürk, 1934

The Turkish government's announcement in 1997 of a proposal to nominate the military landscape to the World Heritage List received an enthusiastic Australian response, with one legislative body seeing these moves as "victories for our common humanity. . . . As a result of what happened, the Turkish community and the Australian community now feel a close affinity with one another" (N.S.W. Legislative Assembly 2003).

Today the Gallipoli legend reinscribes a core national myth, drawing upon collective values that resonate with a domestic audience while asserting the Australian nation's global parity within a league of nations; in some forms, the legend also promotes a vision of world peace and unity. The narrative's evolution exemplifies the process of selection and valorization involved in the national deployment of the international heritage system. However, despite the centrality of concepts of cultural diversity to the heritage system, and despite the integral importance of indigenous values and traditions to Australia's national story, the imple-

1 "Our heritage." *Courtesy of Cathy Wilcox.*

mentation of heritage by the state denies unwelcome claims grounded in culture and history—such as the Aboriginal demand for acknowledgment and restitution for the damage inflicted by colonialism. As the cartoonist Cathy Wilcox has succinctly shown, the former Australian government's endorsement of Gallipoli as the story of a nation forged in battle contrasts with its concurrent refusal to acknowledge more unpalatable aspects of colonial dispossession (see figure 1.1).

"Leave It in the Ground!":
Indigenous Participation in Transnational Processes

The refusal to acknowledge the negative consequences of colonialism has also characterized the development of Australian heritage in promoting a vision of indigenous culture as static, bounded, and shared, and in constructing a celebratory national story centering on progress and consensus. Yet indigenous peoples have also begun to draw upon international heritage discourse to assert their identities, protect their interests, and oppose injustice on the world stage. Some attribute this process to globalization, which has dissolved some boundaries only to strengthen others, namely the assertion of distinctive collective identities and claims to rights. Today minority societies do not simply choose between isolation or assimilation; rather, they seek self-determination "by choosing among various ideas, institutional models, and strategies, originating from dominant societies and global institutions, which hold out possibilities of protecting a distinct community's ability to make such choices in the future" (Niezen 2004: 2–3). Indigenous peoples may now choose to participate in international institutions in preference to national ones.

Such demands do not merely challenge the legitimacy of a state's claim to exclusive jurisdiction over territory, but in fact point toward new transnational modes of political community—what Duncan Ivison (2006a) terms an "emergent cosmopolitanism" that is compatible with universal notions of justice and yet is also rooted in particular, local ways of life. Such demands show how historical injustice can structure our moral concepts, presenting deep challenges to liberal theories of global justice. Appeals to international norms, together with their indigenous revaluation, also reveal a relationship between different levels (local, state, global), "which is pluralist but not state-centric, immanent but also universalist" (Ivison 2006a: 121). Indigenous scholars are showing that conceptions of local culture are changing, shaped by an international context and incorporating a universal notion of human rights without abandoning a sense of local meaning or distinctiveness. For example, the indigenous lawyer Larissa Behrendt (2002, 2003) argues that indigenous people have used the concept of rights to describe their political aspirations, advancing the concept of "internal self-determination" in a vision of increased indigenous autonomy within the structures of the Australian state. Some have also discerned possibilities in new categories of global identity—organizations such as the World Archaeological Congress for example, or the attempts of some indigenous groups to have their traditional countries or sites included on the World Heritage List.

The international campaign led by the Mirarr people of the Kakadu region in northern Australia exemplifies this process, to date successfully preventing uranium mining on the Jabiluka mineral lease. Uranium was widely discovered in the Northern Territory during the 1950s, and in the mid-1970s the Australian government commissioned an inquiry into the issues facing mining in the region. At the same time, legislation was passed that allowed Aboriginal people in the Northern Territory to gain legal title to their traditional land (the Aboriginal Land Rights Act [Cth], 1976). The inquiry's *Second Report* recorded the opposition of the Mirarr people to uranium mining on their land, noting that "some Aboriginals had at an earlier stage approved, or at least not disapproved, the proposed development, but it seems likely that they were not then as fully informed about it as they later became. Traditional consultations had not then taken place, and there was a general conviction that opposition was futile" (Australia Parliament 1977: 9). Nonetheless, the government proceeded against Aboriginal wishes, exempting the Ranger uranium mine at Jabiru from the traditional owner "mining veto" provisions of the Aboriginal Land Rights (NT) Act of 1976. The Mirarr continued to express their opposition to mining, despite the agreement it was pressured to sign in 1978. (For various accounts of these events, see Mirarr 2007; Katona 1998, 2001; O'Brien 2003.)

The Jabiluka Mineral Lease is 230 kilometers east of Darwin, covers 73 square kilometers, and is owned by Energy Resources of Australia Ltd. (ERA). It abuts the northern boundary of the Ranger Mineral Lease, which has been mined since 1980. Both leases predate and are excised from Kakadu National Park, which was inscribed on the World Heritage List in three stages between 1981 and 1992. Kakadu is one of the few sites included on the list for outstanding cultural and natural universal values—including as an outstanding example of significant ongoing ecological and biological processes, of superlative natural phenomena, and for containing important and significant habitats for *in situ* conservation of biological diversity. Its cultural values include its status as a unique artistic achievement and its direct association with living traditions of outstanding universal significance (Department of the Environment and Heritage 2007b). The predominantly Gundjehmi-speaking Mirarr (a group of twenty-seven people) have been traditional owners of this area "since time immemorial" and have always opposed mining on their land. As Jacqui Katona (2002: 29), the executive officer of the Gundjehmi Aboriginal Corporation, explains, "Most important to the Mirarr in defining themselves is their status as traditional owners. This status, authority and power is derived from their land, their relationship to land and each other and has developed over thousands of years." For Aboriginal people, their land is a "humanised landscape which is indivisible and immutable, and every natural feature has a name and meaningful mythological association. Place and person are inseparable, while past and present form a unity of ongoing creation" (John Mulvaney, quoted in Katona 2001: 196). In part, the park derives its preeminent status from its immense archaeological significance (e.g., R. Jones 1985), containing sites such as Malakunanja II (or Madjedbebe as it is called by the Mirarr), where one of the oldest human occupation dates has been recorded (Roberts et al. 1990), and this scientific evidence has powerfully substantiated indigenous claims of cultural longevity.

Despite Aboriginal opposition the Australian government gave approval in May 1978 for Pancontinental to drill at the proposed mine site so as to complete an environmental impact statement (EIS). In 1980 the Mirarr and other Aboriginal people in the region lodged a claim for their land under the Aboriginal Land Rights (NT) Act of 1976. In 1981, Pancontinental agreed with the Northern Land Council not to oppose the land claim if negotiations on Jabiluka proceeded. Under pressure, the Mirarr "consented" to the Jabiluka Mining Agreement entered into by the Northern Land Council and Pancontinental in July 1982. However, in 1983 the Hawke Labor government was elected to office with a policy of halting expansion of the uranium mining industry. The Jabiluka project was caught by this policy, which remained in place for the next thirteen years. In 1991 Pancontinental sold its interest in the Jabiluka mine to ERA, the owner of the Ranger mine. One condition attached to the deed of transfer was that the consent of "traditional owners" would be required before Jabiluka ore could be milled at Ranger. It is generally agreed that unless the ore is milled at the existing Ranger facilities, mining at Jabiluka would be economically unviable. In 1997 the Mirarr formally announced their opposition to this milling.

After the conservative Howard government was elected in 1996, it decided to develop uranium mining by recognizing the fourteen-year-old Jabiluka Mining Agreement. Represented by Yvonne Margarula, the senior traditional owner, and by Jacqui Katona, the Mirarr embarked upon a public campaign to prevent this, involving a speaking tour, public forums, alliances with other Aboriginal groups, and international lobbying, including a submission to the World Heritage Bureau that prompted tremendous media attention. The Mirarr deployed the heritage concept of "living tradition" in their campaign, representing their culture as an ancient survival within the modern world and explicitly contrasting the purity of living indigenous tradition with the vices of modernity. They argued that "the Mirarr communities have had a presence in the Kakadu region for up to 65,000 years. If the mine proceeds, our survival is at risk. . . . Culturally, surviving clans are struggling to hold on to their cultural traditions and pass them on to new generations in the face of the establishment of mines in sensitive and culturally important areas . . . and in the face of alcohol and other substance abuse and the blandishments of the mass consumer culture" (Gundjehmi Aboriginal Corporation 1998: 34–35). In their view, the World Heritage Convention protects "one of the few remaining islands of traditional culture from the relentless forces of development [and constitutes] a legal bulwark defending the integrity of Mirarr society" (Katona 2002: 36). They pointed out that the benefits of modernity as measured in the "quality and length of life of the Aboriginal residents" have not transpired as the result of mining on their land (Gundjehmi Aboriginal Corporation 1998: 36; and see Katona 1998).

In August 1997 the government approved the mine pursuant to an EIS that had been prepared by Energy Resources of Australia, despite widespread public and expert opposition, including serious concerns of the government's own conservation division, Environment Australia, about long-term damage to the environment, Aboriginal people, and World Heritage values.

Jabiluka's "Detour Via Europe"

In mid-1998 the seemingly inexorable pressure toward mining was eased by two key events. First, because the Mirarr continued to withhold their consent for Jabiluka ore to be milled at the ERA's Ranger uranium mine, the government announced approval of the Jabiluka Milling Alternative, whereby uranium would be milled at Jabiluka. Second, Margarula and Katona attended a meeting of the UNESCO World Heritage Bureau in Paris and convinced the bureau to send a mission to investigate the dangers to the Mirarr living tradition and the environment associated with the Jabiluka uranium mine. In October 1998 the UNESCO World Heritage Committee Mission visited Kakadu and Canberra, and the following month handed down its finding that the Jabiluka mine posed serious threats to the cultural and natural values of the Kakadu World Heritage Area (UNESCO 1998). This decision, and the unprecedented threat of placing a site on the World Heritage "in danger" list without permission by the host country, caused huge embarrassment to the Australian government, which refused to comply with UNESCO's resolution. In December the World Heritage

Committee accepted the mission's report and resolved that construction at Jabiluka should cease until the Australian government could prove that the identified threats to Mirarr culture and country were being avoided. It was widely perceived that the Howard government had been ambushed by the globalization of environmental political power, which over the preceding decade had moved from "alternative" to mainstream within European governments. Bob Brown, a Green member of the Australian Parliament, and his colleagues, who were often ignored in national debates, were able to command "enormous entrée" among the coalition Green governments of Germany, France, and Italy, successfully securing the adoption of a Green anti-Jabiluka motion by the European Parliament in Brussels. The federal government had been outflanked by a coalition of international indigenous, social activist, and environmental groups: as one observer noted, "It didn't even see him [Brown] coming, mainly because he detoured via Europe" (Milne 1998).

Nonetheless, following an expensive lobbying campaign mounted by the federal government, in July 1999 member nations of the World Heritage Committee voted overwhelmingly against imposing an endangered listing on Kakadu (Department of Environment and Heritage 2007b). Environmentalists were bitterly angry, but Katona's (1999) response was measured, noting that "the World Heritage Committee has recognised very strongly that there are culture impacts to the living tradition of the Mirarr people. . . . The Australian Government has bound itself to . . . reporting back to the committee and ensuring that there is progressive opportunity back in Australia, to deal with issues of living tradition. . . . It's been an interesting opportunity, because it's one that we haven't had domestically."

The World Heritage Committee emphasized the fact that "whilst fully respecting the sovereignty of States on whose territory the cultural and natural heritage is situated . . . States Parties . . . recognise that such heritage constitutes a world heritage for whose protection it is the duty of the international community as a whole to co-operate." The committee was also of the opinion that "confidence and trust building through dialogue are crucial for there to be any resolution of issues relating to the proposal to mine and mill uranium at Jabiluka. . . . In particular, a more substantial and continuous dialogue needs to be established between the Australian government and the traditional owners of the Jabiluka Mineral Lease, the Mirarr Aboriginal people" (UNESCO 1999).

Throughout 2000 both sides of the dispute lobbied the World Heritage Bureau—the anti-mine coalition to strengthen its hand against the mine, and the Howard government to prevent properties being listed as "in danger" without the government's agreement. In early 2002, Rio Tinto (which had acquired the deposits through its takeover of North Ltd. in 2000) announced that it would "mothball" the project, subsequently filling in the excavation and giving the traditional owners the right to veto future development at the site—perhaps for financial reasons as well as because of criticism for failing to act on discussions concerning sustainability and community relations (Bachelard 2003). No doubt its other, less controversial global mining interests absorbed its attention from this time onward (Heathcote 2003). Although periodic review points remain scheduled for renegotiation between the company and the traditional owners, the Mirarr remain opposed to the mine being developed.

In 2006 the Howard government took steps to increase Australia's stake in the global nuclear energy market, reopening the issue of nuclear energy as a domestic power source, in abeyance since the 1980s. With a change of government in late 2007, it remains to be seen whether this direction will be pursued, in a context of worsening drought and hotly contested debate about a national response to climate change.

Conclusion

Gallipoli and Jabiluka demonstrate the limits, as well as the potentialities, of heritage conceived as a cosmopolitan network of ideas, practices, and policies. As I have described, world heritage discourse acknowledges diverse ways of valuing the past, such as "intangible cultural heritage," while retaining elitist Western values, such as the application of "universal outstanding value" as a threshold of assessment. Conceptually tensioned between a commitment both to universal values and to local cultural meanings, the logical disjunction between universalism and cultural relativism is often framed as an inevitable clash between collective cultural rights and individual rights. Further, emancipatory conceptions of an interconnected world are undermined by the persistent reinscription of narratives that deny indigenous perspectives in the pursuit of national politics. However, in its complex implementation, and the concrete ways that people are drawn into heritage networks, new alliances and practices may transcend the ambiguous dualisms of national and international or local and global. Indigenous participation in the international sphere undermines simple dichotomies of scale, showing that local indigenous culture and identities are interpenetrated by the global community and notions of universal human rights, producing new ways of seeing the past.

As demonstrated by the privileged status of the ANZAC legend in the Australian imagination, national narratives may be given fresh power within a global context. The legend's valorization of a particular vision of the Australian past has been promoted by the federal government, which has even attempted to lay claim to a site on the other side of the world, while at the same time refusing to address internal, Aboriginal experience. In this incarnation Australian heritage has emphasized the nation's collective youth and innocence; the national anthem reminds us that "our home is girt by sea," a geographic boundary that naturalizes this imagined entity, rather than seeing it as a "set of relations that are constantly being made and re-made, contested and re-figured" (Burton 2003: 6–7). But rather than being "young and free," indigenous people are *not* free to choose; rather, they remain constrained by neocolonial myths and processes enshrined in national structures.

By contrast, in mounting their international campaign, the Mirarr asserted their rights as custodians of traditional land and culture through a new pan-global alliance with environmental groups and national and international NGO networks. They created and exploited new international sources of leverage, connecting with the assertion of local commons, expressed through indigenous land rights and conservation values. This multi-scaled form of resistance drew a local place and its concrete resources into a global space of social action, "both inside and outside the imperial core" (Goodman 2006: 165). Key to their campaign was their representation of their culture as ancient and pure, in a narrative of the survival of a living tradition threatened by the ills of modernity. The discourse of world heritage underpinned by a rich archaeological resource fueled demands for the protection of local rights to culture and country; the Mirarr identified themselves as members of a new category comprising "all indigenous people around the world" (Katona 2002: 29), articulating a fluid understanding of culture that accords with notions of universal rights. Despite the problems entailed in balancing the protection of individual rights against collective values, transnational juridical and heritage processes work to undermine relativist notions of difference even as they reemphasize boundaries and strengthen a sense of local identity. In practice, the Mirarr people's participation in transnational linkages and networks, resisting and appropriating according to their need, produced new identities and meanings that nevertheless remain Aboriginal. The Jabiluka campaign shows how the dichotomization of universalism and cultural relativism within transnational networks such as heritage fails to account for the complexity of this cosmopolitan process.

Notes

Many thanks to editor Lynn Meskell for her patience and verve! For comments on early drafts of this paper I am indebted to David Cameron, Jacinta Cubis, William Logan, and Linda Young. In particular I thank Liam Brady for his generosity in sharing his research materials and expert knowledge of Jabiluka with me. I am also grateful to Joan Beaumont and Anne-Marie Hede as conveners of a workshop, "Anzac Day in the New Millennium: A Multi-disciplinary Approach," sponsored by the Academy of Social Sciences Australia and Deakin University, for the opportunity to present my argument concerning Gallipoli. I also thank Barbara Voss and other faculty in the Department of Anthropology at Stanford University for the opportunity to present a shortened version of this paper. I gratefully acknowledge the support of the Centre for Australian Indigenous Studies at Monash University.

    Epigraph quote: "Advance Australia Fair" was composed by Peter Dodds McCormick in 1879; it has been Australia's national anthem since 1984.

  1 See Article 1 of UNESCO, *Declaration on the Principles of International Cultural Cooperation* of 1966; Article 27 of UNESCO, *International Covenant on Civil and Political Rights* of 1966, in force from 1976; Yusuf 2005; and Logan 2008.

Ian Lilley

2 ✵ STRANGERS AND BROTHERS?

Heritage, Human Rights, and Cosmopolitan

Archaeology in Oceania

Archaeologists are archetypal strangers in most if not all of the localities in which they work. This is certainly the case in Australia and Melanesia, where this chapter is set. Can they truly hope also to be brothers,
part of the family, in such places, to the point where the universalizing
scientific tenets of archaeology and heritage management can be reconciled with local perspectives on the past and its material reflection? I
see such reconciliation as a straightforward matter of human rights. It
would be a major step forward if the profession were to treat all those
among whom it works justly, as equals, and in a way that does not simply do them no harm, but also delivers them some good as they define
it. I have no doubt that a cosmopolitan perspective is critical to any
such endeavor. Yet as Kahn (2003: 404) reminds us, cosmopolitanism
as generally conceived in Kantian terms has its problems, most resting
on its embeddedness in the Western intellectual tradition. This position greatly diminishes the claims of universality to which such cosmopolitanism aspires, because "all forms of cosmopolitan thought—those
that following Kant aspire to treat a diverse humanity for 'what they
have in common'—will inevitably begin with culturally-inflected pre-
suppositions about what it is that constitutes that common humanity
(a human essence, whether defined biologically or otherwise)" (Kahn
2003: 411).

Kahn recognizes that the solution is not just for archaeologists to
listen more to "the Other," or help make more "recognition space" for
other voices to be heard alongside ours, vital though such actions might
be. Rather, we should aim to produce *truly* cosmopolitan knowledge
"out of the encounter between representatives of different cultures,"
that is, *new* knowledge that could not "conceivably have pre-existed
the . . . encounter" (Kahn 2003: 411). To do otherwise is to remain

stuck in the unproductive essentialist oppositions of "us and them," "Self and Other." The trick, of course, is to produce this new knowledge in a manner that reduces and, ideally, ultimately eliminates the enormous gulf between the power wielded by Western scholars and that of their interlocutors in local communities (Kahn 2003: 411). The only real means of doing this is to go beyond inviting local people or descendent communities to participate in work in the field and the laboratory, attend conferences, or perform ceremonies on site to ensure spiritual safety and the like. As the succinct overview by Conkey (2005, esp. 15–18) makes clear, it has long been understood that relinquishing power in a politically effective fashion means bringing local conceptualizations into archaeological practice in ways that guide interpretation at a theoretical level as well as field and laboratory studies at the level of technical execution.

The New Frontier

This is where things get disturbing and even intolerable for many in the profession. It is one thing to ask that colleagues consult local descendent communities, but are significant numbers of them really ready to make the conceptual and practical adjustments that are necessary to take the process of power sharing to its logical conclusion? As is appropriate in a discussion of cosmopolitanism, this question can be recast in Kantian terms to ask whether most archaeologists, as outsiders, can make the leap from being visiting strangers to being resident guests in accepting the hospitality of their hosts. As is clear from Scham's contribution to the present volume, making such a move reconfigures the social distances among the parties and so changes how outsiders and hosts alike are recognized and expected to behave. When an archaeologist ceases to be a visiting stranger, the latitude usually allowed owing to the stranger's naïveté is dramatically restricted if it does not evaporate altogether, and he or she is expected to conform much more closely with vernacular custom and practice. If a visitor takes up residence like a guest but refuses to conform in this manner, he or she will be received as neither stranger nor guest, but rather as a difficult and potentially dangerous interloper (Dikeç 2002; Rundell 2004).

Archaeology has long been in this latter position, but global currents of decolonization will inevitably force archaeologists to become guests in the societies in which they work, despite the readily apparent difficulties that this entails. The alternative would see the profession denied access to archaeological resources to a far greater extent than happens now. This struggle for the hearts and minds of archaeologists as well as local communities is not fundamentally different from the upheavals being experienced in a great many other fields of scholarly enquiry, and indeed at the highest levels of international affairs, as the process of decolonization plays out (Lilley 2008). It is worth noting in this context (and in relation to the chapter by Scham, this volume) that Kant thought outsiders should *not* attempt to switch from being strangers to being guests because of the claims that this makes on both the host and the outsider. Moreover, he explicitly excluded nonstate societies from those among which his "universal" rules of hospitality should apply, because they were too different from states to be included (Dikeç 2002; Harvey 2000). Such questions of difference are still the crux of the matter, insofar as dealing with state-level actors generally entails dealing with institutions that despite inevitable cultural differences share basic characteristics that reduce the uncertainties of cross-cultural communication (as attendance at—indeed, the very possibility of—any successful international conference instantly makes clear). Dealing with nonstate or substate actors, though, and especially indigenous minorities, frequently entails encounters with profound difference for all parties, despite the long-term and ever more intense cross-cultural interaction of the post-Columbian period.

When we focus on indigenous societies as an exemplar of such difference, we see that the difficulty for archaeologists who try to "go native" (or the reverse for Native scholars) is that there is a strong chance they will fall between the two stools they aim to straddle—the indigenous one and the Western scientific one. This is because they could give up the intellectual and technical positives of science to attain a goal they might be unable ever to reach owing to the "blood and soil" factor well known to scholars of identity: their lives lack some experiential dimension or, in even more essentialist terms, the "single drop of blood" that is critical to an authentic indigenous perspective (Conkey 2005: 26–29). For Native scholars the matter would be to achieve a truly Western standpoint (e.g., Atalay 2006; Cachois 2006; Dugay-Grist 2006). Archaeologists making the attempt thus risk becoming marginalized as neither fish nor fowl, like Naipaul's (1964) unfortunate Mr. Biswas. If they pull it off, though, they should gain the sort of mongrel cosmopolitanism paraded so provocatively in exactly such terms by the likes of Salman Rushdie (e.g., 1989). This hybridity is both founded upon and most effectively able to produce truly cosmopolitan new knowledge of the sort envisaged by Kahn (2003). It should also provide an appropriate vantage point from which to deploy such knowledge ethically to the benefit of all parties involved (Lilley and Williams 2005).

Looking Up from Down Under

The latter prospect has led *inter alia* to the idea that archaeologists should become "discrepant" (Clifford 1992), "rooted" (Appiah 2006a), or "vernacular" (Bhabha 1996) cosmopolitans. As the other contributions to this volume all discuss, this means archaeologists should acknowledge their inevitably Western roots and decolonize their practice to make it meaningful in the varied local settings into which they insert themselves (see also L. T. Smith 1999). This process has gained a lot of momentum over the last decade and now reaches well beyond the settler societies in North America and Oceania where most headway has been made (e.g., Atalay 2006; Bedford 1996; Bernardini 2005a; Byrne 2003, 2004; Colwell-Chanthaphonh and Ferguson 2006; Conkey 2005; David and McNiven 2004; Lilley 2000a; Lilley and Williams 2005; McGuire 2004; Nicholas and Andrews 1997; Sand 2000a; Sand et al. 2006; Watkins 2000). It now encompasses places as diverse as the more isolated parts of Great Britain (e.g., S. Jones 2003) and at least some Asian countries, such as Japan (Mizoguchi 2004) and Taiwan (e.g., D. Blundell 2000). Australia, though, seems to be at the cutting edge. This is not simply self-serving chauvinism on my part, as the words of my North American colleagues such as Atalay (2006) and Silliman (2005) make clear. As I have described elsewhere (Lilley 2006a), pictures like those painted by Atalay and Silliman are reinforced by concrete evidence from the world of international cultural heritage management. The World Bank leans heavily on the Burra Charter of Australia ICOMOS (http://www.icomos.org) for guidance on the "world's best practice" in its management of "physical cultural resources" (http://www.lema .ulg.ac.be), as did the Chinese government in its recently promulgated "China Principles" (http://www.icomos.org/australia). Much the same is happening in Iraq, where "world-class site management plans based on the Burra Charter" are being developed (http:// hnn.us).

The Burra Charter was originally designed to deal with historical non-indigenous built heritage, but it has evolved along a trajectory that has seen its wording and applications expand to accommodate pre-European indigenous heritage as well as shared colonial heritage. The transformation of other aspects of the country's archaeological practice has advanced at the same time. This is most emphatically not to say that Australian archaeology and cultural heritage management are flawless paragons of cross-cultural virtue, a question to which I presently return. Nor is it the case that individual colleagues elsewhere in the region, such as New Zealand or New Caledonia, or for that matter elsewhere in the world, such as Canada or the United States, lag appreciably behind Australia in any critical respect. For the moment, though, it seems that as an institution Australian archaeology is enjoying unparalleled success in bringing archaeological and indigenous interests together as a matter of conventional professional practice at a national scale (Lilley 2000b).

Just why this is so remains a matter of conjecture (Lilley 2006a; Smith and Jackson 2006). It seems plain, though, that it hinges in significant part on two factors. The first is the profession's recognition beginning in the early 1980s that decolonization raises profoundly important questions about archaeology's relations with descendent communities. The second has been the pragmatism of the discipline's response (i.e., calling a spade a spade and doing what was needed to make things work). This pragmatism is typically quite creative and at times even radical by global standards, as Smith and Jackson's (2006) recent contribution leaves in no doubt. Yet all is not as rosy it might seem, if Thorley's (1996, 2002) periodic interventions are anything to go by. On the basis of his extended experience with remote desert people, Thorley (1996: 10) points out that even in situations where archaeologists (as well as ethnographers, linguists, and the like) have endeavored to practice reflectively in a manner that is sensitive to issues of authority and representation, indigenous people usually have other priorities. If they value research at all it is because of the social and economic opportunities it offers and in fact the value to them of such opportunities can make it hard for them to challenge researchers or their findings. Thorley (1996: 10) observes that "interest in the relationship could be misinterpreted as approval of the researcher's findings while from an Aboriginal point of view the content of the research may be seen as unimportant. Different values are assigned by each side. As a society without a Western tradition of impersonal academic debate there is little incentive to argue with the researcher and risk the relationship; in fact there may be a tendency to defend the researcher in order to preserve the relationship, no matter how misguided the representation."

Elsewhere Thorley (2002: 110) draws attention to a similar question of values in connection with notions of cultural heritage management in remote settlements. He is specifically concerned with the idea that the value of material items often lies in their intangible qualities, which might require them to decay physically to be preserved, what Colwell-Chanthaphonh calls the "preservation paradox" in his contribution to this volume. Thorley (2002: 110) notes that while indigenous Australians use archaeology and heritage management for their own purposes, this does not mean that they invest in Western archaeological or heritage management values. For Thorley (2002: 110), "This raises the question of whether the transmission of new cultural forms and practices must include a corresponding transfer of meaning. It could be argued that rather than the internalisation of Western values, adoption of contemporary heritage practices by Indigenous groups reflects a conscious manipulation of terms of their own priorities and interests."

There is significant variation in the wider indigenous Australian community, which means that issues like those Thorley raises apply to greater or lesser degrees in different places. Nonetheless there is a very high level of physical (and virtual) mobility within that wider community, and so a great deal of communication about values and the like, both from the remote areas to more settled regions and vice versa (e.g., Lilley and Williams 2005: 237–38). This means that attitudes such as those Thorley describes exhibit a strong underlying continuity across the continent despite the above-mentioned variation. Thorley does not think the gap between indigenous and Western approaches can be bridged. "While there has been growing support for Indigenous perspectives," he writes (2002: 123), "it is doubtful whether wider recognition will be sufficient to resolve underlying conflicts of value." In his earlier article (Thorley 1996: 11) he pointed out that "both Byrne . . . and Hodder . . . have put forward arguments for 'indigenous archaeologies' in Australia, but neither have described how these might translate into practice. Despite the best of intentions, the notion of indigenous archaeology is itself the product of an external and more powerful society. This is particularly ironic, since it would seem that the basis of such approaches would draw from Aboriginal forms of identification, rather than a framework not of their making."

Talking the Talk

Thorley (1996: 11) believes the way forward is to accept that the foregoing intellectual differences are too great to span and to get on with things using approaches that respect the reasons for the differences. I understand perfectly well what he means, having worked in remote parts of Australia and the Pacific for many years. I am not yet convinced, however, that all is lost. Language is a large part of the issue for Thorley. He (1996: 9) points out that English is not the first or even second language of choice in much of remote indigenous Australia. I would add that Standard English is not even the language of choice among indigenous Australians in most rural and many urban areas, where either some local form of "Aboriginal English" or the Kriol of northern Australian and the Torres Strait is commonly used in everyday contexts. The barriers to effective communication created by such linguistic variation should be apparent, especially as they reflect often profound differences in worldview.

One obvious way such barriers might be breached, though, is for more archaeologists not only to take care with the academic language that they use so that they can avoid neocolonial overtones (e.g., Smith and Jackson 2006; Watkins 2006), but also to learn to speak local languages or lingua francas, and indeed to produce appropriate written material in local languages, too. This idea goes a long way beyond simply being able to translate for basic comprehension: in my experience it can have crucial social and political implications in cross-cultural encounters. Clendon (2006: 50) underscores how important the matter is in much of northern Australia, for instance, where a "religious mandate linking land and language" underpins "a positive social expectation that visitors . . . should speak the language of their hosts if they can."

Numbers of archaeologists around the world do this now, of course. I do not speak any of the myriad local indigenous languages of Oceania, but I do speak Papua New Guinea's lingua franca, *tok pisin*. So do most of my colleagues who work in the region. This gives us reasonable linguistic access in other parts of Melanesia, where related but slightly different creoles and pidgins are spoken. It helps in Torres Strait and Aboriginal northern Australia, as well, where the related Kriol is used. The same obviously applies in reverse for colleagues working in these varied areas. I have not yet produced an academic or even a popular publication in any of these languages, though I have presented informal written reports to community authorities in *tok pisin*. Others are in the process of producing school texts, primers for heritage rangers, and the like (e.g., Kaltal et al. 2004). Just as Anglophone colleagues working in Latin America or Francophone Africa frequently learn Spanish, Portuguese, or French, I have also learned (still rudimentary) French to help with research I am developing with local and expatriate colleagues in the Francophone Pacific. I will endeavor to learn at least enough of the language of the island on which we work to allow me to follow conversations among community members and my multilingual local colleagues as the project advances. The issue of language is crucial to this particular study, a matter to which I will return.

Being conversant with the vernacular of their research areas would help archaeologists get their message across, but there is much more to it than using a bit of "restaurant French" to get by. The latter is necessary but obviously far from sufficient. Whatever language they use (though the more locally specific the better), the heart of the problem is that archaeologists need to frame their research in terms that makes sense to the communities with which they pursue their research. In Thorley's terms, they must appeal to the sorts of values and perspectives local people are likely to bring to the matter. As described elsewhere (Lilley 2006b; Sheehan and Lilley 2008), my current approach to this question takes off from Merry's (2006) discussion of the vernacularization of transnational ideas concerning human rights and violence against women. Like these ideas, archaeology has been resisted to varying degrees by indigenous people around the world as "an alien, Western import not suited to local normative systems" (Merry 2006: 38). If archaeologists are to engage local people with the discipline in their local context, the discipline's universalizing scientific conceptual apparatus needs to be "framed and presented in terms of existing cultural norms, values and practices" (Merry 2006: 39). Merry (2006: 39) calls this process "indigenization," which she defines as the "symbolic dimension of vernacularization." The term applies regardless of whether the recipient population is indigenous in the sense commonly used to refer to colonized native minorities.

One problem with orthodox approaches to vernacularization and indigenization can be that they seek "resonance" on the seemingly sensible grounds that a "frame needs to be resonant with cultural traditions and narratives to be appealing" (Merry 2006: 39). Research summarized by Merry (2006: 41) shows, though, that "resonant discourses are less radical than nonresonant ones . . . [so] resonance is a costly choice because it may limit the possibility for long-term change." This is because "frames" can restrict who may and may not speak and what can and cannot be said, and thus they can flatten variability and downplay dynamism and contestation (Merry 2006: 41). On these grounds, Merry (2006: 41–42) advocates "a more dialogic analysis" that recognizes variation and competition between views. This fits closely with my experience of the interactions between archaeology and local and especially indigenous communities over the last few decades. If we recognize rather than avoid this reality we will be better equipped to benefit from the conceptual and technical opportunities a dialogic—or, in Appiah's (2006a) terms, conversational—process has to offer.

To gain maximum leverage from these insights, vernacularization and indigenization must proceed from one specific end of a range of variation in the degree to which "local cultural forms and practices are incorporated into imported institutions" (Merry 2006: 44). This end is that of hybridization, an interactive form of cross-fertilization "that merges imported institutions and symbols with local ones, sometimes uneasily" (44). Merry (2006: 48) describes the novel phenomena that result as being "thickly shaped by local institutions and structures." At the other end of the range, where many past and some contemporary attempts at collaboration by archaeologists are still lodged, there is "replication," which is only "thinly adapted to local circumstances" (Merry 2006: 48). Although she makes no mention of vernacular (or any other form of) cosmopolitanism, the link between Merry's line of thought and Bhabha's is obvious and compelling.

Creating functional and mutually rewarding hybrids will not be easy. To paraphrase Merry's comments about international funding for human rights NGOs, the funding and permitting agencies that facilitate archaeology are still strongly oriented toward hard science and are thus likely to react skeptically to thickly indigenized research proposals. By the same token, the local (and especially the indigenous) communities with which archaeologists work are likely to remain skeptical about the discipline owing to continuing historical grievances or the imperatives of contemporary identity politics. We must try, though, if we believe that vital matters of mutual interest are in the balance (Lilley and Williams 2005). Though this issue cuts in both directions, archaeologists should make the greatest effort at this stage, given that they still have by far the most institutional power (despite the passage of NAGPRA and so on). The first steps are to show our colleagues that there are other ways of seeing the world and on that basis train them to think outside the square.

I know some archaeologists will react badly to this suggestion, but there is nothing "fringe" or "New Age" about such thinking. It is just good anthropology. As Geertz (1983: 70) taught us a generation ago, "Accounts of other people's subjectivities can be built up without recourse to pretensions to more-than-normal capacities for ego effacement and fellow feeling." As he went on to say, though, "Normal capacities in these respects are, of course, essential, as is their cultivation, if we expect people to tolerate our intrusions into their lives at all and accept us as persons worth talking to." Applied anthropologists have been putting precisely these sorts of ideas into practice in this fashion for at least a decade (e.g., Sillitoe 1998a, b). Furthermore, as Strathern (2006) recently pointed out, approaches like the one I am advocating are ontologically not appreciably different from the "ideas trade" entailed in the interdisciplinary approaches to research that everyone is being encouraged to pursue these days and, we might add, with which archaeologists have long been acquainted (cf. Warren 1998). To quote Strathern (2006: 192) quoting Galison (1996: 14), the idea in all of these varied areas of endeavor is to "work out an intermediate language, a pidgin, that serves a local, mediating capacity" (also see Osborne 2004).

The following examples from Australia and New Caledonia discuss how my colleagues and I are trying to develop such mediating intermediate languages of this sort. Both projects are in their infancy and so may appear somewhat underdeveloped here. My descriptions should be read as "dispatches from the front" rather than reports on mature case studies. Moreover, the two projects involve very different researchers and descendent communities in very different historical, linguistic, and current sociopolitical contexts. This means that what we are trying to achieve, the way we are going about it, and the language and tone

I use here to describe the projects all differ markedly between the two cases. In particular, the Australian example can be described in Merry's language as seeking to frame archaeological approaches in terms that are resonant with Aboriginal perspectives, whereas the New Caledonian project takes a more radical, nonresonant tack to bring archaeological and local views together.

Aboriginal Ways of Seeing

I have previously described some of the efforts in which I have been involved to take such matters forward in Australia (Lilley and Williams 2005). These projects place indigenous concerns uppermost, but otherwise they entail relatively straightforward collaboration between Aboriginal and archaeological interests. More recently I have tentatively headed off at more of a tangent with an indigenous nonarchaeological colleague to explore the deployment in archaeology of contemporary indigenous visualization of landscape (Sheehan and Lilley 2008). I stress that it is still very much work in progress that remains largely at the experimental conceptual level. We hope it will ultimately build on the advances of landscape archaeologists such as Bender (1993), Bradley (2000), Thomas (2001), and Tilley (1994). Their approaches incorporate ethnographic information about hunter-gatherer perspectives on landscape, but they do not, themselves, apply it to the landscape archaeology of hunter-gatherers rather than of agriculturalists. Our focus on landscape is intended to complement the attention to matters of history that has characterized much of the effort to indigenize the discipline so far (e.g., Bernardini 2005a).

We advance the general proposition that the way that the physical landscape appears to Aboriginal people—its visual organization or structure—contains spiritual information concerning the organization or structure of the landscape that constrains people's behavior. This means, to give a simplified example, that if the landscape in a particular place looks like a snake, it actually is, in its spiritual guise, that snake and must be approached as such. Different sorts of sites will occur in particular places along the snake's body in accordance with the spiritual information inhering in this or that locality. Moreover, the investigation of those sites requires them to be treated as part of that specific sort of living organism (in this case a snake), which will be related as kin to at least some of the local indigenous community. Digging, in particular, but also other forms of study such as mapping and photography need to be undertaken with this fact in mind.

In some parts of Aboriginal country, whole landscapes form images representing the meaning embedded in those localities. Faces might be discernable in vegetation patterns or rock exposures, for instance, because that country contains stories concerning the people whose faces can be seen. This sort of imagery is usually considered of profound significance to Aboriginal people because ontologically it is a manifestation of the ancestral knowledge of all the relationships between people and their environment that is held within the land (see also Godwin and Weiner 2006: 128–32). The nature and distribution of sites in such locations, and the archaeological work that can be done there, will depend on what the stories are about and whom they concern. The challenge for archaeologists is to learn to see what is there, just as they all once had to learn to see with "an archaeological eye" when they were students, so they could distinguish stone artifacts from natural rocks, or agricultural terraces from natural rotational slumping. Bender (2006: 313, original emphasis) describes learning to see in the Aboriginal way as coming "to recognise the *animate* nature of the . . . world" (cf. Bradley 2003).

Intellectual property negotiations prevent us from discussing specific landscape images at this stage, but opportunities are arising to develop a visual archaeology that can reveal what my co-researcher calls "these edifices of Aboriginal culture" to a wider audience. Furthermore, we have not yet developed our position to the point where we can carry out field trials. We have, however, described initial visualization experiments undertaken as classroom exercises in undergraduate courses for mainly non-indigenous university students in Aboriginal and Torres Strait Islander studies. Though lack of space prevents detailed discussion here, the results are very encouraging (see Sheehan and Lilley 2008, for initial findings). Other Australian archaeologists are doing broadly similar sorts of research. Some of the most innovative work is that led by David and McNiven in the western islands of Torres Strait, between mainland Australia and New Guinea. These researchers and their indigenous and non-indigenous collaborators have sought to "historicize the spiritual" by archaeologically examining various sorts of sacred sites, including ritual mollusk-shell arrangements (David et al.

2005), dugong ("sea cow") bone mounds (McNiven and Feldman 2003), intertidal stone alignments (McNiven 2003), and caches of turtle-shell masks (David et al. 2004). Building upon contemporary Torres Strait Islander knowledge and belief, they are beginning to show how "chronological changes in the use of these sites inform us about historical developments in Islander ontology and their ritual orchestration of seascapes and spiritual connections to the sea" (McNiven and Feldman 2003: 169). David (e.g., 2006) has done similar work elsewhere in Australia.

Godwin and Weiner (2006) also provide some excellent case studies of how such opportunities are changing the way archaeology is being done in Australia, in this instance in cultural heritage management. They remind us how Aboriginal people read their country and the distribution of sites upon it in terms of past and present actions of ancestors and Dreamtime entities. This contrasts with the attention archaeologists would normally pay instead to the distribution of resources, though the latter is directly linked to Dreamtime activity and so is encompassed by Aboriginal perspectives in any event. Understanding this as a general principle means that archaeologists can develop appropriate analogical models that can guide research even if the specifics of the Dreamtime stories relayed by contemporary Aboriginal people differ from those in the past. The idea is not simply to replace conventional models based on past environmental patterns and the like, but rather to add a dimension to such models so they can better account for more of the complexities of past human behavior in modes that make sense to local indigenous people.

Godwin and Weiner also underline techniques by which meaning is negotiated through dialogue and conversation rather than imposed in such readings, highlighting the difference between Aboriginal and Western approaches to the creation and management of knowledge. If Aboriginal people working on a project were uncertain about the meaning of a particular site, landscape feature, or occurrence during fieldwork (such as the unusual activity of a swarm of native bees, in one instance), they took their questions to more knowledgeable people (Godwin and Weiner 2006: 132–35). The sites in question were usually unexceptional archaeologically, but their indigenous meanings had to be fathomed if their occurrence was previously unknown to the Aboriginal field crew or if they exhibited some noteworthy feature, such as a particular richness of worked stone.

As mentioned earlier, I am also involved in indigenizing research in the French Pacific, specifically the Loyalty Islands in New Caledonia some 1,200 kilometers off the northeast coast of Australia. The project includes local archaeologists of Kanak and European descent as well as colleagues from metropolitan France. It focuses on Tiga, the smallest of the inhabited islands in the Loyalties. Pilot studies concluded in 2006, laying the foundation for more intensive studies in years to come. To avoid continual highly repetitive citation, I note that the following is abstracted from our recent successful proposal for further work, which drew heavily on the extended treatment of the issues in question by Sand et al. (2006).

The project is motivated primarily by the fact that New Caledonia is unique in Pacific prehistory. The founding Lapita occupation some three thousand years ago differed in several critical respects from that elsewhere in the distribution of the Lapita cultural complex, while the ensuing trajectories of change produced levels of cultural diversification unparalleled anywhere in Remote Oceania, the region beyond the main Solomon Islands chain, uninhabited prior to the Lapita dispersal (Kirch 2000: 148; see Lilley 2004 for general discussion of Lapita; and Sand 1998, 2000b for overviews of New Caledonian prehistory). The problem for archaeologists is that their interpretations of New Caledonia's dynamic human history conflict with local Kanak views. The latter are largely either based on or a reaction to Eurocentric historical and ethnographic pictures developed before modern archaeology began in the region. These scenarios portray "traditional" Kanak society as small-scale and semi-nomadic, and governed as petty chiefdoms. Such descriptions have been completely undermined by the archaeological demonstration that the last millennium before European contact was actually characterized by a densely inhabited landscape based on labor-intensive horticulture organized by strong chiefdoms that collapsed as a result of massive demographic and cultural disruption between initial European contact in 1770 and the French takeover in the 1850s.

This dramatically nonresonant archaeological reappraisal of "traditional Kanak culture" as it has been understood for generations does not sit well with politicized indigenous New Caledonians, the bulk of whom receive their higher education in metropolitan France, or indeed with the expatriate scholars who have promoted it. Nor do scientific archaeological explanations of the often dramatic cultural changes that occurred over the preceding three millennia of human settlement in the archipelago. As much of the work of the New Caledonian Department of Archaeology makes clear (e.g., Sand 2000a; Sand et al. 2006), just what archaeology is "for" in New Caledonia remains as unclear to most Kanaks as it does to many indigenous people in other settler societies. The nub of the matter is that like those in other colonial societies, pre-archaeological settler interpretations in New Caledonia ascribed all evidence for pre-European change to successive waves of invasion much like the one represented by European colonization. The political effect of this approach is to diminish indigenous people by characterizing them as just another group of migrants who have no more claim to special land and cultural rights than any other group in the modern population. In reaction, Kanak activists and their European sympathizers have attacked the entire concept of history and long-term cultural change as an oppressive neocolonial device. As in other settler societies, the offending pre-archaeological interpretations have been replaced with a simplistic two-step model in which a static indigenous past where everything was peaceful and well organized was suddenly destroyed by Western colonization. In this scenario, the population of New Caledonia is polarized as "indigenous" or "invaders." This division emerged in the late 1970s. It led to a major political emergency, including periods of undeclared civil war in the 1980s, the aftereffects of which have not entirely dissipated.

The finality with which this stark and highly politicized model was asserted almost completely stifled Kanak interest in history, as witnessed by the almost complete absence of historically oriented research conducted by Kanaks, except the handful working in the New Caledonian Department of Archaeology. This reveals how difficult the indigenous community still finds it to replace the recent ideologically motivated two-part account with a more complex archaeologically informed conception. The principal criticism of archaeologists in this context is that they place too much emphasis on historicizing the past and not enough on validating models of stasis that in the view of indigenous activists provide the basis for historical rights. Although rooted in profoundly different approaches to history, this divergence in perspectives has been exaggerated by synchronic ethnographic models that left Kanaks and other native peoples "outside the realm of world historical experience" (Peterson 2000: 27).

Ironically, because archaeology underwrites a diachronic view of indigenous societies, some indigenous people are adamant that their past—as described ethnographically—and the authenticity of identities built upon such pre-archaeological descriptions will be completely undermined by the historicization that archaeology entails. Contemporary political considerations are thus pivotal to the debate, because all nonliterate societies have oral traditions that clearly illustrate the dynamism of their pasts. A significant part of the problem is that the materiality of archaeological evidence is much harder to dismiss on political grounds than oral-historical testimony, which is often disputed within and among local communities, not to mention by settlers. Archaeology's "solid" data thus fuel the fires of contemporary competition over land and other resources and archaeologists are inevitably drawn into current political maneuverings.

These internecine struggles belie the claims of those Kanak activists who contend that there is a unified "Kanak people." Contestation of this sort also generates practical and intellectual difficulties for archaeologists and friction between them and sections of the Kanak community. Coping with such complications will be a small price for archaeologists to pay if the melding of a vibrant, archaeologically informed history with contemporary perspectives can produce cosmopolitan new knowledge that helps modern indigenous communities show that they have never been "people without history" at the same time that it renders archaeological interpretation more nuanced at the human level. In addition to any direct positive impact it may have on local conceptions of history and long-term change or on archaeological approaches to analysis and explanation, new knowledge that situates indigenous people well and truly within "world historical experience" should also improve the light in which they are perceived by non-indigenous people in multicultural settler societies such as New Caledonia. Western and other cultures that place a high value on "progress" and material acquisition still generally portray the alterity of indigenous peoples as a marker of moral and intellectual deficiency. By demonstrating that archaeologists have as much to learn from indigenous people as the reverse, the successful production of hybrid new knowledge should provide local people with additional ammunition in their fight for social and political justice.

To the foregoing ends, our project on Tiga aims to produce cosmopolitan new knowledge by integrating archaeological field and laboratory research with an understanding of how local people conceptualize and mark culturally important sites and landscapes today, including the sites under archaeological investigation. A still embryonic methodology is being developed in collaboration with the Tiga community to integrate the results of the two parts of the study in this manner. At its most basic level, archaeological results and contemporary Kanak histories and conceptualizations of cultural landscapes will be brought together as the project proceeds, through constant dialogue between the local community and the professional archaeologists and oral historians (who include Kanaks from the Loyalties and elsewhere in New Caledonia). The extent to which a single, new, hybridized cultural history is feasible can only be determined through continual conversation as the results from the two different facets of the project become known and can be compared, contrasted, and where possible reconciled.

An exploratory project of this sort would be unnecessary if it were already known just how this process would advance. As is the case in the Australian work discussed earlier, though, we aim eventually to go well beyond the use of oral history or tradition to augment archaeological interpretation along the lines advocated by Whiteley (2002). There is certainly no cookbook to follow, but we envisage a procedure similar to the constant negotiation described earlier among the Aboriginal people working with Godwin and Weiner (2006). In accordance with the principles outlined by Merry (2006), the idea is to foster conceptual hybridization that is "thickly shaped by local institutions and structures," rather than replication that is only "thinly adapted to local circumstances." Language will be a critical factor in this process. We work not only in French, New Caledonia's lingua franca in the absence of pidgins like those used elsewhere in Melanesia, but also in the local Kanak language(s), as made possible by working with local Kanak archaeologists and oral historians. This last should allow us to get much closer than we otherwise would to native conceptualizations of the past and the role(s) played in the present by archaeological materials as well as other tangible and intangible facets of local cultural landscapes.

A Concluding Note of Cautious Optimism

The projects I have outlined above all pivot on the proposition that archaeologists cannot remain as visiting strangers rather than resident guests if they want to reduce the distance between their interpretations and those of the local and especially indigenous communities in which they work. In this the projects I have sketched here share a great deal with the post-processual approaches of Bender, Thomas, Tilley, and others. Recent appraisals of their work, such as Brück's (2005) assessment of the rise of phenomenology in British archaeology and Fleming's (2006) critique of post-processual landscape archaeology, therefore raise issues that are also of relevance to the sorts of research with which I am involved. The issue of most concern in both cases is "whether contemporary encounters with landscape . . . can ever approximate the actual experience of people in the past" (Brück 2005: 54). To my mind, this question subsumes or is at least closely related to many of those Whiteley (2002) raises regarding the evidential reliability of oral tradition. As archaeologists should know better than anyone else, people and their values change, as do physical landscapes. It should therefore be clear to us that "describing our own [or contemporary indigenous people's own] embodied encounters with landscapes tells us more about contemporary perceptions and preoccupations [and the modern environment] than it does about the past" (Brück 2005: 57).

Despite this reservation, Brück (2005: 65) applauds the fact that the approaches of Tilley, Thomas, Bender, and others have forced archaeologists to "reconsider the social significance of landscape and to explore concepts of the person that are very different to modern Western models of the individual." The studies I have described are intended to take this process further by according non-Western models a centrality that is absent from the sorts of post-processual approaches that Brück canvasses. Intriguingly, Fleming's (2006) altogether more pointed review takes an unexpected turn to argue much the same thing as Brück in this regard. After lambasting Tilley and others for visiting a postmodernist methodological nightmare upon the discipline, Fleming concedes that "it is good that landscape historians who work in prehistoric periods are exploring the potential of cognitive approaches, experimenting with new ways of writing, and have been reminded of the ever-present issues of 'the dearth of people.'" Even more fascinatingly, though, he argues that conventional landscape archaeology has done this sort of thing all along. In his estimation (Fleming 2006: 271–72, original emphasis), this is because it is about doing "*work* in the field . . . in the open air. An outsider at first, the landscape archaeologist has no choice but to become engaged in the landscape, to become an insider as a consequence of acquired knowledge. . . . Landscape archaeologists are not obsessed with the attainment of hard-edged objectivity always and everywhere, and our field discourse always and necessarily involves thinking about the intentionality and mindsets of people in the past." As Fleming (2006: 272) himself recognizes, this contention is a far cry indeed from "Binfordian scientism," despite what would seem to be their shared intention to debunk post-processualism and, by extension, the sort of approaches with which my colleagues and I are experimenting. In this connection, it is salutary to return to Wylie's (1992: 16–17) discussion of the manner in which the "conceptual and methodological commitments of scientific archaeology . . . have tended to direct attention away from what Binford . . . has vilified, in his most uncompromising defenses of processual approaches, as 'ethnographic,' internal variables . . . he considers explanatorily irrelevant and scientifically inaccessible, such as gender . . . [and] other symbolic, ideational, social, and broadly 'ethnographic' dimensions of the cultural past."

Conkey's (2005) recent consideration of the "intersections" of feminist and indigenous archaeologies updates us on many of the questions Wylie took up in that landmark essay. I would expect scholars of Wylie's and Conkey's reputations as theoretical innovators and activists to have left processualism far behind in recognizing that greater attention to "relational dialogues" and other issues of language should make it "an easier step to engage with oral traditions and oral accounts as a viable line of evidence in the interpretation of archaeological materials and the cultural past" (Conkey 2005: 29–30). I am still somewhat disbelieving of the possibility that we have come so far that an "anti-post-processualist" as red in tooth and claw as Fleming not only explicitly distances his position from Binford's but also asserts that the orthodox approaches he esteems have "always and necessarily" involved ostensibly post-processual perspectives. It gives me great hope, though, that far more of my colleagues than I imagined might be prepared to take the leap from outsider to insider, or, to return to Kant, from visiting stranger to resident guest in their relations with local communities. They might say they are comfortable with the sorts of approaches I have sketched out here because they have always done such things, if under other names. I am certainly not going to split terminological hairs if it helps archaeology take local conceptualizations of history seriously. Ultimately this is the only way the discipline can live up to its obligations to advance the human rights of the people among whom it seeks to work.

Note

First thanks go to the descendent communities I have worked with in Australia and Melanesia, especially the Aboriginal and Kanak communities with which I am currently involved. I am grateful to Lynn Meskell for asking me to contribute to this volume and to my director, Michael Williams, for supporting my work through thick and thin. I also greatly appreciate the friendship and collegial support of the co-researchers on the projects discussed here, particularly Norm Sheehan in Australia and Christophe Sand, Jacques Bole, and John Ouetcho in New Caledonia. The research I have described has been funded by the University of Queensland Aboriginal and Torres Strait Islander Studies Unit, the New Caledonian Department of Archaeology, the Centre National de la Recherche Scientifique, the Embassy of France in Australia, the Academy of the Social Sciences in Australia, and the Australian Research Council. Versions of this chapter have been presented in Brisbane and Stanford and it benefited from discussion in those venues as well as from the insights of this volume's peer reviewers.

Denis Byrne

3 ✹ ARCHAEOLOGY AND

THE FORTRESS OF RATIONALITY

If environmental conservation conjures its own global spatial universe out of a deliberate focus on the needs of biodiversity rather than the needs of people living in or near protected areas (Hughes 2005: 157; Tsing 2000), archaeological heritage conservation might be said to conjure a global spatial universe of its own. This latter is an order of space defined by the discourses of archaeology and heritage. It exists in the imaginary of national and international archaeology and heritage practice and is largely unknown to local people despite the fact that they dwell in it. It is unknown to them insofar as the old objects and places that populate this space—the equivalent of nature conservation's biodiversity—are known to them in other terms.

Practitioners of archaeology and heritage conservation who are committed to a cosmopolitan view seek to accommodate these local realities via a "values approach" that endeavors to canvass, document, and assess the multiple meanings that old objects and places can have (e.g., Avrami et al. 2000; Byrne 2008) using such value categories as the scientific, the social, the aesthetic, and the historical. A parallel values approach is employed by many nature conservationists who reject the "fortress conservation" approach (Borrini-Feyerabend et al. 2004; Brockington 2002, 2004; Colchester 2004: 94; Harmon and Putney 2003). As the name implies, fortress conservation seeks to protect national parks from local people, who frequently become the subject of expulsion and forced resettlement (see chapter 4 by Meskell, this volume; Phillips 2003: 12).[1] They join the ranks of the world's "conservation refugees."[2]

My geographic focus here is Southeast Asia, a region where forced resettlement of people from archaeological conservation zones is by no means unknown today. There is, however, another dimension to fortress conservation in the Southeast Asian heritage field that, though less traumatic for those on its receiving end, is far more pervasive. I refer to a discursive barrier, erected by archaeologists and heritage practitioners, that excludes serious consideration of popular religion as a means by which old objects and places are contextualized within the world of everyday life. Citing the case of Thailand, I describe the ways in which people attribute magical supernatural qualities to the material past. I argue that we are prevented from acknowledging, let alone accepting, this situation because of the way our discourses are constituted in a secular-rationalist Western worldview that grew out of the Protestant Reformation and the Enlightenment. This worldview not merely rejects the magical supernatural; to a significant extent it was founded upon this rejection.

For the most part we do not find practitioners of archaeology or heritage conservation actively blocking people from interacting with the material past via the magical supernatural. What we find instead is an effacement of that whole contextual frame. This effacement is clearly incompatible with a cosmopolitan respect for plurality; but how do you respect a plurality that you cannot see? I propose that a thick cosmopolitanism requires history: we need to be willing to excavate our own practice in order to know how it is constituted.

The Local, the Popular, and the Magical

Before embarking on a history of the effacement of the magical supernatural in the specific case of Thailand it seems advisable to make some general observations about popular culture and popular religion. As a belief system and field of practice, the magical supernatural in Thailand is spread across all segments of the population, albeit not evenly. The belief in the supernatural empowerment of certain objects and places appears to be shared by farmers, construction workers, upcountry Buddhist monks, politicians in Bangkok, waiters in the tourist hotels of Phuket, pop singers, noodle stall owners, and taxi drivers, among others. It transcends the rural-urban divide and the class divide, as well as the divisions of gender and age. And yet it is absent from the school curriculum, will not be found in modern orthodox institutional Buddhism, and tends not to be mentioned in heritage impact assessments, heritage inventories, government museums (except as a relict phenomenon), or at those other sites that have their origin in the formation of the modern Thai nation-state (beginning in the mid-nineteenth century).

Thai popular religion includes the often overlapping practices of animism, non-canonical Theravada Buddhism, Hinduism, and elements of Chinese popular religion. Animism in Thailand is centered on the *phi*, those territorial spirits associated with particular trees, fields, forests, swamps, and other natural landscape elements. Described as "nature spirits" by Tambiah (1970: 316), they inhabit road intersections, bridges, and mountain passes. Turton (1978: 124) shows how "non-specific forest spirits" become specific when forest areas are cleared for houses or cultivation. *Phi* commonly occupy archaeological sites and ruins (e.g., Wijeyewardene 1986: 147–48). When the ruins of temples are discovered in the jungle it is assumed they are occupied by *phi* and mediums may be brought in to attempt to channel the spirit and thus identify it. The many millions of spirit shrines that continue to be erected in Thailand map the tangible presence of the supernatural but so do the tens of thousands of Buddhist stupas, the physical fabric of which is frequently considered to be empowered and miraculously efficacious. At a popular, non-canonical level, the realms of animism and Buddhism overlap and entangle.

In addition to the localized cults of territorial spirits there are those cults that have a virtually unlimited spatial spread. The emergence in the 1980s of the cult of the former Thai king, Chulalongkorn (Rama V, reigned 1868–1910), exemplifies this phenomenon. At the spatial epicenter of the Rama V cult is the equestrian statue erected to honor him in the Dusit area of Bangkok. While amulets and images of Rama V appear not to have originally been associated with rituals seeking supernatural assistance (for example, in providing invulnerability), the cult's more recent popularity among rural and urban laborers has led to the incorporation of these ritual objects within established patterns of Thai supernaturalism (Jackson 1999a: 168). Cult objects of Rama V have jumped the national borders of Thailand and are now to be found, for instance, on the *hing bucha* (worship shelf) of Thai restaurants all over the world.

Almost any object that is old is likely to be considered *saksit* (supernaturally empowered). The historian Lorraine Gesick (1995: 62) cites a case from southern Thailand where the remains of an old dugout canoe were excavated by villagers who placed them in the local temple. But, "gradually," she tells us, "as villagers took away slivers as talismans, [the canoe] almost entirely disappeared." It was said that some of the people who took the wood died because they could not withstand its supernatural power.

A key principle in Thai popular religion is that of contagion, the belief that supernatural power transmits via physical contact. This is seen in the way caves once occupied by famously empowered forest monks become empowered places and in the way powerful monks transmit efficacious power to amulets and statues of the Buddha by praying over them while linked to them via sacred cotton threads. Similarly, the efficacious potential of an ancient stone adze is transmitted to the water in the earthenware jar in which it is kept and protects those who drink the water against illness and lightning strikes (Sorensen 1988: 4). To think of such objects as having agency is not to imply they have intentionality (Gell 1998; Meskell 2004: 77); it is we human agents who initiate the "causal sequences" that give objects the power to act on us (Gell 1998: 16). Within these limits, however, the magical agency possessed by a great array of objects and places in Thailand means that they are not available to be "managed" by us in the conventional mode of heritage management. The agency they have means that they have the capacity to act upon us as much as we have the capacity to act upon them. We might usefully think of local people being in dialogue with old objects and places; we might consider the appropriate relationship of conservators to these objects and places as also one of dialogue (Byrne 2005: 59–60).

The magical supernatural is better thought of as a geographically unbounded discourse than a localized practice. Particular cults may be quite localized, but the magical supernatural, as a way of giving meaning to the material past, constitutes a kind a lingua franca that exists across the whole of Southeast Asia and beyond and arguably brings into being a transnational community. I would guess that the cosmopolitan urge, to the degree that it currently exists in archaeology, takes the form of an openness to the particular meanings that different cultures give to old objects and places. It is cosmopolitan at the level of culture. The magical supernatural, however, is a discourse in the sense that archaeology is a discourse. It is global in its reach and it characterizes the relationship that the greater proportion of humanity has with the material past. The sheer prevalence of the magical supernatural in Asia, Africa, and Latin America alone, as against the very restricted penetration of archaeology and heritage discourse into the realm of everyday life in these areas, urges us toward a cosmopolitanism that is comfortable with magic.

Western Disenchantment in Southeast Asia

By the time it achieved a significant presence and influence in Southeast Asia, the West had rejected the existence of the magical supernatural. Yet even in the case of those Southeast Asian lands that, unlike Thailand, were acquired as colonies, the West never enjoyed sufficient influence to significantly influence the practices and beliefs of popular religion. What it did achieve was a significant influence on elite society in these lands and on the path these elites took to modernity. It profoundly influenced the discourses of archaeology and heritage as and when they developed in Southeast Asia. In this section I offer a brief overview of the West's experience of "disenchantment" and its influence on Thailand's modernity.

In European medieval Christianity God was a living presence in the landscape, manifest in the miraculous efficacy flowing from saintly people, sacred relics, and sacred places (Bender 1993: 253–55). In part this was a reflection of the way early European Christianity had assimilated elements of preexisting religions. Many of the sacred sites of paganism were physically overlain with churches, altars, and shrines. Wells and springs were named for Christian saints and martyrs and their water became "holy water" used in Christian rituals (Strang 2004: 88; K. Thomas 1971: 48). Christianity's scheme of the supernatural consisted of the ordered realms of the diabolical, the natural, and the divine supernatural, the first governed by Satan, the second two governed by God (Le Goff 1988: 12). The character of the divine supernatural came to be heavily informed by the cults that formed around saints and their relics (Geary 1986; Meskell 2004: 45–46). The sites of saints' graves and the relics themselves were believed to be animated by miraculous efficacy and were a target of appeal by the faithful for favors in this life as well as in the next. There are a great many parallels between medieval Christianity and contemporary Thai popular Buddhism. These include the latter's syncretic overlap with animist belief and ritual, the superimposition of stupas and monasteries onto animist sites such as hilltops and rock outcrops, the cults that form around saint-like "magic" monks (Jackson 1999a), and the ascription of miraculous power to Buddha images, consecrated amulets, and the physical fabric of religious structures, including stupas (Byrne 1995). The key characteristics of the world of Thai popular religion should thus be familiar to us, in the West, as they are so much a part of our own past. The Protestant Reformation, beginning in the sixteenth century, had the effect, however, of distancing us from our medieval selves. I suggest that it is the Reformation in us that makes it so hard for us to accept the validity of the magical supernatural as a way of making sense of the material past in today's world.

In the Protestant view, particularly the Calvinist view, religion was to be a matter between one's soul and a God who dwelt in heaven (Eire 1986: 312). This is Latour's (1993: 32–35) "crossed-out God," the God of modernity, relegated to the sidelines. In repudiating belief in the presence of magical and sacramental forces in the landscape, the Reformation effectively removed God from nature as an active, causal force, opening the natural world up to understanding through learned inquiry via discourses such as natural history and archaeology. Counter-Reformation Catholicism, for its part, validated the worship of holy images but warned against regarding them as possessing power in their own right. It did not exactly resile from the miraculous—this was hardly possible, given the central place in Catholicism of the sacramental act of transubstantiation, in which the bread and wine are magically transformed into the body and blood of Christ. Instead, it sought to carefully manage popular engagement with the miraculous. We see this at Lourdes, where pilgrims are discouraged from treating the spring water as magically efficacious (Eade 1991: 55–68). The revolution in European scientific thought that took place in the seventeenth century complemented key tenets of the Reformation: "The notion that the universe was subject to immutable natural laws killed the concept of miracles" (K. Thomas 1971: 643).

One thus speaks of the "disenchantment" (Weber 1946: 155) of the post-Reformation world. One problem with this proposition is that for many of Europe's Christians, God continues to be immanent in nature—for them, the relics of the saints continue to be miraculous. Nor have other manifestations of the supernatural entirely faded from modern life experience, as Jay Winter (1995: 54–77) shows in relation to the First World War. Another problem is the common assumption that post-Reformation disenchantment encompasses the non-European world, Asia for instance. While, as described in the next section, most Asian countries have experienced state-driven campaigns against "superstition," nothing similar to the Protestant Reformation ever actually occurred there. Contrary to the Weberian "rationalisation thesis," in Asia capitalism and modernity have not been accompanied by disenchantment. On the contrary, Asia's rapid economic development in the last decades of the twentieth century has been accompanied by a surge in popular religion (Keyes et al. 1994; Jackson 1999b).

The first Europeans to arrive in Siam, toward the end of the seventeenth century, set foot there nearly two hundred years after Martin Luther (1483–1546) formulated his ninety-five theses in 1517. The first to reach Siam were Portuguese explorers and traders in 1511; Portuguese Dominican missionaries followed in 1567. The Dutch opened factories at Patani in the south of Siam in 1602 and six years later at the capital, Ayuthaya, where Japanese traders, many of them Christians who had fled persecution in their homeland, were already established (D. Hall 1981: 380). The British East India Company followed in 1612. In 1664, during the reign of King Narai (reigned 1657–88), French missionary priests were allowed to build a church and a seminary at Ayuthaya and they were soon carrying out missionary work elsewhere in Siam. The other Christian missionary project of the most influence in Siam was that of the American Protestants beginning in the mid-nineteenth century.

The Protestant missionaries were particularly concerned to attack what they saw as the idolatry of popular Thai Buddhism and they used every opportunity to try to demonstrate to Thais that images of the Buddha and other deities were not imbued with divine power. On occasion this involved destroying the images in order to demonstrate their powerlessness (e.g., Perkins 1884: 452), a strategy in the iconoclastic tradition of Calvinism. At around the same time that Western missionaries were attacking "idols," Western art historians were appropriating them to the discourse of aesthetics. While the outcome was the reverse—the physical fabric of the idols was privileged and preserved for aesthetic edification—the discursive shift was in other ways the same. That is to say, it moved away from the idea of religious objects as divinely empowered and toward the idea of them as cultural property or cultural heritage. Being perhaps the most obvious "collectible" in Thai material culture, statues of the Buddha began to be acquired by Western traders, travelers, and missionaries as early as the seventeenth century though it was not until the second half of the nineteenth century that the European discourse of art history began to inform this collecting. In 1917 George Coedès, formerly director of the Ecole Française d'Extrème Orient in Hanoi, was appointed to the National Library in Bangkok and it was only then that art history and archaeology began to be practiced on a professional basis in Siam. Unlike most missionaries, the art historians and archaeologists would treat the images of Buddha respectfully or at least "neutrally" though still via a discourse that focused purely on their formal materiality. It was a discourse that was immune, so to speak, to the divine power and efficacy of the objects.

This discursive shift would be manifest spatially as thousands and then, by the twenty-first century, hundreds of thousands of images of Buddha began their migration out of Asia toward the museums, the mantelpieces, and the glass coffee tables of the West. Some of these images are ancient, some are modern sacralized images, and many are unsacralized images produced specifically for the Western market. Not all of these images, however, have moved into the purely secular realm of art history; many have been acquired and displayed by westerners who, though not Buddhists, do appear to invest them with some degree of spirituality. Interesting here is Meskell's (2004: 177–94) view that the modern collecting of ancient Egyptian religious objects (and reproductions of them) does not entail a leaving behind of their original spiritual, magical properties. She observes the "quasi-ritual piety" with which many modern consumers "revere" them (2004: 178) and she notes that while "consumption may to some degree cheapen the grandeur of religion . . . commodities can also democratise the spiritual" (2004: 182). In the case of Thai images of Buddha, an added permutation of their migration westward has been that this transfer has been accompanied by a movement in the same direction of Buddhism itself. Beginning in the nineteenth century, many in the West have been attracted to a certain construction of Buddhism emphasizing holistic thought (Bruce 2002) and meditative, transcendental practice. But the Buddhism championed in the West tends to be "a religion without gods, a type of spiritual self-effort totally dependent upon the will of a determined practitioner" (J. Holt 2003: 112). This could hardly be further removed from the kind of popular religious practice in Thailand that mediates local relations with the material past. As Jackson (1999a: 251–52) observes:

In popular religiosity—whether practised within an animist, Brahmanical, or even a Buddhist symbolic frame—neither the clerical bureaucracy of the Buddhist *sangha* nor notions of non-self (*anatta*) or transcendent salvation (*nibbana*) play a significant role. In Thai popular religion it is the 'self' of the spiritually powerful personality that is of paramount importance, and spiritual practice centres on establishing a strong personal relationship between the devotee and that personality. This is the case whether the spiritual personality is a Buddhist monk, a Hindu god, a former king of Siam, a Chinese deity, or a locality spirit believed to inhabit an old tree, a cave, a mountain top, or other natural feature.

Returning to the nineteenth-century missionaries, we observe that they brought more than religious faith with them to Asia; they also traveled with the science of medicine, the technology of the printing press, and an enthusiasm for modern education. Apart from their undoubted altruistic, humanitarian aspect, the medical services provided by missionaries were intended to help undermine superstitious beliefs (e.g., Cort 1886: 318). On the whole, Thais accepted the efficacy of modern medicine, but it seems unlikely that they saw it as canceling out the efficacy of the magical supernatural as recourse against illness and injury. In present day Thailand, where modern medicine is almost universally employed, invulnerability tattooing and recourse to the spirits and deities, channeled by mediums, are both extremely common in the remedy and prevention of bodily harm as well as spiritual assault (Kitiarsa 1999). Even more prevalent in contemporary Thai society is the wearing of invulnerability charms, many of which are small stamped clay amulets (Chirapravati 1997; Turton 1991). They are ritually sacralized by powerful monks and are frequently "archaeological" in the sense of having been dug up from archaeological sites or "released" from stupas that have been broken open (Byrne 1999: 276; Tambiah 1984: 204).

What the above discussion indicates is that in Thailand, as in many other parts of the non-Western world, the discourses of science and the supernatural can be practiced simultaneously, and by millions of people they are so practiced. The practice of one does not necessarily lead to the collapse of the other; the idea that they are antithetical is one of the conceits of Western modernity. I would argue that in a similar way and in the course of everyday life Thais participate in and practice the public discourse of heritage while simultaneously practicing

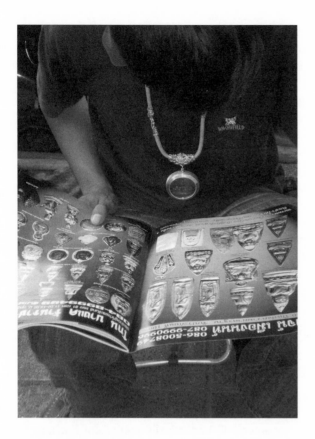

1   An amulet stall-holder in central Bangkok is reading
an amulet collectors' magazine. He is wearing one of
the currently popular Jatukam Ramathep amulets.
Photograph courtesy of the author.

supernatural Buddhism. For example, people visiting the iconic heritage site of Sukhothai in Central Thailand participate willingly in the
state-sponsored narrative of this ancient religious center as the first capital of the Thai nation (Peleggi 1996) while at the same time venerating
and propitiating individual structures and objects within the complex
as supernaturally empowered entities. This display of cosmopolitanism on the part of ordinary Thai folk stands in contrast to the manner in which archaeologists and heritage practitioners tend to police a

strict taxonomy aimed at preventing the archaeological meaning of the material past from being contaminated by supernatural meaning. Like the nineteenth-century missionaries, we archaeologists put our faith in the incompatibility of science and the supernatural. One effect of this is that it prevents local practice from having a say in heritage management, but another is that it denies heritage practice the richness of discourse plurality and contributes to the experiential and intellectual aridity and blandness that characterize heritage practice.

The interest taken in the natural history of Siam by Western travelers and sojourners from around the middle of the nineteenth century was similar to the advent of modern medicine in that natural history constituted a self-contained, explanatory system with no interest in integrating existing indigenous forms of knowledge to itself. Its self-consciousness as a modern science insulated it from traditional knowledge. Natural history embodied a classificatory approach based on observable physical attributes (Foucault 1973). It detached observed objects such as plants, animals, trees, soils, and rock formations from their local social and religious settings, moving them into the new global setting represented by geological tables and biological taxonomic systems. "Natural" objects might be acknowledged to have quaint meanings assigned to them in local custom and folklore, but this had nothing to do with their essential meaning as "natural" phenomena. Taxonomic systems such as Linnaeus's could accommodate the biological species and other natural phenomena of Asia as easily as those of Europe. As Mary Louise Pratt (1992: 30) observes, circumnavigation of the globe by Europeans brought into being not just a "planetary consciousness" but a "European global or planetary subject": "One by one the planet's life forms were to be drawn out of the tangled threads of their life surroundings and rewoven into European-based patterns of global unity and order. The (lettered, male, European) eye that held the system could familiarize ("naturalize") new sites/sights immediately upon contact, by incorporating them into the language of the system" (Pratt 1992: 31).

The Western sojourners who made up most of the membership of the Siam Society, founded in Bangkok in 1904, traveled widely in Siam, sometimes resided in the provinces, and were in a position to make just the kind of firsthand observations valued by natural history. The indefatigable Colonel Gerini (1904), in his exhortation to his fellow members of the Siam Society, suggested 217 topics that warranted their interest. Under the letter "a" were to be found Aboriginal, agriculture, alchemy, alimentation, amulets, ancient cities, animals, Annamese, anthropology, archaeology, architecture, arms, arts, and astrology. "Every casual observer," he urged, "even if not interested in the subject, can help by merely noting down such facts as fall under his knowledge" (1904: 1). The Siam Society, under royal patronage, functioned somewhat like its sibling learned societies in the surrounding European colonies, including the Malayan Branch of the Royal Asiatic Society and the Ecole Française d'Extrême Orient. It served to gather and centralize knowledge that was made available to various branches of the sciences and humanities in the metropolitan centers. These forms of knowledge—for example, archaeology, botany, ethnology, geology, zoology—had no precedent in the indigenous cultures of the region, which they marginalized by creating authorized bodies of knowledge whose center of gravity was situated in Western centers of learning. In relation to these centers, places such as Siam, Malaya, and Burma constituted the "field."

Much more was involved, though, than the simple collection of knowledge and the channeling of it into Western repositories. As Foucault (1967, 1973) was at pains to point out, the great classifiers of eighteenth-century Europe strove to transform the disorder of preclassical knowledge into a new type of order. The "disorders of illness," for instance, were transformed "into something akin to the order of plants" (Elden 2001: 127). It is tempting, by analogy, to see the classificatory schemes of art history and archaeology, which arranged Buddhist stupas and other structures into types and subtypes, as an effort to remedy and displace a similar disorder. This disorder was the perceived madness of a system of popular knowledge that ordered these monuments according to their record of miraculous efficacy or according to the spirits and deities known to reside at or in them, information that was recorded in shrine chronicles as well as being the subject of a vastly detailed and continually updated body of oral local knowledge.

Art historical and archaeological taxonomy is based on visual observation of material fabric and form. Popular religious knowledge is not indifferent to materiality but is interested primarily in materiality's effects. It finds evidence of these effects in dreams and apparitions and messages channeled by mediums. It carefully observes the flow of good fortune emanating from places and objects actively venerated or propitiated; equally, it registers the flow of ill fortune consequent upon the neglect or mistreatment of the same objects and places. These two knowledges coexist, but while the former is legitimated as proper knowledge by national and international institutions, the latter, though it flourishes at a popular culture, is denied this legitimacy.

Western knowledge systems operating in Siam rendered local popular religion as quaint rather than real. As noted at the beginning of this section, this discrediting has had little or no impact on the belief in and practice of local religion and the way it contextualizes the material past. What it has done is move it to the periphery of our view. But at least as important in the way the popular has become largely invisible has been the emergence, beginning in the mid-nineteenth century, in Siam-Thailand[3] of the nation-state. This highly centralized form of government necessitated the crafting of a new national history (Reynolds 1991), one that spelled the "nationalization" of archaeological heritage sites and the emergence of a discourse of heritage that—somewhat incidentally, somewhat tactically—was disarticulated from popular culture.

Marginalization of the Popular by the Centralized State

There are strong parallels between the development of the nation-state in Southeast Asia and the development in that region of archaeology and archaeological heritage management. This is not happenstance. As numerous archaeologists themselves have noticed, the nation-state, particularly in its project of national identity building, has profoundly shaped the form that modern archaeology has assumed in most parts of the world (e.g., B. Anderson 1991; Diaz-Andreu and Champion 1996; L. Jones 1997). There was no precedent in Southeast Asia for the type of space the nation-state would require for its existence, and archaeology, along with historiography, cartography, demography, education, museums, and transport infrastructure, would be among the programs or technologies that would help make this space available (B. Anderson 1991).

The centralization of knowledge that has occurred in the course of the formation of nation-states in Asia is well illustrated by the production of Thailand's new national history, beginning in the late nineteenth century. The production of this history does not imply the absence of prior historiography. Premodern "traditional" historiography, known as *tamnan* (Wyatt 1976), was a localized form of history, each locality having its own body of *tamnan*, oral or written, closely associated in an explanatory way with local sites (built and natural) and local landscapes. Royal capitals had their own *tamnan*, which, like those of outlying places, blended mythology and history, and the premodern state also maintained archives of royal edits that were themselves sacred objects. Then there were Buddhist cosmological texts such as the Traiphum, which was compiled as early as 1345 BCE from the Pali canon and commentaries and was preserved and kept current by the kings of Siam, who periodically commissioned recensions of it (Reynolds 1976). The nature of premodern Siamese historiography was thus continuous from the local to the state, from the village to the center.

The move to the creation of national history is documented at a local level in a case study by Gesick (1995). She describes the situation in the Songkla area of peninsula Thailand where, traditionally, *tamnan* manuscripts written on palm leaf were regarded as sacred objects in their own right (Gesick 1995: 20). Curated in local temples, they were charged with power in a way that made them dangerous to read. In 1902 Prince Naris toured the Siamese provinces of the Malay Peninsula in his capacity as the minister of post and telegraph in the government of King Chulalongkorn. While visiting a famous old monastery in the Songkla area, he was shown a set of old manuscripts that had been in the care of a local woman (Gesick 1995: 5–6). Gesick interviewed two elderly sisters who were descendants of the curator of the manuscripts during Naris's time and who related the story of how the manuscripts had been removed to Bangkok.

> Reading the manuscripts, they say, was extremely dangerous and was rarely if ever done, and then only with ceremonial precautions. The manuscripts, they agreed, could only be read—the clear implication is "read aloud"—from the back of a white elephant. Otherwise, whoever attempted to read the manuscripts would cough blood from the larynx and die. Upon questioning, they explained that the "white elephant" was a symbolic white elephant constructed out of cloth over a bamboo frame. They also said the "royal servants" (*kha ratchakan*) who took away the manuscripts took them on a white elephant. Without the white elephant, the manuscripts "refused to go." (Gesick 1995: 20)

The removal of the manuscripts to Bangkok "signals" the ascendancy of scientific "national history" over sacred local history (Gesick 1995: 15).

The collection of local source material to build national history had its counterpart in archaeology. What Prince Damrong Rajanuphab (1862–1943) accomplished for the government as the minister of the interior under Chulalongkorn, establishing and administering the new provincial bureaucratic infrastructure, he also did for the past of the new nation: he centralized it (Craig Reynolds, personal communication). Damrong personally recorded numerous ancient sites, mainly religious monuments, during his frequent travels across the country. Provincial governors and other officials were requested to put out feelers and to report finds to Bangkok and they were instructed to collect and conserve antiquities. The resulting inventory served to give these sites a new coherence as the physical imprint in the landscape of the emergent national narrative. Unlike the case of the *tamnan*, this project of mapping, which helped to bring into being a national space, had no interest in the supernatural attributes of the sites. It might indeed be argued that these places could only play their nation-building role once they were freed from the web of magical supernatural power relations that contextualized them within popular culture. Similarly, in the master plot of the new national history, the old narratives of kings that explained their rise and fall in terms of their religious merit were replaced by ones in which the kings were nation builders (Thongchai 2000: 544).

The interrelatedness of the various components of the nation-building program is seen in the relationship between archaeology, history, and transportation. By 1907 some 550 miles of railway track were in operation in Siam (B. Anderson 1978: 225). Railways, new roads (replacing buffalo and elephant tracks), and telegraph lines allowed the center to be present at the periphery, permitting the centralized national government to be a tangible reality in all parts of the country and to control minutely life across the country in a way that had never been possible previously. If the railway and then the highway system made even the far-flung reaches of the nation governable it also made the physically dispersed heritage sites visitable. Successive Thai governments have developed iconic monumental sites such as Ayuthaya, Sukhothai, Pimai, and Phanom Rung as historical parks for visitation by both Thai and foreign tourists. As Ivy (1995) has shown in the case of Japan, the railway helped introduce the public to the idea of national space as well as promoting the idea that national culture was a visitable, consumable entity. In Siam, as in India, China, and elsewhere, the building of the railways required huge volumes of "ballast" for use in constructing the bed of the line and this was often acquired in the vicinity of the line by demolishing the ruins of old stupas and other monuments. Among other places, this occurred in the area of the old capital, Ayuthaya (Vella 1978: 203–4). One author even claims that railway contractors were actively encouraged to use temple ruins as a source of "ballast" (Graham 1924: 178). There is a sense then in which those sites that nationalism raised to iconic status became visitable by the new national community in a process that consumed non-iconic sites of purely local-popular significance.

In Benedict Anderson's words (1991: 173), across Southeast Asia in the second half of the nineteenth century, the surveyors were "on the march to put space under the same surveillance which the census-makers were trying to impose on persons." Whereas previously the power of the king only extended as far out from his capital as he was able to project military force, now the writ of government extended across the whole country to its very borders. But the borders themselves had to be created for the purpose. Previously there had been no need to know precisely where the kingdom began or ended geographically—at their peripheries, the kingdoms of Siam, Burma, and Cambodia gradually merged into each other. The modern topographic survey map of Siam, first produced at the end of the nineteenth century by Western surveyors employed by King Chulalongkorn, displaced a preexisting notion of a sacred landscape that consisted of sacred centers, such as princely capitals, surrounded by unmeasured space (Thongchai 1994). This space was depicted in the murals painted on temple walls in which "the universal land of the Buddha" (Thongchai 1994: 22), consisting of stories from the Buddha's life, was shown as being set in the local landscape surrounding the temple. It was a spatial order in which the cosmological and the terrestrial tied together. Henceforth, however, it was only the confines of the Buddhist temples across the country that were recognized by the center as constituting sacred space, not the landscape surrounding them, which was subsumed into the new "geobody" (Thongchai 1994) of the nation.

Prince Damrong's nationalization of ancient monuments, alluded to earlier, was part of a larger move to invent a whole new notion of Thai "culture," which became particularly marked in the 1930s and 1940s.

The thinker, writer, and politician Luang Wichit Wathakan (1898–1962) played a key role in this invention, convinced as he was that the new nation must be "a tangible entity which individuals could identify with and love" (Barmé 1993: 87). This tangibility included new ritual behavior in relation to national symbols (for example, the flag and the national anthem), a whole new raft of performing arts (sponsored by the Fine Arts Department, founded in 1933), a new style of dress and deportment, and the promotion of Thai language at the expense of Chinese languages (Barmé 1993: 144–63). Popular religion had no place in this new cultural domain.

The construction of the Thai nation-state thus affected popular religious practice in a variety of ways. An attempt was made to confine religious belief to a segment of life that was defined by institutional Buddhism. The supernatural was taken out of history (by the new national historical narrative), taken out of nature (as an explanation of natural phenomena), taken out of the landscape (displaced by modern cartography), taken out of the very notion of "culture," and taken out of the material past, where it would be displaced (at an official level) by the discourses of archaeology and heritage. At least this was the program: it would be more accurate to say that popular religion was taken out of visibility.

It is impossible to separate the creation of archaeological or heritage space in Thailand from either the influence of Western secular-rational modernity or the internal nation-building project. One might say that the magical supernatural context of the Thai material past has been stratified below these developments and obscured from view. I mean specifically the view from "above," the perspective one has of Thai society when one's view is mediated by official institutions and discourse. Archaeology has benefited from the disenfranchisement of popular religion as a form of legitimate knowledge and practice insofar as it has allowed us to promote the illusion that ordinary Thais see the material past the way we do. A space has been opened up for us to occupy, but our occupation of it is always at the expense of a disengagement from the world of our fellow citizens in places like Thailand. To dwell in this space is to live an illusion.

Finally, in this section, I turn to briefly consider the role that religious reform in Thailand has played in the disenfranchisement of the popular. King Mongkut (Rama IV, reigned 1851–68) came to the throne after living twenty-seven years as a Buddhist monk, during which time he learned English and read extensively about Western religions and Western science, himself becoming a knowledgeable astronomer. But he also studied the Pali canon of Buddhism and turned his energies to promoting an orthodox practice of Buddhism that eschewed belief in magic and the supernatural. In 1829 he founded the Thammayut order of Buddhist monks, who aimed "to purify the religion by restoring to it the outstanding qualities of rationality and objectivity that had characterized early Buddhism but had been lost with its popular acceptance" (Ishii 1986: 156). Before and after his ascension Mongkut was a vocal defender of Thai Buddhism against those Westerners, particularly Protestant missionaries, who denigrated it as a primitive, superstition-ridden religion. In doing this he stressed the rationality of orthodox Buddhism: "His discussions with the missionaries made him realize that it was the folk beliefs appended to Buddhism that underlay their contempt for his religion. He became firmly convinced that in order to defend Buddhism from the pressures of Western civilization, he must strip it of those heterodox accretions" (Ishii 1986: 159).

Monastic reform and the "modernization" of religion continued throughout Mongkut's eighteen-year reign and during that of his son, Chulalongkorn. Several Brahmanistic and animistic court rituals, such as the Giant Swing ceremony, were discontinued and a radical reform of the Buddhist *sangha* (the monkhood) was instituted. The highly dispersed nature of the monastic structure was reinvented as a centralized system, controlled by the Sangha Council in Bangkok, that was not unlike the new civil service and that paralleled the newly centralized Thai state. *Tamnan* were removed from local monastic education but the Sangha reforms also involved a very direct intervention in monastic ritual and the way that monks lived their religion. The modern state has always had a problem with mobile populations of pastoralists and hunter-gatherers and it is significant that one of the key measures of the reform package was a concerted campaign to stop the wandering existence led by many of Siam's monks, an existence that saw them roam from one forest monastery, pilgrimage site, ancient ruin, or meditation cave to another. Under the terms of the 1902 Sangha Act monks were required to register at a particular monastery (J. Taylor 1993: 71).

The spiritual power possessed by monks meant that it was natural for local people to rely upon them in their various dealings with the *phi* and other non-canonical spirits and forces (Tiyavanich 1993). To counter this, a program of surveillance on the part of the Sangha Council aimed to curtail the extent to which village monks were enmeshed in non-canonical religious practices centered on the local cults.

It is questionable how much effect any of this has had in the long term on the practice of popular religion in Thailand. The emergence in the 1980s of "prosperity cults" headed by "magic monks" (Jackson 1999a, 1999b) suggests that non-canonical Buddhism is enjoying a resurgence. Jackson notes that "from the 1980s to the mid-1990s, the Thai state withdrew from its historical role of controlling expressions of Buddhist religiosity and that its place was increasingly taken by the market" (Jackson 1999a: 258). The orthodox-conservative leadership of the *sangha* has also suffered a loss of prestige. A run of financial and sexual scandals in recent decades has eroded the position of the monkhood in general, and the supreme patriarch's alignment with the conservative military side during the democracy massacre in 1992 was also damaging (J. Taylor 1993: 74). At the same time the state has to some extent relaxed its highly centralized power structure and has implemented the policies of decentralization that are now common to governments in most parts of the world. This has been concurrent with a resurgence of interest in local history, which, in places, even includes a relegitimization of *tamnan* (Thongchai 1995: 111).

Cosmopolitanism and Conservation

I would stress the point that popular religious culture does not require our consent in order to flourish in its relationship with the material past. It is principally we who stand to gain by taking a cosmopolitan approach. Our choice is over whether we want to live and work in the world of actual social practice or in the imaginary world our discourse has furnished us with.

It seems wishful thinking, however, that the Western conservation movement will bring down the walls and engage with local practice anytime soon. To date, the real gains made by socially inclusive conservation management, both in the natural and cultural domains, are almost entirely confined to the developed world. In places such as Australia, New Zealand, and North America, indigenous people have gained a real degree of control over their heritage, resulting sometimes in embargoes on archaeological research and sometimes in collabora-tive research. In the developing world the gains have mainly been at the level of the case study. In Thailand, for instance, ICCROM has a proj-ect to promote the engagement of heritage professionals with local communities and their value systems.[4] The regional intergovernment heritage body, SPAFA, also promotes community engagement, but this usually turns out to be focused on educating local communities to adopt state-endorsed heritage values, ignoring the local systems of value that already exist. In the cultural heritage field, as in nature con-servation (Brockington 2004: 414; Igoe 2006: 73, 76), a combination of the desire of proponents of the community conservation approach to want to believe it works and the "loudness" of the positive spin put on the approach by international conservationists obscures the shal-lowness of its penetration.

We need to go beyond the sort of community engagement programs that aim to give locals a better appreciation of their heritage. They al-ready appreciate it. The problem for us is that their appreciation often does not amount to "conservation" in the restricted sense in which we use that term, a sense in which "*things* trump people at every turn" (see Meskell's introduction to this volume). Our restricted understanding of what a *thing* can be blinds us to alternative forms of conservation. For example, historically and in the present day, Thais often "restore" the crumbling ruins of old or ancient stupas by completely encasing them within the form of a new stupa constructed on top of and around them. What they achieve in this way, at considerable financial cost to themselves, is the conservation of the meaning of the stupa as a divine object (Byrne 1995). The divine nature of the stupa is by no means com-promised by such an intervention; it can only be enhanced.

And yet there is hope to be had from the pressure that continues to build within the fields of archaeology and heritage conservation for the implementation of the "values approach" mentioned at the opening of this chapter. There is particular pressure to give adequate weighting to the contemporary social value of the material past. The social turn in heritage management consists at least as much of rhetoric as action, but this simply underlines the problem for cultural heritage: one can only foreground social value at the level of principle for so long before people begin to notice the way it is effaced at the level of professional practice. My guess is that this will eventually lead archaeologists and heritage practitioners to an engagement with popular religion: the religious simply cannot be extricated from the social and the social, it would seem, is here to stay.

Cosmopolitanism draws heavily on the mind-expanding benefit of cross-cultural conversations. A cosmopolitan archaeology is one whose "researchers will have to engage in wider social and political conversations," the outcomes of which we cannot control (see Meskell's introduction to this volume). According to the philosopher Kwame Anthony Appiah (2006a: 57), while value judgments may differ, "Cosmopolitans suppose that all cultures have enough overlap in their vocabulary of values to begin a conversation." However, when it comes to the possibility of dialogue between local practitioners of popular religion and professional practitioners of archaeology and heritage, we have to question whether such overlap presently exists. Can it exist in the face of our rejection, as rational modernists, of the existence of the magical supernatural?

In pondering this we might note that the type of conversation Appiah refers to would be based on the principle of tolerance and that this principle does not necessarily *require* us to accept the truth of the magical supernatural. Indeed, as Habermas (2003a: 3) observes, "Toleration first becomes necessary when one rejects the convictions of others: we do not need to be tolerant if we are indifferent toward other beliefs and attitudes." It is not belief we need, then; it is tolerance, tolerance as a deliberate position that we take up and tolerance that proceeds from our disbelief.

Notes

1 Environmental conservation projects funded by the World Bank alone, in the decade between 1986 and 1996, entailed the forcible relocation of an estimated three million people (Colchester 2004: 30).

2 http://www.conservationrefugees.org (accessed November 2006).

3 Following the coup of 1932, which ended the absolute monarchy, the military government changed the country's name from Siam to Thailand in 1938.

4 See http://www.iccrom.org.

4 ✹ THE NATURE OF CULTURE

IN KRUGER NATIONAL PARK

South Africa was subject to colonial occupation and more recently apartheid repression until the 1990s, leaving a legacy of decimated indigenous archaeological heritage. Archaeologists played crucial, albeit detrimental, roles in the fabrication of archaeological narratives and subsequent history making that remain inescapable today, and they have had the particular effect of diminishing the importance of an archaeological past for the majority of the nation's populace. Focusing on Kruger National Park—the flagship of South Africa's conservation, biodiversity, and wilderness heritage—I underscore the current tensions surrounding the privileging of nature over culture and the continuing sacrifice of historic recognition and restitution for the "greater good" of conservation. An archaeological ethnography based around heritage sites and projects across the park exemplifies the displacement of an archaeological past and exposes the implications for black descendant communities today. I argue that, irrespective of leadership or regime change, the mobilization of state power continues to devalue the archaeological past and its indigenous histories. What subsequently emerges as a dominant concern in the new South Africa is a distinctive articulation of nature in the cosmopolitan discourse of biodiversity.

Globally, biodiversity is positively viewed as an ecological workhorse, essential raw material for evolution, a sustainable economic resource, a font of aesthetic and ecological value, a global heritage, genetic capital, and the key to the survival of life itself (Hayden 2003: 52). Given this enormous potential and the future-geared, promise-based rhetorics of rescue, is it surprising that archaeological pasts seem weary and moribund ruins that are not living up to their earning potential? Perhaps as a result of this disinterest, and given the recent volatile struggles over land claims in Kruger and elsewhere, narratives of *terra nullius* or "empty lands" have resurfaced in dangerous and familiar ways (see also the chapter by González-Ruibal, this volume). The now discredited discourse has become sutured to the celebratory discourses of conservation and biodiversity: both pertain to global desires for pristine wilderness, minimal human intensification, the erasure of anthropogenic landscapes, the primacy of non-human species, sustainability, and so on. Without recognition of the complex and continued human history in Kruger's landscapes there is little chance of historical justice and restitution for indigenous South Africans.

Narratives of *terra nullius* hitch to the imaginings of powerful international bodies and regulations, including the World Wildlife Fund (WWF), the United Nations (UN), the World Conservation Union (IUCN), and the Convention on International Trade in Endangered Species of Wild Flora and Fauna (CITES), that want to privilege and preserve flora and fauna over and above people (or even the evidence of people) in the name of a common humanity and the global commons. Biodiversity and conservation may today be global constructs, but they are imagined in South Africa in very specific, historically charged ways. They are distinct yet related discourses and both are enshrined in a "protected areas" strategy developed largely on a U.S. model of national parks and wilderness reserves that historically bifurcated humans and nature, nature and culture (W. Adams 2005; Adams and Mulligan 2003b: 10). While synonymous with nature in the form of dramatic wilderness and exotic game, South Africa is also renowned for its natural degradation, environmental troubles, pollution, and toxic landscapes (McDonald 2002). Human occupation and intensification are thus negatively inflected from the outset, whether in precolonial, colonial, or postcolonial contexts, and are similarly positioned with poaching, mining, deforestation, resource depletion, and so on.

The case of Kruger reveals the cosmopolitan frictions among transnational organizations, funding agencies, state projects, heritage bodies, and indigenous communities in and around the place of culture in a nature reserve. Both natural and cultural heritage are imagined in particular local and national ways, and each is influenced and effected by global organizations and mandates. Funding for the running and research of Kruger National Park and its outreach is supplied by North American government agencies, private foundations, international organizations, universities, research grants, NGOs, and state and private revenues (McKinsey Report 2002). Nongovernmental organizations ultimately do much of the work of the South African state. Many assert that they float the nation, the danger being that they become de facto agencies for service delivery and devolved responsibility for government (Cheah 1998: 322). Notions of local, state, global, and indigenous are all pieced together from this complex mosaic of sources, resources, inspirations, and agendas. The research I present here is based on several years of work in Kruger National Park, and my research has been both archaeological and ethnographic (Meskell 2005a, 2006a, 2007a). Based at Skukuza, Kruger's research station, I have had sustained interactions and interviews with park managers, research scientists and technicians, ecologists, service workers, rangers, heritage officers, and those forcibly removed from the park during previous regimes. What began as a project of tracking the progress of archaeology after ten years of democracy has necessarily come to embrace the fraught relationship between cultural and natural heritage, and to ask why it is that nature trumps culture. In fact, it would be impossible to conduct either archaeological or ethnographic fieldwork outside the confines of the parastatal pressures that prioritize the flora and fauna of Kruger National Park, as they are taken up in global imaginings of salvage, development, empowerment, and the good.

Parastatal Relations

In scores of interviews around the park borders, dislocated residents of the park see Kruger as the state, irrespective of its former management by the apartheid-era white National Party or its current management by the black ANC. Kruger is a parastatal organization; it operates as an arm of government, is answerable to the minister for Environment Affairs and Tourism, and yet is primarily financially self-sustaining. But more than its programmatics, Kruger operates likes a state and has always exercised a significant degree of juridical and disciplinary power. Its central administrative node and main tourist hub is Skukuza. The name Skukuza is telling. It means "to sweep clean" or "to strip bare" in Tsonga, and it was the name conferred upon the first warden of the park, Stevenson-Hamilton, in the early 1900s, by the local Shangaan people (Carruthers 1995, 2001). His measures to rid the park of its indigenous inhabitants became synonymous with the structure and identity of the park, particularly with systematic histories of erasure. Elders whom I interviewed from the northernmost park border at Pafuri south to regions around Orpen and Lilydale, who once lived inside the confines of the park and were evicted between the 1920s and the 1960s, still refer bitterly to the organization of Kruger National Park as "Skukuza." The name Skukuza, the action of stripping away all that existed before, has come to represent the politics of the park to this day. Skukuza, as both noun and verb, continues to have a strong resonance.

The complex relationship between people and nature that developed through colonial and apartheid regimes continues to haunt South Africa, specifically concerning what sorts of people serve nature versus those who are afforded its bounty. Historically, these have always been lines of tension, of circumscription and discrimination—and they continue to be a potent social and spatial determinant. The "fences and fines" approach, also known in its stricter guise as fortress conservation (Brockington 2004a), has always been in operation in South Africa, although prior to 1994 it was manned, quite literally, by the white elite and their soldiers. Kruger National Park was always considered a military buffer zone, a wilderness corridor that shielded the state from political resistance and insurgency during apartheid and now safeguards it from illegal immigration. As one might imagine, social transformation has still a vast way to go in the traditionally white, racially segregated preserve of national parks. Moreover, there has still been no recognition of the thousands of black workers whose labor created the park and whose forced sacrifice of land, livestock, and cultural lifeways made it possible for the fortunate to enjoy the spoils of biodiversity and conservation today.

Kruger comprises some two million hectares of fenced land and is bordered by Mozambique and Zimbabwe. Together the three countries have allowed the creation of a transfrontier or transboundary park (Great Limpopo Transfrontier Park), sponsored by the Peace Parks Foundation—a conglomerate of international development agencies, private donations, and corporate involvement. The whole notion of an international park that traverses three countries experiencing in their own particular ways dire poverty, the HIV-AIDS pandemic, unemployment, violence around immigration and displacement, and so on seems to test the limits of possibility. Some of my work has been conducted in Limpopo province where the three countries intersect. That intersection ominously known as Crooks Corner is testament to the histories of exploitation, both human and animal, that southern Africa has suffered through European colonialism, in the brutal regimes of apartheid South Africa and the former Rhodesia, through war-torn Mozambique, and in the forced relocations and displacements of people more recently (Connor 2003). This point of triangulation, a no-man's land of sorts, also witnessed some of the most aggressive poaching and illegal trading of animals, gunrunning, movements of military and insurgents, and untold numbers of refugees. For over a century this has been a stain on the map—a lawless area that has defied containment. It should not then be surprising that it was from this region, to the extreme north of Kruger National Park, that apartheid forces launched chemical weapons assaults into Mozambique against the resistance forces, the FRELIMO (Cock and Fig 2002), using perhaps the nation's most positive emblem of heritage as a staging ground for crushing the resistance across national borders. Kruger's origins and history have been deeply implicated in the consolidation of Afrikaner nationalism and later apartheid, bolstered by extensive military force. Army and air force bases were dotted across the landscape, on its fragile borders with the rest of South Africa and, more importantly, with Mozambique. Some of these remain operative today while others have been reappropriated, such as the military barracks on land currently leased by the luxury five-star resort of Singita (Meskell 2006a) that now houses its black service workers.

The Nature of Biodiversity and Bad Citizens

As a result of ongoing fieldwork, I have become increasingly concerned with the current understandings of and ambition regarding the concept of biodiversity in South Africa. The global Convention on Biological Diversity (CBD) defines biodiversity as "the variability among living organisms from all sources including, inter alia, terrestrial, marine and other aquatic ecosystems and the ecological complexities of which they are part; this includes diversity within species, between species and of ecosystems" (Orlove and Brush 1996: 329–30). "Biodiversity" as a construction entered the stage of science and development in the late 1980s, while its textual origins can be traced to the CBD in 1992, the Global Diversity Strategy (fostered by the World Conservation Union, the United Nations Environment Program, and the World Resources Institute) in 1992, and the Earth Summit in Rio in 1992 (Escobar 1998: 54). For South Africa, the end of apartheid and the shift to a democratic neoliberal state came at the very moment that the mandate of biodiversity achieved global recognition, and this synchronicity is particularly salient. One senior scientist in Kruger explained it in an interview as "an intersection between a political opportunity or a window of policy change that we've seen right through just about all the legislation in South Africa, and these changes in ecological thinking." While biodiversity has "concrete biophysical referents, it must be seen as a discursive invention of recent origin. This discourse fosters a complex network of actors, from international organizations and northern NGOs to scientists, prospectors, and local communities and social movements'"(Escobar 1998: 54). And this ties neatly into developments in South Africa from the mid-1990s onward, when the new democratic nation first became enmeshed in this series of international networks.

In South Africa biodiversity is packaged as modern and forward-looking. It is entrepreneurial, economically indexical, and global, whereas cultural heritage is backward-looking, politically fraught, and signifies potential loss to the nation under the specter of land claims. Yet conversely, material heritage cannot always be sutured easily to living communities today given apartheid's victory of historical erasure. Biodiversity is conceived as cosmopolitan and neutral, belonging to no single person, group, nation-state, or corporation (Litzinger 2006: 69) but instead to a common humanity, coercing us all to participate in its mandate. In reality its immediate beneficiaries are often few and occluded. I should point out that Kruger itself is *not* a biodiversity hotspot and the park was proclaimed for very different historic reasons, including aesthetic value and the prevalence of game for hunting. Embarrassingly, scientists and researchers agree that there is more actual biodiversity in the poverty stricken rural sprawl that constitutes Bushbuck Ridge on Kruger's western boundary (see also Fairhead and Leach 1996, 2003).

In asking why diverse nature offers a more compelling suite of concerns, as opposed to cultural diversity and preservation, a number of differences are laid bare. Nature is neutral, supra-racial, existing and entreating protection beyond race: it can be embraced by the new, multicultural concept of South Africa as the Rainbow Nation (Meskell 2005b, 2006b). Nature is immediately legible with real-time collective consequences for the planet if we fail to meet our protective agendas. Thus, a truly cosmopolitan engagement is required, whereas the archaeological and historical past requires decipherment, translation, and education and is packaged in South Africa as peculiarly local. Cultural heritage is identity-specific and factional, and while seemingly important for crafting a new national identity, archaeological remains are currently configured to particular communities in partial, exclusionary, and politically divisive ways. Multiple stakeholder sharing of the past is understandably difficult given the repressive histories of colonial and apartheid rule. Species diversity is universally recognized and consumed, irrespective of race, nation, religion, gender, ethnicity, and so on. It is also globally supported by an organizational and fiscal infrastructure that further operates an index of modernity, civilization, and alignments to the priorities of the first world. The language and scope of biodiversity is inherently modernist and cosmopolitan, neoliberal in ethos, and positively configured as scientific, sustainable, developmental, and experimental. Here neoliberalism refers to a set of policies and practices marked as privileged modes of governance for addressing social, economic, and environmental problems. Nature has increasingly been treated by development agencies, national governments in the North and the South, organizations regulating global trade, and some conservationists as a public good in the name of one worldism. From the 1980s onward, development and conservation discourses reframed economic development and "modernization" in terms of environmental "sustainability"—commonly defined as development that meets the needs of the present without compromising future generations' ability to meet theirs (Hayden 2003: 48–49). Private and state-sponsored environmental education programs, especially those targeting school children, throughout and beyond the borders of Kruger exemplify these hallowed concerns for creating good environmental subjects whose primary goal is conservation for the future. Conversely, no such programs exist for cultural or archaeological heritage.

Understandably, the ANC wants to trump the poor environmental record of the apartheid regime and the most expedient and globally recognized avenue is through high-profile nature conservation, which lies at the intersection of science, development, and neoliberal internationalism. Additionally, there are huge monetary incentives from overseas scientists and funding agencies. Archaeology and cultural heritage strategies cannot hope to match these resources or fiscal potentials. Given that the most famed archaeological site in the park, the Iron Age site of Thulamela, is not generating notable tourist traffic or revenues (Meskell 2006a, 2007a) despite being generously funded by corporate sponsors and international development funds in the 1990s (WWF, NORAD, Gold Fields Foundation), it is unlikely that other sites will be considered for recognition and development by SANPARKS in the near future.

Cori Hayden (2003: 33) has eloquently argued that we are in the midst of a powerful set of turns pertaining to international development and conservation, biodiversity conservation, market-oriented sustainable development initiatives, and (endangered) cultural diversity. Several of these forces are at play in and around Kruger, although cultural diversity remains almost invisible within the park and is only lightly marked outside its borders by a flourishing market in tourist-oriented cultural villages. Since the 1990s the United Nations has a mandated register for biodiversity, and South Africa is a signatory to the international Convention of Biological Diversity, which outlines the need for its promotion in a range of sectors. Other international organizations, including the National Science Foundation and the Mellon Foundation, both of which are based in the United States, are operating in South Africa to fund research and inventory natural resources. Meanwhile, the same governance has since been applied to cultural heritage, as the South African Heritage and Resources Agency has now formed its own register. There are numerous overlaps between the two management systems. In the specific context of *cultural* heritage, Francisco Bandarin, the director of the UNESCO World Heritage Center in France, recently chose to stress that it was "the natural beauty of Africa and the remarkable biodiversity of its ecosystems [that] are of special importance to humankind, not only for the enjoyment of visitors but also for their scientific value and their critical importance for sustaining global biodiversity" (Russouw 2006: 15). Biodiversity trumps cultural heritage, particularly in the context of Africa, as opposed to the acclaimed cultural sites of Europe. As Bandarin makes clear, there is "an under-representation for Africa and the developing world" in the cultural realm. With biodiversity, alternatively, there are so many more potential economic sources for funding as well as strategic potentials for development. And it is precisely the cosmopolitan nature of nature's potential that makes it ripe for such transnational attention and implicates us all in its ambitions.

Building on Foucault's notion of governmentality, the notion of "environmentality" (Agrawal 2005) offers a provocative terrain for investigation into the recasting of SANPARKS under the ANC, particularly in terms of the kinds of subjects and subjectivity implied therein. Hayden (2003: 83) rightly asks what kind of participation and subjectivity is being recognized, impelled, forged, and articulated through the promise of biodiversity. Such promises tend to revolve around future-geared common goods that must be guaranteed by the continued participation, sacrifice, and self-monitoring by those very disadvantaged communities who have ultimately paid the price for conservation. While good environmental subjects are strongly desired, with an emphasis on the indigenous populations surrounding Kruger Park, their own knowledges and practices cannot be interpolated into park management strategies.

Many black South Africans, long excluded from the park on racial grounds (other than as service workers or guides), have understandably seen Kruger as an exclusive enclave catering to the cultural and recreational tastes of the white and the wealthy (Beinart and Coates 1995; Brockington 2004a). Numbers of black tourists visiting national parks have risen from 4 percent in 2002 to 19.7 percent in 2005 according to the director of SANPARKS. The reasons for these low numbers are both historic and economic (McKinsey Report 2002). The park system's discourse of stakeholding and community involvement is aimed at creating the appropriate disciplined environmental citizens. And coincident with the "rhetoric of stakeholding comes a certain provisional language of representation and participation, expressed through the intertwined idioms of compensation, investment, and incentive-building" (Hayden 2003: 8). In South Africa, as elsewhere, rural people, researchers, and governments are "all encouraged to buy in to the globalizing project of biodiversity conservation and protected areas with the promise of dividends dangling in the future" (Hayden 2003: 8). Throughout many interviews, I have enquired whether people are proud of the park as a national treasure, an international icon, a beacon of biodiversity, and the pinnacle of conservation. Most reply that they still await an explanation for their eviction, for compensation, and for the right to freely enter the park, to see the animals, to visit the graves and sites of their ancestors, and to have their children and grandchildren given employment by the park. Many more are angry that dangerous animals that escape the park's confines destroy their crops, attack their cattle, and threaten their personal safety and that nothing is done to protect or compensate them. If they retaliate and kill the animal, they face possible prosecution. Yet Kruger takes no responsibility for such destruction (in 2006 Kruger was deemed legally responsible rather than the state). So common is the damage inflicted by the animals that researchers refer to their rogue escapees as DCAS (Damage Causing Animals). Much of the "human cost" of wildlife has been elided from the preservationist discussion (Fortmann 2005: 202). In a similar vein, many of the poorest people interviewed do not understand what biodiversity entails and yet most representatives for South African National Parks believe that they do and are in essence supportive of this united venture (Meskell 2006a). Most of the people living in the area see little or no social or economic benefits from having one of the world's great conservation enclaves at their doorstep, but rather applaud the more tangible benefits provided by private reserves such as those run by Conservation Corporation Africa. Moreover, people living on the edge of the park clearly understand that hunting in nearby private game farms by rich tourists is differently configured to traditional hunting practices. The taxonomies of "hunting" for sport or survival might seem porous to an outsider, but they have serious legal ramifications to those who once lived inside the park and are now very much on the outside. One man, jailed numerous times for poaching in Kruger put it well: It's all about money, about who can afford to hunt and who cannot. He connected this immediately to the indices of race and power: being white means killing an animal has different significations and ramifications. How might such "disaffected" individuals, the bad subjects of conservation, and their descendents be brought into line, so to speak, with preservationist efforts? This question resides very much at the heart of Kruger's didactic efforts and outreach programs.

Putting Archaeology in Its Place

Relations between the park and its forcibly relocated neighbors have improved since the democratic elections of 1994, however, and an entire unit known as People and Conservation was established with education, development, and employment as its mandate. Importantly, this is the unit that also manages cultural heritage, although SANPARKS has at present no qualified archaeologists on its staff in either its administrative offices or across its twenty-one national parks. We might well ask where Kruger's rich archaeological heritage falls in this new landscape of cosmopolitan biodiversity and development. Some of the answers are reflected in interviews with the park's senior management. The tension between cultural and natural heritage is ever present among senior black ANC government employees who chose to privilege nature and the conservation effort over and above the economic and spiritual needs of their own people. In this regard I am not suggesting that cultural heritage necessarily be a primary concern, but rather that pressing social or cultural issues tend to be considered secondary. It was frequently said that Kruger is not a development agency.

The new black leadership continually highlights the international biodiversity mandate, trading it "off against social needs such as health care and other welfare services," stressing that "to achieve the 10 per cent IUCN ideal, some 50,000km² of additional land (2.5 times the size of Scotland) must be acquired" (Magome and Murombedzi 2003: 109) for protected, conservation areas. It should be said that land reform during the ANC's rule has been slow and heavily criticized for the reformers' reluctance to disrupt nationally profitable white farms. In 2005 more than seventeen thousand land claims had yet to be processed: most successful claims entail financial compensation rather than land settlement. The potential losses to Kruger—dramatized in terms of local black communities turning wilderness into theme parks and casinos—featured heavily in the *2005 State of the Nation Report* (Walker 2006: 68).

When interviewed, the director of Kruger National Park revealed that he had never visited the nationally celebrated site of Thulamela and, when pressed on the scale of Kruger's cultural heritage, resorted to stock answers from the park's public relations materials. With its impressive stone walls and dramatic discoveries of smelted gold (Grigorova et al. 1998; Küsel 1992; Steyn et al. 1998), the site has been used in speeches by cabinet ministers and presidents (Jordan 1996), and yet it has quickly fallen from public and park interest. There is a general feeling that safari tourism, featuring charismatic mammals (faced with threats and danger and extinction), offers a more reliable fiscal return. The success of UNESCO's Ukhahlamba Drakensburg Park, with its rich rock art and heritage ecotourism, suggests that culture can be capitalized upon. If anything has been forefronted in Kruger it is the white history of exploration, discovery, trekking, trading, and hunting that have been visibly celebrated by historical markers. One need only think of the proliferation of memorial sites dedicated to Jock of the Bush-veld—Jock being the faithful dog in Sir Percy Fitzpatrick's story of 1907—that occupy pride of place in Kruger and still dominate park maps. One can easily imagine apartheid park wardens and administrators privileging nature and wilderness at the expense of the historical cultural achievements of the black South Africans they victimized. Less easily envisaged is that the recent black ANC management has similarly chosen to downplay archaeological heritage and marginalize human history within the park, which is palpably felt by communities along the park's edge. Willingness to address the past, or better still, to ethically recount its specificities, is a necessary condition for justice and reconciliation in the present. But as is indicated here, people of various political commitments and affiliations in South Africa today disagree profoundly over the details and consequences of historical injustices for thinking about future reparation. These disagreements impinge upon their respective notions of justice, and those of responsibility, freedom, and identity (Ivison 2002: 93–94). One third of Kruger's land is now "threatened" by indigenous claimants in South African courts, and since Kruger is the jewel in the crown of African parks, and the most financially viable national park across the nation, black management is in a predicament, and future reparations are going to be inflected with volatile public negotiations about justice, identity politics, and common goods.

A complex example of the tensions between natural and cultural heritages and agendas can be traced through the negotiations around developing San rock art for the purposes of tourism and indigenous development. In recent years attempts have been made to publicly showcase the significant paintings within the park, attempts that I have observed as both an archaeologist and an anthropologist. Some two hundred rock art sites have been located and mapped, with hundreds more awaiting discovery within the two million hectares that constitute the park. There has always been great public interest in San rock art in South Africa, even during apartheid times, and there has been a recent resurgence of support with the collaborative interventions of the Rock Art Research Institute (RARI) at the University of the Witwatersrand (G. Blundell 1996, 2002, 2004; Smith et al. 2000). A management plan was devised by RARI in conjunction with the ongoing recording project and an intensive stakeholder survey was designed to maximize collaboration, inclusion, development, and tourism. With support from the People and Conservation Unit, rock art specialists proposed several walking trails that would be led by qualified guides and rangers that would ensure protection of visitors and fragile rock art and promote greater understanding of the long and interwoven histories of occupation in Kruger. Instantly this proposal was met with strong disapproval by section rangers who, for the most part, did not want to be responsible for visitors' safety (despite the long history of walking trails in Kruger) or have any number of people in the southern sector of the park since it was considered a prime "wilderness" zone. Traffic of any sort was considered unwelcome due to the close proximity of Kruger's private game lodges—private fee-paying concessions that operate quasi-independently within Kruger but pay SANPARKS handsomely for long-term leases. Even when the team was recording rock art around Afsaal, members were admonished for having left a vehicle on a dirt road in plain sight of tourists who were paying hundreds if not thousands of dollars per night to experience a "wilderness area." Visitors to these luxury lodges were afforded walking tours that included visiting rock art with the aid of an armed escort, but such experiences were not open to regular visitors to the park. Rangers with rifles were necessary for all such visits, including our own, as we were on foot in the park and thus at the mercy of all manner of wild animals. During mapping researchers frequently encountered elephants that had no difficulty traversing the steep rocky slopes and outcrops where much of the paintings were located. This was given as another reason why a rock art trail was dismissed by rangers: they were short staffed, had to patrol great swathes of territory alone, monitor their black field rangers, and be on call for fires, animals, tourists, accidents, and other incidents. It was simply not going to be possible. A solution came in the form of a rock art specialist and tour guide who was a trained ranger himself and had worked extensively both inside and outside Kruger at several exclusive private game lodges. He could handle the rifle and the narrative about San history and cosmology. This option too was rejected on the basis of funding.

Ambivalence toward the archaeological past is palpable in Kruger National Park. An elderly retired ranger who spearheaded the recording of the art some decades ago told me that he still refuses to publicly present his materials to his colleagues at Skukuza because he fears reprisals for his focus on cultural heritage. He cautiously remarked that he still had a son working in Kruger and he worried that speaking out would negatively effect his future in the organization. In the next breath he lectured me that Kruger was *not* a cultural park, but a natural one, and should not be developed with its archaeological resources in mind. He certainly did not want to see archaeology form the basis for successful land claims or have people return to living in the park. This same man took me to numerous archaeological sites, spanning Paleolithic to recent historical times, lamenting the state of their preservation, their lack of recording or research, and their ultimate loss to memory. While he had no archaeological training as such, he was one of the only park employees I have met to date who expressed any interest in the archaeological past or its public presentation.

Just as the mapping and development project foundered, so did the attempts by young black researchers from RARI to glean information concerning relevant stakeholders and their concerns, ideas, and needs. Arrangements within Kruger were fraught, meetings with various SANPARKS representatives were cancelled, questionnaires were not distributed at gates and lodges, interviews were sometimes hostile, and there was little access to the communities who may have had most to gain. Some park workers felt threatened that the researchers were there to replace them and the overall impression was that of disregard for cultural resources and development across Kruger as a whole. At present the project is at an impasse and no concrete steps have been taken to consolidate the work done or the prospects for developing rock art in the future.

My lasting impression of archaeology's place in Kruger National Park crystallized in the Skukuza archives. There, after much sorting and shredding since the bad old days of apartheid, two boxes labeled "Argeologie" were filed among hundreds containing meeting minutes, field rangers' notebooks, reports on biophysical research, boundary issues, and prosecutions. And what constitutes archaeology in the park? — certificates granting mining rights, petitions for cinnabar prospecting and mica prospecting, and permits to dig for "buried treasure" no less. And there is some justice in this conceptualization; the negative inflection of mining, of depleting resources, of stripping, and of poaching is probably deserved given the particular history of our discipline in South Africa. It reminds me of another connection to biodiversity, namely bioprospecting, the global economic element of nature that similarly conjures the specter of centuries-old images of the mining of gold, diamonds, and minerals (Hayden 2003: 51) from the colonies that became nations like South Africa.

Dreams of *Terra Nullius*

John Locke is largely blameworthy for the trope of *res nullius*, the idea of the globe as a common possession that effectively disregards historically existing property rights. In his teleology, *private property* follows from *private appropriation*, namely from the work of one's hands, the labor of one's body, and so on. European expansion deployed Locke's treatise to justify colonial appropriation of lands. In the first instance indigenous lands were considered given to all "in common" and in the second they were worked by the industrious and thrifty (read European) for the benefit of all, so thus doubly possessed (Benhabib 2004: 31–31). Just as native fauna in South Africa have been proclaimed *res nullius*, or belonging to no one, the eco-enclave of Kruger has been branded as *terra nullius*, an empty land before the onset of white exploration and settlement. An attendant moral absolutism attaches to *terra nullius*, as it does to the constructs of nature and wilderness, with humanity being oppositionally and negatively juxtaposed. Nature, in this binary equation, is intrinsically valued whereas people and their material histories are intrusive, destructive, artificial, and devalued (Soper 2000: 19). Deep ecology and green politics have further bolstered these hierarchies, divisions, and narratives of blame. Despite the green movement's nods to indigenous knowledge and participation, the remnants of colonial conservation ideologies remain. Neutral nature trumps the greed, waste, and devastation of people and societies, past and present.

Myths of emptiness have been vigorously dismantled in Australia and North America, yet have significant resilience in South Africa, whether due to lack of education or the association of archaeology with the apartheid state. Whatever the causes, Kruger's indigenous history remains a deep wound in the landscape and one that is painfully ever present for the indigenous communities that live on Kruger's borders. These groups have the most to lose, or win, in the recognition and restitution that might logically follow archaeological acknowledgment. Without an admission of the human past, recognition premised upon historical and genealogical grounds cannot move forward in the present.

In cosmopolitan terms we need to counter South Africa's continued residual racism that imputes that certain people do not matter (Appiah 2006a: 153) and realize that particular histories do matter.

To underline the continued diminished position of the archaeological past I draw upon its recent rendering in Kruger National Park's public documents. It is puzzling that in 2007 they still claim:

> Bantu people entered about 800 years ago, gradually displacing the San. The available evidence suggests that humans occurred at low density and were mostly confined to the more permanent river-courses. It is reasonable to assume from the continuous presence at some sites (Pafuri, for example) that humans and wildlife existed in harmony, with no major impact of humans on wildlife or the reverse. The arid nature of the environment, together with an abundance of predators and diseases (e.g., malaria) would have played a role in preventing large-scale human population growth and settlement. Nevertheless, sophisticated cultures already existed by the 16th century.[1]

The first myth is that Bantu-speakers (read black Africans) arrived at the recent date of eight hundred years ago, which is challenged by archaeological evidence that suggests at least two millennia (Mitchell 2002). The former still participates in the apartheid mythology of roughly joint arrival of black and white immigrants to South Africa, specifically when they reached the Western Cape. These deeply flawed constructions of history and culture have had a lasting legacy, felt to this day, but most palpably felt over the apartheid years since they were used to create racial hierarchies and structure unequal living experiences for both black and white South Africans.

Furthermore, the myth of low density is highly speculative as so little systematic fieldwork was done during the apartheid regime. Moreover, the archaeology within the park, for example the Iron Age sites of Thulamela, Makhahane, Shilowa, and Masorini, suggests significant industrial activity and occupation. These are material facts that are never engaged with, even by the researchers in Scientific Services or the foreign scientists who come to conduct research on the flora and fauna of the park. For the scientific community in Kruger, population density is determined teleologically: not by archaeological investigation but by current observations about impacts and modifications on the landscape. As Hayashida (2005: 45) points out, because of the time lag in ecosystem response to disturbance and environmental change, current ecosystem structure, function, and composition cannot be fully understood or explained without a historical perspective. The lasting effects of past human actions (termed "land-use legacies") include changes in species composition, successional dynamics, soils, water, topography, and nutrient cycling. Many seemingly natural areas have a cultural past that is part of their ecological history; their conservation today requires knowledge of that past and assessment of the value of continuing or replicating past cultural practices.

Given the forced relocations of people who lived in the park over the last century, the determined efforts to reinstate something imagined as a pristine wilderness, and the absence of any serious systematic archaeological survey, the lack of substantive human trace is undoubtedly in the eye of the beholder. Yet we know that there are over a thousand sites across Kruger's vast expanse: early hominid, Paleolithic, San rock art, Iron Age, historic, and recent. Ironically, even under the rule of the National Party several publications recorded early and continued black history in the park, by way of documenting early European explorers passing through the original area. More than 170 historic place names have survived to reflect indigenous settlement, industrial or sacred sites (Kloppers and Bornman 2005), undoubtedly a mere fraction of the original.

Finally, the old apartheid fables of aridity and predator activity are spuriously given as reasons for the lack of supposed landscape intensification and modification. Historically, indigenous people are thus refused the role of "ecological agents" in their own right (Plumwood 2003). The South African national parks system must dismantle the devastating myths of empty lands and late arrivals that deprivilege indigenous South Africans and erase their historic achievements in the materiality of the past and present.

There is a growing movement that recognizes that even at colonial contact many landscapes were as fully anthropogenic as those found in Europe (Clark 2002). Recognition of this point would, however, be troubling for the mandate and ambition of SANPARKS, which needs to preserve the more barren notion of Kruger as predominantly pristine. While culture is all about fluidity and movement, nature is ideally meant to stand still: culture is a process, nature an object. And when humans enter the fray, as below, they are typically cast as destructive agents of change. According to recent park documents, the positioning of humankind in the "natural" debate has attracted as much debate and usually settles out on a statement along the lines of "effects of pre-industrial people are considered natural" or the IUCN's comment, "where people have less effect than any other species." Each of these have potential flaws. For instance, many pre-industrial civilizations collapsed because of overexploitation of resources, and ecosystems with influential species (for example, elephant) leave more scope, in the IUCN's definition, for human impact. Conceptually, many sustainable use systems place humans quite explicitly in the ecosystem. In modern times, society's decision to proclaim parks at all is testimony to an agreement that people living elsewhere in more altered systems will strive to keep parks less altered for a different (usually far less altered) mode of usage (South African National Parks 2005).

Why is the peopled past so repeatedly undercut or erased from the landscape, even after the apartheid years? During 2005 I was asked by scientific researchers to participate briefly in a collaborative interdisciplinary project about disease landscapes in Kruger, this time assuming my role as an archaeologist. When I presented the established evidence for early and continued human occupation in the region this evidence was greeted as both unheard of and slightly unwelcome. Eagerly I pointed to Kruger's own apartheid-era Parks Board publication from the 1970s that assembled historical accounts of the first Europeans in the area and their encounters with significant black populations (see Punt 1975). Archaeological and historical evidence was deemed peripheral or speculative at best in the face of biophysical science. Years of sedimented disinterest within the nation; the lack of any archaeologists employed in South African national parks or within Kruger; the prioritization of the biophysical sciences; researchers, rangers, and trackers with other tasks and no interest in cultural resources; the residual inertia of racism; and the lack of education are just some of the foundational reasons why the past remains problematic. There is a long way to go in terms of site management, tourism development, upgrading museums and displays, curation, creating inventories, and even securing the return of archaeological objects. Positive steps are gradually being taken, but the disparity between management of nature and culture remains troubling terrain. The work of heritage in South Africa is

1 The Mkhabela family at the grave of Chief Nyongane, Kruger National
Park, 2005. *Photograph courtesy of the author.*

always in process; it is future perfect. Heritage agencies like the South
African Heritage Resources Agency (SAHRA) or the National Heritage
Council (NHC) are forward looking, forever making recommendations
for the future, and workshopping future projects. They are ultimately
caught in this double time, backward dependent while forward-looking
(Farred 2004). This leads us into the double bind of historical injustice
and its moral consequences in the present. Without a past, one cannot
hope for recognition or restitution. While the passing of time changes
facts on the ground, in the case of South Africa this is a very recent and
remember-able history, effectively ending with the elections of 1994.
Historical injustice goes hand in hand with reparations, of which Ivison
(2006b) outlines three modes: restitution, compensation and recognition, or acknowledgment. These can take the practical forms of financial payment, apologies, affirmative action, constitutional provisions,
and so on. Most importantly, recognition acknowledges the victims
and the harm enacted against them and involves the act of restoring

or compensating those who have suffered. Recognition can also take the form of public apologies and forms of collective remembrance, as has become commonplace in post-apartheid South Africa, which are themselves political acts.

Around Kruger numerous communities have petitioned for various kinds of reparation. For example, some like the Mkhabela family have suggested a change in the name of the park gate, Numbi, to Nyongane, the name of the mountain nearby, a symbolic change that would cost little in financial terms. They have asked for acknowledgment of the burials of their elders and of some 350 cattle situated within the new borders of the park (figure 1). Recently People and Conservation at Skukuza successfully organized an inscribed commemorative plaque, for which the Mkhabela paid. Financial restitution has also been suggested, though it has not been forthcoming from SANPARKS. Part of this compensation would be for the death of a female relative killed by buffalo in 1988, previously denied by the park since she was not a SANPARKS employee. The Malatji have been more vigorous in launching a land claim that might entail a financial compensation. Elders told me they would be looking for a share in the Phalaborwa gate takings, but on a more pragmatic level they would like some decision-making power in the development of their ancestral site, Masorini (Meskell 2005a). In 2005 after consultation, community members were employed in reconstructing some of the huts and furnaces at the archaeological site, although the final negotiations between the tribal authority and SANPARKS were fraught. Alternatively, park authorities can always provide alternative scenarios to dismiss notions of sustainable use, much less resource development. "The issue of conversion of natural capital is intriguing, some countries or operations depleting their natural capital without successfully creating manufactured capital or social capital (the latter meaning human capacity and trust) in its place" (South African National Parks 2005). Not all reparations are costly or financial. It is the process that is often crucial in the spaces of reconciliation and potential restitution. The challenge for postcolonial liberalism, as Duncan Ivison argues, is to orient ourselves toward the local, while similarly providing an account of the conditions and institutions that distinguish this effort from merely deferring to existing relations of power (Ivison 2002: 22). This seems key in an emergent nation like South Africa where regime change may have replaced racial oppression, yet it has not erased local issues of ethnic, indigenous, and political difference that remain central vectors of inequality, nor has it erased pressing concerns for a new redistributive economy. Working at the interface of indigenous justice in the postcolonial, settler nations of Canada and Australia, Ivison's (2002: 89) modest aims are for fostering "better conditionality" and remaining open to the future to come. While this entails acknowledging the impossibility of justice, our continued attempts to navigate a just course are the appropriate ethical tactics for keeping viable the possibility of new modalities of politics, identity, and justice.

Skukuza: State without History

Why would an archaeologist be interested in the narratives of conservation, biodiversity, sustainability, or development? Moreover does a heritage perspective have anything to offer scholars and practitioners in these other fields? Suffice to say that archaeologists need to recognize more fully our epistemic genealogies and the interwoven threads binding understandings of natural resources and nature conservation to cultural resources, landscapes, and values. Conservation and biodiversity mandates are cosmopolitan concerns in South Africa, while heritage remains a troubled and very local affair. Yet on a wider, world stage the discourses of nature and culture conservation share a legacy and are now mobilized through cosmopolitan networks, as argued in the introduction to this volume. Resource use and sustainability inform to a great degree cultural heritage concerns about site usage, occupation, and lived traditions, often undervaluing them when it comes to indigenous owners and stakeholders. We tend to see the past as both raw material and finite resource, a "fossil fuels" template of the world that wants to restrict utilization and save our stocks for future generations. Conservation is seen very much as a global good for a common humanity, whether natural or cultural. The language of sustainability, so prevalent in nature conservation, is fast becoming the rallying cry for heritage development as an economic growth industry worldwide.

As this chapter demonstrates, however, land use legacies and human histories are sometimes erased in the productions of place. In the conservation equation human interventions are destructive, dangerous, and undesirable. Just as some of my colleagues in Kruger National Park are concerned that any sort of natural resource utilization is the beginning of the end and refuse to allow sustainable harvesting of flora and fauna, heritage agencies the world over typically struggle with the realities of human occupation, encroachment, ongoing traditional practices, visitation, and appropriation in and around significant sites. There are exceptions at the local level, though these struggles have often been hard won such as in Australia (Lilley 2000b; Lilley chapter in this volume; Lilley and Williams 2005), or are ongoing sites of contestation between local and international bodies, as seen in issues of preservation and management of sites across Southeast Asia for example (Byrne 1991, 1995, the chapter by Byrne, this volume). Just as animals, plants, and landscapes have been deemed part of the national estate for moral and scientific uplift from the Victorian era onward (see Ritvo 1987), archaeological and historic sites are often wrested from their immediate inheritors for the benefit of others, all in the name of the global good. The convergences of both natural and cultural protection and management undoubtedly culminated in the colonial occupations of Africa, Asia, Australia, and so on by British and other European empires.

Many authors have pointed to the continued colonial, national, and governmental overtones of conservation and management (e.g., Adams and McShane 1996; Adams and Mulligan 2003a; Brockington 2004a; Duffy 2002; Greenenough and Tsing 2003; Honey 1999; Keller and Turek 1998; Moore 1998, 2005; Moore, Kosek, and Pandian 2003; Neumann 1998; West 2006). More recently some impute that, discursively, biodiversity does not exist, rather it conveniently "anchors a discourse that articulates a new relation between nature and society in global contexts of science, cultures, and economies" (Escobar 1998: 55). Yet much of its networks of models, actors, theories, strategies, and objects remain hegemonic. Over the years I have come to view Kruger National Park as a state within a state. One park officer explained her idea for a passport system with entry stamps for Kruger and, despite the obvious marketing ploy, she had succinctly captured the nationalist spirit of the place. Kruger is cumbersomely bureaucratic and juridical, with its own policing and border enforcement powers. It considers itself a business, but also a charitable organization and a national trust. It flirts with the notion of development, embarks on education programs for HIV-AIDS, and minimally entertains notions of sustainable resource use. Kruger is reliant on international funding agencies, philanthropy and donor aid, and assistance from NGOs: it operates on American and European support. Is it any wonder that various researchers from very different disciplines I have interviewed have used the descriptor "schizophrenic" to describe Kruger's workings? During my own fieldwork I have continually struggled to find coherence in the philosophies and management strategies for natural and cultural heritage within the park. Kruger is a lumbering beast that refuses to be brought into line with the nation's other parks and the wider organization of SANPARKS. Its history of triumphal nationalist conservation coupled with long-term successful policies of human removal and erasure has made it near impervious to development and, ironically, adaptation.

From a hut on the N'watshisaka River I would daily observe monkeys causing havoc amid our rubbish and hear elephants tramp through the dry riverbed nearby (threatening biodiversity in their wake), and I fully understand the lure and grandeur of the park that is frequently touted as "the size of Israel"—"Skukuza." A visiting ecologist asked me recently whether I considered Stevenson-Hamilton a genius for founding Kruger, "for leaving us *this*," he exclaimed, looking around in wonder. That is one perspective I ventured; another would be offered by the countless residents along the park border who saw Skukuza as stripping them of their land, their livelihoods, and their history. His bemused look suggested he had not entertained these "other" histories of the park. As outlined above, archaeological and cultural assets continue to remain low profile and low priority. Capturing that dimension of biodiversity has been roundly overlooked, and natural heritage remains privileged and paramount in the hearts and minds of those who research, manage, and represent the park "for the benefit of all South Africans."

Notes

I would like to thank the entire staff at the People and Conservation unit, especially Sibongile Van Damme, Edgar Neluvhalani, and Thanyani Madzhuta, as well as the researchers at Scientific Services in Skukuza. As always, logistical support came from the Rock Art Research Institute at the University of the Witwatersrand and particularly Heidi Hansen, Ben Smith, Geoff Blundell, and Thembi Russell. This research would not have been possible without the generosity of people in Musunda, Benndemutale, Tshikuya, Numbi, Lilydale, Justicia, and Welwediene and this chapter is about their pasts in the park. I owe other debts to Glynn Alard, Martin Hall, Nick Shepherd, Eric Makuleke,

Leonard Luula, Donald Moore, Liisa Malkki, Paulla Ebron, Miyako Inoue, Ian Hodder, Denis Byrne, Conrad deRosner, Nikhil Anand, and Lindsay Weiss. The National Science Foundation, the Andrew W. Mellon Foundation, the Institute for Social and Economic Research and Policy at Columbia University in New York, and Stanford University provided financial support for my fieldwork. Versions of this chapter were presented in Leiden, Vancouver, and Stanford and benefited greatly from discussions and debate.

1 http://www.sanparks.org/conservation. This same text also appears in the newly commissioned brochures for the Great Limpopo Transfrontier Park.

Alfredo González-Ruibal

5 ✸ VERNACULAR COSMOPOLITANISM

An Archaeological Critique of Universalistic Reason

Eïa pour ceux qui n'ont jamais rien inventé
pour ceux qui n'ont jamais rien exploré
pour ceux qui n'ont jamais rien dompté
mais ils s'abandonent, saisis, à l'essence de toute chose
—Aimé Césaire (1956 [1939])

Throughout this chapter I argue that our concern for others, as archaeologists, has been caught up in the neoliberal rhetoric of development, which helps to maintain and justify, in the long term, the inequalities it purports to alleviate. Moreover, some archaeological preconceptions in the past and some research strategies in the present have helped, in a conscious or unconscious way, to construct indigenous communities as dispensable or improvable. Here I propose another sort of archaeological engagement, drawing upon the work of Žižek and Bhabha among others, which is both cosmopolitan and vernacular in its scope. This archaeology excavates the present in order to understand from within the destructive effects of globalization, modernism, and development, and it explores the genealogies of collaboration between the discipline and universalistic theories of progress. In so doing, it intends to provide a more radical critique of the modern world than it is usually offered in our field of research. The work presented here is a mixture of archaeology and ethnography that has been carried out in Ethiopia and Brazil.

The Archaeological Rhetoric of International Cooperation

I am suspicious of some community-oriented, multicultural, and multivocal archaeology that is being carried out nowadays. I am totally convinced that many archaeologists are truly serious in their concern for others, but it is hard not to see something of a fashionable attitude behind many projects that purportedly pay attention to local communities. We should be helping people and collaborating with them without any specific interest in mind, but it seems hard for us to put our academic agendas aside. What I find compelling about a cosmopolitan practice is its statement that we have *obligations* and *responsibilities* with regard to others (Nussbaum 1996; Appiah 2006a). It is an ethic imperative of Kantian resonance, not a choice that we graciously make: there is nothing to boast about an obligation. Doing cosmopolitan archaeology ought to mean that we take for granted that others matter. However, even when we are doing humanitarian work, dialoguing with stakeholders, or reflecting upon the social consequences of our research, we have a very particular, although somewhat unconscious, academic interest in mind.

Slavoj Žižek is a scathing critic of the humanitarian activities that many scholars practice today: "Many Western academics cling to some humanitarian ritual . . . as the proof that, at the core of their being, they are not just cynical career-oriented individuals but human beings naively and sincerely trying to help others. However . . . what if this humanitarian activity is a fetish, a false distance that allows them to pursue their power struggles and ambitions with the clear conscience that they are not really 'that,' that their heart is 'elsewhere'?" (Žižek 2004: 178–79). His critique is pertinent to archaeology, too. I distrust much engaged archaeology because it seems to be translated in the condescending language of charity, which entails a sense of superiority and an inability to see underlying structural problems. Again, Žižek (2004: 179) pitilessly attacks this attitude by saying that "the developed countries are constantly 'helping' the undeveloped (with aid, credits, etc.), thereby avoiding the key issue, namely, their complicity in and coresponsibility for the miserable situation of the undeveloped." The way we help the people with whom we work, as archaeologists, recalls too much, too often that of other well-meant private or public agencies devoted to the promotion of welfare in third world nations. The vocabulary of many NGOs and some archaeologists unwittingly resonates with the (neo)colonial rhetoric of development.

It seems that there is some naïveté in the way public archaeology is often portrayed in specialized publications. Tales of archaeology and development generally end with a self-praise, both of the archaeological team and archaeology in general. It is possible to detect a certain unabashed heroization of the discipline in this kind of discourse. Take an excerpt from a typical heroic archaeology: "In conclusion, the benefits from our contributions to public archaeology in a small Andean community have been fruitful for both local communities and archaeologists. . . . Such experiences place communities in positions to receive benefits (i.e., employment) from future archaeological projects and open the door to the possibility of economic development through tourism. . . . Thus, local communities and officials now have a better understanding concerning the process of archaeology, the important archaeological sites that exist on their land, and the need to protect them" (Duwe 2006: 6). Similar projects, couched in a comparable language, can be found during colonial times in different places of the world. A good example is that of Sir Henry Wellcome's excavations in the Anglo-Egyptian Sudan (Addison 1951). Wellcome was an American millionaire who sponsored excavations and development projects in Sudan between 1910 and 1938. His excavations in the site of Jebel Moya gave work to hundreds of Sudanese peasants, whose training in "industrial habits" favored the transformation of their "wild spirit" into "more peaceful attitudes," as Sir Henry noted (Abdel-Hamid 2000). He promoted a series of development projects in the area, including a model village, roads, new farming systems, forestation, training in diverse crafts, and health services. A mixture of paternalism and hard discipline characterized the whole enterprise. Wellcome was considered by archaeologists and politicians alike to be a true philanthropist and a "world benefactor." His was a "loving and compassionate imperialism" (see Scham chapter in this volume) imposed on the locals without dialogue or consent.

The aim of bringing up this example is to reveal comparable agendas and rhetorics in colonial and modern (neocolonial) archaeologies: we find similar well-meant attitudes among archaeologists and a not much different self-heroization as saviors of an underdeveloped community. The real "thinliness" of the engagement is also very typical. I had the occasion to confirm that nothing is left of the development projects started by Wellcome in a visit to the place in January 2000. The most durable element is the monument that Sir Henry made to himself: the House of Boulders. Colonial and neocolonial archaeologists work on the short term, on the surface. They rarely address structural problems and their projects are meant to fail (cf. also Hodder 2003: 65).

It is widely accepted now that community archaeology should start by acknowledging indigenous perceptions of history, instead of portraying Western science as the only way of engaging with the past

(Y. Marshall 2002; Wobst 2005). This comes along with a wider awareness among social scientists involved in development projects of the
relevance of local knowledge (Escobar 1994). However, when it comes
to cooperation, it still has to be accepted that a thorough critique of the
situation of that community (why things are the way they are) is necessary, too. Local knowledge, without an understanding of global historical processes and the overall political context, has little use. Otherwise,
by focusing on temporary (mainly economic) remedies, we help, in the
long run, to reinforce the image and the existence of the "other" as per-
petually dependent and undeveloped. Andre Gunder Frank (1996: 24)
admitted that development studies such as those he used to carry out
were not part of the solution, but rather part of the problem, because
they helped to deny "the real problem and the real solution, which
lay in politics." The apolitical rhetoric of cooperation implies that the
problem is always with them (Bauman 2004: 43–44): they have the
problem and lack the knowledge. Nongovernmental organizations,
international agencies, and even archaeologists drop from the sky, as
dei ex machina, with knowledge and solutions to the local problems
(which are rarely local). A reflection on how our own archaeological
practice and theory may be a problem, instead of a solution, is urgently
needed.

My point is that our critique as engaged intellectuals can be more
useful in the long term, as Bourdieu (2001: 37–38; 2004: 44–45) imputed, than our stopgap solutions as (bad) NGOs. Instead of interrogat-
ing the operations of international agencies and development policies,
as anthropologists and sociologists have already done (among many
others, J. Ferguson 1990; Escobar 1994; Chew and Denemark 1996;
Arce and Long 2000; Edelman and Haugerud 2003), we have taken
for granted that aid for development is the right thing to do, and we
have uncritically followed the path of international agencies, putting
plasters where open-heart surgery was needed. Thus, many cooperation works undertaken by archaeologists (and not only archaeologists)
are at best temporary remedies, in some cases applied without the
consent of the victims: this is just papering over the cracks of global
disorder. Archaeology endows us with a way of reasoning and reflecting upon the problems of humanity that is original and powerful: we
work with material culture—development, the state, and modernity
are about material culture, too—and with the long term—conflicts

and problems in a given area are rarely new. It is up to us to make the most of our discipline to understand and criticize the world or keep being mediocre imitators of other specialists. Actually, some of the most thought-provoking and reflexive public archaeology has dealt seriously with the social and historical causes of present troubles (e.g., Leone 2005). I do not see why we should be doing something different in third world contexts (cf. M. Hall 2000). This, of course, does not preclude any other kind of more "practical" and direct help in heritage management or in any other field, but it is essential to problematize the figure of the archaeologist in the role of voluntary worker, the concept of development, and the idea of "cooperation" itself.

Vernacular Cosmopolitanism: Archaeology on the Border

Can cosmopolitanism be the answer to the colonial rhetoric of international cooperation and development? It might be, but probably not in the way many intellectuals have outlined cosmopolitanism. Wallerstein (1996: 124) thinks that the stance "citizen of the world" is deeply ambiguous: "It can be used just as easily to sustain privilege as to undermine it." There are basically two kinds of cosmopolitans: the powerful and the disempowered, those who have chosen to live with others in different countries, and those who have been forced to do so (such as labor migrants and refugees) (Werbner 2006; Beck and Sznaider 2006: 7–8). The people in the first group, in which those archaeologists working in foreign countries are to be included, are allowed to be cosmopolitans, because they (or their states and societies) have made the *kosmos* into their *polis*, the *orbs* into their *urbs* (Pollock 2000: 602). It is easy to be cosmopolitan when power is on one's side.

Appiah's theories (2006a) are a good example of the elite-centered, self-satisfied streak of cosmopolitanism (see other chapters in this volume for more positive readings of the author). The cosmopolitan experiences that inform much of his work are those of a member of a privileged Westernized upper class who feels as much at ease in a royal palace in Kumasi as at Princeton University. Appiah states throughout his book that we have obligations and responsibilities to others, but they are "not monstrous or unreasonable. They do not require us to abandon our own lives. They entail . . . no heroism" (Appiah 2006a:

174). Not if heroism is understood in the neoliberal-individualist way criticized above. But when one thinks, for example, of all the activists who have lost their lives defending indigenous and peasant rights, Appiah's statement cannot but sound outrageous.

To say that the world today does not require heroisms because we are much better off implies a sanction of global capitalism and the status quo. That is a kind of a comfortable cosmopolitanism that allows Western(ized) elites to keep their lifestyles and worldviews, while at the same time it appeases their consciences: "What would the world look like if people always spent their money to alleviate diarrhea in the Third World and never on a ticket to the opera?," asks Appiah (2006a: 166). The answer is simple: a much better world indeed. I do not only find his ethical standpoint wanting, to say the least, but also the theoretical basis of his cosmopolitanism, which leaves the question of the "other" largely unproblematized—the same with Nussbaum's (1996) romantic vision of difference. Slavoj Žižek's recent essay on otherness is much more thought provoking. Drawing on a critical reading of Judaism, Levinas, and other sources, Žižek (2005: 140) emphasizes the "alien, traumatic kernel" that forever exists in the "inert, impenetrable, enigmatic presence" of "my Neighbor." He goes beyond Levinas though by trying to grasp the "inhuman Otherness itself" (Žižek 2005: 160). However, this troubling engagement with the Neighbor does not restrict our "infinite responsibility" to the other. Both Levinas and Žižek stress the unboundedness of our responsibility, in striking contrast to Appiah's complacent limitations.

Furthermore, Appiah (2006a: 109–13) espouses the fashionable theory among anthropologists today that globalism is not homogeneity, but leads to endless creativity (cf. Inda and Rosaldo 2002). This, again, overlooks global structural inequalities, long-term processes of oppression, and the real and traumatic impact that Western culture and politics exercise over the third world. The anthropologists of globalization dehistoricize the phenomenon and naturalize neoliberalism (see critiques in Graeber 2002; Edelman and Haugeraud 2003; Žižek and Daly 2004: 139–66). This is the problem too with multiculturalism, which Appiah (2006a: 104–5) criticizes with regard to identity but reproduces in other ways—for example, by ethically leveling discrepant voices: victims and tyrants, rich and poor, master and slave. Archaeology, with its long-term historical standpoint and its focus on destruction and ruins, may offer counternarratives to the anthropologists' positive view of globalization.

Although there are some general ideas in which I agree with Appiah and other cosmopolitans of the same breed, I find this cosmopolitanism flawed, yet not the idea of cosmopolitanism per se, which I consider a way of articulating a concern for others without couching it in universalistic or paternalistic terms. A qualified cosmopolitanism, as proposed by Homi Bhabha among others, could be a starting point.

Bhabha (2001: 42–43) defines a vernacular or marginal cosmopolitanism based upon three main points: 1) it is a cosmopolitanism that stops short of the transcendent human universal and provides an ethical entitlement to the sense of community; 2) it is conscious of the insufficiency of the self and the imperative of openness to the needs of others; and 3) it finds in the victims of progress the best promise for ethical regeneration. Vernacular cosmopolitanism is equivalent to Julia Kristeva's (1997: 274) "cosmopolitanism of those who have been flayed." Vernacular cosmopolitans, says Bhabha (Bhabha and Comaroff 2002: 24) "are the heirs of Walter Benjamin's view of modernity, that every act of civilization is also an act of barbarism."

I believe, with Bhabha, that it is possible to be committed to the specificity of the (traumatic) event and yet to be "linked to a transhistorical memory and solidarity." The way this cosmopolitanism works is illustrated by Bhabha through a poem by Adrienne Rich, in which a repetitive first person recounts different tragedies occurring in different locales and times. The same procedure was used before by Aimé Césaire (1956: 39) when he wrote "I shall be a Jew-man / A Kaffir-man / a Hindu-from-Calcutta-man / a man-from-Harlem-who-hasn't-got-the-vote." According to Bhabha (2001: 44), "The 'I' that speaks [in Rich's poem]—its place of enunciation—is iteratively and interrogatively staged. It is poised at the point at which, in recounting historical trauma, the incommensurable 'localities' of experience and memory bear witness, side by side, but there is no easy ethical analogy or historical parallelism." Rich's work is presented as the "atlas of a difficult world," articulated in a series of traumatic juxtapositions. Vernacular cosmopolitanism is to be more than in dialogic relation with the native or the domestic: it is to be "on the border, *in between*, introducing the global-cosmopolitan 'action at a distance' into the very grounds—now displaced—of the domestic" (Bhabha 2001: 48). It also implies a critique of liberal individualism that excludes communities and individuals that do not fit liberal secularism. It might be a way of challenging universalism. Žižek notes that every universality is hegemonized or particularized, but there is a sort of universality (as there is a sort of cosmopolitanism) that can be redeeming: it is the universality of those who are "below us," the neglected and outcast. It is a negative universality to be opposed to Western universalism (Žižek and Daly 2004: 160).

My archaeological research in Ethiopia, Brazil, and Spain focuses on the effects of globalization, modernity, development, and universalistic policies. That the local contexts in which I work are not isolated, traditional, disengaged, or disconnected from larger processes, as Lynn Meskell reminds in the introduction to this book, is more than obvious in the communities where I work. In Ethiopia, I explore the archaeological remains of Cooperazione Italiana, USAID, and interventionism by the Soviet Union (González-Ruibal 2006b). In Brazil, a railway funded by the World Bank crosses the rainforest where the Awá hunter-gatherers live, through which tons of bauxite are transported, every two hours, to the coast, and from there to Europe and the United States. The Awá, then, are hunter-gatherers whose life experience is inseparable from the World Bank, the European Union, agribusiness, aluminum industries, and illegal loggers. The peasants I work with in Galicia are connected with diasporic communities in the United States, Germany, and Argentina (González-Ruibal 2005). My research might be considered a sort of cosmopolitan archaeology from a threefold point of view: it explores international engagements and the application of universalistic policies; it is triggered by a true concern for others; and it juxtaposes three different localities shaken by international forces. Brazil, Ethiopia, and Spain are the poles of my own cosmopolitan agenda of action and research—they form my own "atlas of a difficult world." At the same time, my work is also a vernacular undertaking, because it takes domesticity, culture, tradition, identity, and roots seriously into account.

The communities I work with share many points in common, but I make no attempt to even them out. As in the poems of Rich and Césaire, it is the juxtaposition of traumatic, singular experiences and their articulation with transhistorical memories and global troubles that interest me. I work on the border—the marginality of minority groups in third world countries, but I bring the border to my own homeland.

By doing that, I dissolve the concentric circles that Martha Nussbaum (1996: 9) imagines emanating from one's home and subvert her cosmopolitan hierarchy. As a matter of fact, I do not want to make all human beings more like my "fellow city-dwellers" (Nussbaum 1996: 9); on the contrary, as recommended by Said (1996: 514), I prefer to "annihilate my place," which does not imply a rejection of primordial affects, but an elaboration of them (Said 1996: 515; also Kristeva 1997: 274). And, with Žižek (2005: 163), I am against the "ethical 'gentrification' of the neighbor" and the ethical leveling of the other. Nussbaum's (1996: 13) statement that "politics . . . will be poorly done if each thinks herself equally responsible for all, rather than giving the immediate surroundings special attention and care" goes against the radical ethics proposed here, following Žižek (2005). If there is any hierarchy in our responsibilities toward others, it should be dictated by the urgency of the situation, not by national ties.

I am an archaeologist who works with living peoples, their material culture, and the remains of their contemporary past—a kind of research that may be labeled "archaeology of the present," a term that tries to blend those interests in a meaningful way (González-Ruibal 2006a). In the rest of this chapter, I will deal with two of the areas in the atlas of the difficult world I have been mentioning—the most troubling ones: Brazil and Ethiopia. I will try to show what flawed notions of development and evolution, in part supported by an archaeological metanarrative, have implied for the communities in which I work.

Ethiopia: Development in *Terra Nullius*

In my first trip to Sudan and Ethiopia, in January 2000, both countries were the poorest nations in the world according to the UN listing and both of them were at war. Armed conflict and extreme poverty made those countries, at that time as well as today, very cosmopolitan countries—in a very particular way. International agencies and institutions, governmental and nongovernmental, large and small, American and European, populated then and populate today the tortured landscapes of the Horn of Africa.

The panorama is cosmopolitan too from an archaeological point of view. Sudan and Ethiopia host a sizeable community of Western researchers. Their agendas, however, are more universalistic than cosmopolitan. While cosmopolitanism implies a concern for others, for difference and diversity, universalistic archaeology has a Western interest camouflaged under the vocabulary of globalism—much like that of many international institutions. According to Beck and Sznaider (2006: 19) universalism "does not involve any requirement that would arouse curiosity or respect for what makes others different." Archaeological research in Ethiopia is polarized around human origins and the state. Ethiopia usually hits international news for two issues: famine and human fossils. For different reasons, they both capture Western imaginations and create an image of the country as a barren land where early hominids once roamed and dispossessed humans die en masse today. For palaeoanthropologists, Ethiopia is an accident. They could well be doing the same work in Utah or Bavaria, if there were such wonderful sites there. Admittedly, they could not show the stunning photos of the jeep stuck in the sand, the beautiful (black) women smiling, or the fierce ancestral warrior with an AK-47. The epics of palaeoanthropological research in sub-Saharan Africa certainly deserve a good ethnography that is to be done some day. By now, we just have a romantic account from the point of view of those great gentlemen adventurers (for example, Johanson and Edey 1981; Kalb 2001). Palaeolithic specialists are barely interested in the (too parochial) history of the Horn of Africa because they aim higher: they want to reveal the Origins of (all) Humankind. The search for origins that bypass indigenous interests is certainly not something that affects Ethiopia alone (cf. Shepherd 2002; Wobst 2005: 25). In Ethiopia the situation is perhaps more poignant because the Euro-American search for origins takes place in one of the poorest nations in the world. The Afar pastoralists, who live in the area where most hominid fossils are found, kill each other for securing a waterhole for their herds (Gebre 2004: 252–54) and their nomadism is more and more restricted by development projects and the national park that occupies part of their traditional lands—which feature in the World Heritage list as the cradle of humankind. The state is striving to transform them into "'law abiding,' modernized and productive citizens" (Kassa 2004: 224). Meanwhile, archaeologists and physical anthropologists struggle for a new fragment of a yet older Australopithecus that might make it to the front page of *Science* or *Nature*.

The other important focus of attention by international scholars and institutions is Ethiopia's history as a state. This includes the Aksumite civilization (early first millennium AD), the churches of the Middle

1   One of the seventeenth-century castles of Gondar, a World Heritage monument. *Photo courtesy of the author.*

Ages (Lalibela), and the castles of the Abyssinian court of the seventeenth and eighteenth centuries, based at the city of Gondar (figure 1). International interest in Aksum (Munro-Hay 1991) has been fostered for two main reasons: its outstanding monumentality and its connections with other parts of the world—Egypt, Greece, Rome, Yemen, and India. Later, the medieval and Gondarine periods are also marked by an outstanding architecture and art with obvious foreign resemblances: Gondar has been called the "Camelot of Africa" (Ramos and Boavida 2004). Ethiopia, then, is valued as are other third world nations for being a strategic crossroad, attractive for its hybrid nature. This vision of Ethiopia's history is reflected on the World Heritage list. The Ethiopian sites that have been incorporated are mainly related to the origins of humankind (Awash and Omo valleys) or the history of the Abyssinian state as a unified and cosmopolitan nation (Aksum, Gondar, Lalibela). In incorporating such sites, the complexities and intricacies of Ethiopian history are lost, whether because they are bypassed wholesale (human evolution) or because only the state perspective is given. This has to be related to the colonialist, modernist bias of the concept of world heritage (Meskell 2005d: 128).

Modernity sanctions the role of the state and its works as progressive, and it considers nonstate societies as backward and anarchic. Archaeology has played an important role in justifying the works of the state and forgetting the people at its margins (Meskell 2005d: 130–32; Wobst 2005: 28). With Appiah (2001: 225), I am against "Africa as a fancied past of shared glories—the Africa of Diop and the 'Egyptianists.'" I am, on the contrary, with that of Aimé Césaire (1972: 23), in his (admittedly idealized) defense of the societies destroyed by imperialism. Instead of undermining the concepts of progress and cultural achievement developed by the Enlightenment, some pan-Africanists appropriated them and used them to strike back. The merit of these interpretations lay in bringing attention to the intellectual creativity of sub-Saharan peoples. At the same time, however, this means accepting the rules of the game as presented by those in power: cultural success is based on state polities, strong inequalities, wide (and usually unfair) economic networks, and large monuments and infrastructures, all of them made possible by social exploitation (Stahl 2004: 254–55). Other intellectuals, such as Aimé Césaire, have resorted to a more radical weapon of resistance: changing and challenging the rules of the game—the roots of colonial discourse—altogether. By praising "those who have invented nothing," Césaire (1956) created a new structural metaphor that broke with Western assumptions of historical success. The same occurs with Clastres's "societies against the state," for whom failing to achieve "social complexity" is not a failure but a political act of resistance (Clastres 1989).

The project in which I have been involved in Ethiopia since 2001 is an alternative to prevailing universalistic approaches. It deals with communities at the border of the state, in an area lacking remains from the deepest past. I will refer here to the history of one of the groups that inhabit the borderland of Ethiopia, the Gumuz of Metekel. Metekel is located north of the Blue Nile, near the frontier between Sudan and Ethiopia. The annexation to Ethiopia was only completed around 1901 (Abdussamad 1999). Although originally conceived as an ethnoarchaeological project, our concern for the situation of the people with whom we worked led us to rethink our principles of engagement and reconsider our research under more cosmopolitan and postcolonial lines. What I will try to show here is that the Gumuz's present situation of disempowerment with regard to national and international development projects is just the final step in a long history of dispossession and marginalization.

Since at least the middle of the first millennium AD the Gumuz have been considered *homines sacri*, in Agamben's (1998: 71–80) apt terminology, a sort of humans liable to be massacred, enslaved, and deprived of their lands: "If someone kills the one who is sacred according to the plebiscite, it will not be considered homicide," says the Roman law. The killing of a *homo sacer* is a sort of banal death without the aura of a sacrifice—this is why Agamben rejects the concept of Holocaust for the extermination of the Jews by the Nazis. The existence of the *homo sacer* is bare life (*nuda vita*) at the will of sovereign power. The justification for the inferiority of the Gumuz resonates with other colonialisms elsewhere: they are heathen, flat-nosed, black, nomad, and uncivilized (Pankhurst 1977). Their land is a *terra nullius*, available for more industrious peasants, living in sedentary villages and worshipping the true god, or for capitalists involved in development projects.

It is very likely that the slave raids in this territory, along with expeditions in search of gold, were carried out already in the Aksumite period (Pankhurst 2001: 28–30). After the thirteenth century the documentation about the slave raids grows steadily and significantly reaches a peak during the period of splendor of the Abyssinian Kingdom, from the early seventeenth century to the mid-eighteenth century. The Gumuz, pejoratively called Shankilla ("slave"), were captured and killed by the thousands during those centuries (Pankhurst 2001: 351–72). That the Shankilla were regarded as little better than animals is demonstrated by the hunting expeditions carried out in the late nineteenth century and the early twentieth by noble Ethiopians, in which elephants were killed and Gumuz were captured (Abdussamad 1988). Slavery continued until the Second World War, when Fascist Italy put an end to it—and presented the achievement as a moral justification for the conquest of Ethiopia. The Italians, however, undertook most development projects in the heart of the country, leaving only military posts in lowland areas. Fascist rule in Ethiopia was organized on racist lines, and the Gumuz were too black and too primitive to be able to benefit from progress, unlike the Caucasian-looking highlanders (Amhara, Agaw). Over the centuries, the Gumuz were gradually expelled from their original territory and banished to the margins of their homeland, the least healthy and fertile lowland areas (Wolde-Selassie 2004a: map 8-11). Many Amhara and Agaw settlers came from the highlands, giving rise to the complex ethnicity of the area today. As a matter of fact, the process has not come to an end, and each year new families descend to the lowlands in search of new cultivable land, escaping from the wasteland in which the Abyssinian plateau has been transformed by the feudal politics of the same state that built Gondar (Girma 1992).

Even today, the land of the Gumuz is somewhat perceived as a *terra nullius* by the state, the neighboring groups, and the West: they see it as an underpopulated territory that deserves better exploitation. We may think that the relegation of the Gumuz, based on their culture and race, is something of the distant past, with no effect in the present whatsoever. Yet ancient beliefs have not withered away. The journalist Alan Moorehead (2000 [1961]: 6) tells that the land of the Gumuz "is a country of conical grass huts and oppressive heat that creates a sort of woolliness in the mind, and of long, slow, uneventful days that have stunted human ambition from prehistoric times." This racist perspective is still shared by many developmental agencies, missionaries, and sanctimonious, well-educated Westerners. The "woolliness in the mind" prevented the Gumuz from building splendid palaces that may deserve inclusion in the World Heritage list or even attention by archaeologists. Unambitious and uncreative, they have been unable to make history, and their lives have been condemned to the same hollow nothingness since the dawn of times. The land of the Gumuz is a great place for an ethnoarchaeologist, where he or she can see prehistory alive. Unfortunately for such prehistoric relics, "There was never any possibility that these undeveloped people would be left alone in their slow dull round existence," states Moorehead (2000 [1961]: 9). When the author wrote that, slavery had ended two decades before, but new adversities were still to come for the Gumuz, this time from beyond the Horn of Africa in the shape of development policies. The treatment of the Gumuz and their land was going to be very much the same.

In 1985, as a late response to the terrible famine and drought that killed one million Ethiopians, the Communist state decided to establish a development program and resettlement scheme in the land of the Gumuz (Wolde-Selassie 2004a, 2004b). They were spared by the famine, as were most inhabitants from lowland areas, because their "primitive" swidden agriculture and egalitarian politics were much less aggressive to the environment and had not caused the large-scale deforestation of more "advanced" cultivation methods and political economies based on heavy taxation. The scheme—the so-called Tana-Beles Project—was developed in the Beles Valley, where 250,000 hectares of land were to be occupied by 48 villages and several agricultural projects. Over 82,000 highlanders were displaced to the area (Wolde-Selassie 2004b: 76) and 73,000 hectares of tropical forest were cleared (Yntiso 2004: 92). The enterprise was made possible thanks to funds and technical assistance provided by the Italian government. Thousands of indigenous peoples were uprooted from their ancestral lands and banished to less fertile areas. Perhaps because the locals were not starving, nobody thought that they should receive any benefit from the development project. Thus, my Gumuz informants often complained that they did not have access to the health and education services offered to the newcomers or to free seeds and agricultural machinery. This embittered the relations between the Gumuz, the central state, and the highlanders, a situation that ended in overt ethnic conflict after the fall of the Communist regime in 1991.

The situation has improved with the implementation of federal policies that grant more political power to the indigenous inhabitants of Metekel (and disenfranchise the settlers). However, multicultural federalism has not helped the Gumuz as much as it could be expected to. At least in part, this is due to the terrible legacy of the Tana-Beles project. As we have had the occasion to see during our fieldwork, those Gumuz communities that are located around the premises of the development scheme suffer from acute social problems: violence within the community and between clans is widespread, with frequent killings and feuds; there is a high ratio of female suicide; traditional working parties and celebrations have given way to alcoholism; the authority of the elders seems undermined by youngsters whose new means of legitimation is the possession of automatic weapons (cf. also Wolde-Selassie 2004a: 111). Other problems brought by the new political situation, however, are not inherited. They are the result of the introduction of new modernist strategies under the sign of capitalism, which also considers the land a *terra nullius*. The new local elites are eager to develop their region at any price, usually to the detriment of their own inhabitants. Thus, agro-industries flourish, the Gumuz are still being displaced from their homeland, and deforestation increases every year (Wolde-Selassie 2004a: 126).

In March 2006, when we were looking for a village where we could carry out fieldwork, we discovered a huge deforested area, extending for dozens of kilometers along the road. As we found out later, the deforestation was carried out by a Dutch multinational company that planned to cultivate oil palms for biodiesel in that area. It cut down eighty thousand hectares of tropical trees, expelled the local population, and brought in laborers from the neighboring villages, most of them highlanders recently settled in the area. Once again in their long history of abuse, the Gumuz have been decreed disposable and their lands stolen or rented for nothing. However, in macro-economic figures, this agribusiness project will appear as a sign of development and probably contribute a bit to the rise of the federal GDP. At a global level, the production of biodiesel—itself a dubious alternative energy—will be depicted as an eco-friendly solution to the fuel crisis.

My point is that, by being only concerned with glorious monumental pasts and the history of the state (preferably a well-bounded nation-state) as an evolutionary success (cf. the chapters by Lydon and Byrne, this volume), archaeologists and heritage managers are sanctioning the crude modernist vision of many development agencies. By studying the history and material culture of "those who have invented nothing," another discourse, one that challenges evolutionism and concepts of progress, can be produced. The archaeology of Metekel is also about monuments, the state, and international contacts, as much as the castles of Gondar or the obelisks of Axum. The monuments of Metekel are not inherently different from those sanctioned by the World Heritage Organization or by the interests of Western archaeologists. The difference has to do with time only. The archaeological remains of Metekel are the ghostly ruins of the Tana-Beles project, which failed and was abandoned in 1991 (González-Ruibal 2006b), or the rusty carcasses of tanks and trucks ambushed on the road to Sudan during the last civil war. Archaeological sites are also the palaces built by slave traders, impressive brick buildings, now abandoned, boasting an incongruous solidity in a land of "conical grass huts and oppressive heat" (figure 2). The monuments of Metekel are trenches and arsenals constructed by fascist Italians, who dealt with this area as though it were an empty battlefield and protected the frontier with human waste: indigenous troops, *askaris*, because the life of an Italian soldier was too valuable

2 The ruined palace of the slave trader Banjaw Abu Shok, built in the 1930s in the town of Gubba. *Photograph courtesy of the author.*

to be lost in a *terra nullius*. Metekel, too, is a crossroad of civilizations. But this is the dark side of all cultural crossroads. The state, development, progress, history: from the border, things never look the same.

Brazil: Order and Progress

"The settler and pioneer have at bottom had justice on their side: this great continent could not have been kept as nothing but a game preserve for squalid savages," said Theodore Roosevelt (quoted in Maybury-Lewis 2002: 45). Despite the years that have passed since that statement, the viewpoints and beliefs have not changed substantially: development projects for the progress of the nation-state trump indigenous communities everywhere in the world. In some cases, like Brazil, the means of exterminating squalid savages and getting hold of their lands have not changed much either. In chapter 4 of this volume, Lynn Meskell says that myths of emptiness have been vigorously dismantled in Australia and North America, but not in South Africa. Myths of

3   A group of Awá during a hunting expedition. *Photograph by permission of Almudena Hernando.*

emptiness are still very much at work in the Brazilian cultural and political imaginary, also, with terrible consequences.

The Awá or Guajá are a small group of hunter-gatherers, numbering around three hundred individuals, who inhabit the Amazonian forest in the state of Maranhão, Brazil (Cormier 2003b) (figure 3). Officially contacted by white Brazilians for the first time in the early 1970s, their population was dramatically reduced by that contact, which included the invasion of their land by impoverished peasants, loggers, and landlords, the spreading of diseases, and the development of colossal projects cofinanced by international institutions (Treece 1987). The Awá were by no means the only group affected by the arrival of "order and progress" at the southeastern edge of Amazonia. Other communities were heavily damaged, including the Tenetehara, Krikati, Ka'apor, Gaviões, and Ramko-Kamikrá (Coelho 1987; Treece 1987: 128–38). The work of progress here has been a "systematic history of erasure" (see chapter 4 by Meskell, this volume), with the difference, with respect to South Africa's natural reservations, that erasure in Brazil has not been dictated for the preservation of nature, but for its more thorough exploitation. The Awá are a clear example of *homines sacri*. People only make sense if comprised within the concept of citizenship. The Indians are not citizens and they are considered legally minors, forever surveilled and protected by the National Indian Agency (FUNAI). Not being Brazilians, they lay "outside the sanctioned universe of obligation" (Fein 1984: 11). "I have never been in Brazil," To'o, an Awá Indian, told me during my first visit to his reservation, and he did not know how right he was. It is counter-cosmopolitanism that it is at work here.

Indians are the most disposable of all peoples. Some of the peasants who invaded the Awá forests in the 1970s and 1980s commented with astonishment, when they met with an Indian family, "They almost look like humans" (Elizabetha Beserra Coelho, personal communication 2005). The similarity was incomplete, sufficiently incomplete to unleash a genocide when the invaders gave the Indians infected clothes or poisoned food or simply shot at them (O'Dwyer 2000). Local politicians who agree with Roosevelt's words and with a liberalism that grants rights to individuals alone (Ivison 2002) consider that a handful of savages should not be occupying thousands of hectares of primeval forest that could be developed and benefit many more people. Development has to come first by the slash-and-burn agriculture of miserable peasants, then by the large-scale cattle raising that takes hold of the land after the initial clearing. That is the normal evolution of things: savagery as represented by the indigenous hunters, barbarism in the shape of poor but hard-working laborers cutting down the jungle, and civilization brought by agribusiness, ranching, mining, and industry.

As in the case of the Gumuz presented above, we have to understand the disenfranchisement of the Awá in a long-term perspective. The contact between the Awá and the European colonizers probably started in the early seventeenth century, when the Portuguese conquered the coasts of Maranhão, previously settled by other European colonists (Cormier 2003b: 3). The Portuguese invaded indigenous lands, enslaved Indians, and brought about the dislocation of many communities. Several pandemics during the seventeenth and eighteenth centuries decimated the native population of the region and seriously damaged the social fabric of several indigenous communities (Cormier 2003b: 5). It is probable that the Awá were a group of swidden agriculturalists who lost their knowledge of cultivation after their persecution and enslavement by the colonizers (Cormier 2003b: 4): the Awá would have turned to hunting and gathering in isolated forests to escape from whites. The Cabanagem civil war (1835–41), which wiped out entire Indian groups in Brazil, has also been suggested as the motive for the "involution" of the Awá (Forline 1997: 30; also Mércio Pereira Gomes, quoted in O'Dwyer 2000: 34). Ironically, then, it was the white man's development and progress that "underdeveloped" the Awá.

After a period in which news about the Awá come from a few casual encounters in which they were described as foragers (Nimuendajú 1949), the Awá suffered the massive encroachment of Brazilian society by the end of the 1960s and the beginning of the 1970s. As with the territory of the Gumuz in Ethiopia, the Awá forests were considered "land without men for men without land" by the Brazilian state (Forline 1997: 16). We find again the concept of *terra nullius* used to the detriment of indigenous communities. The personal dramas of the Awá, chased and killed by the hundreds, their families broken and dispersed, amounted to a veritable genocide. Some individuals, isolated from their families after a confrontation with ranchers or peasants, trekked hundreds of kilometers alone for a decade or more. The resettlement program of the FUNAI was likewise traumatic. Out of ninety-one individuals settled in a village by the Indian agency in 1976 only twenty-five were alive in 1981. Most of them died due to an ill-advised vaccination campaign (O'Dwyer 2000: 69). The establishment of four FUNAI villages for the Awá was carried out with disregard to family and group ties.

Nonetheless, the implementation of the Grande Carajás project was the single most traumatic event for the local communities. It was devised to occupy an area similar to that of Britain and France combined and it consisted of several mining projects (iron, gold, and bauxite), roads, dams, and railways (figure 4). The two largest investors were the European Union and the World Bank. Even before the program began, contracts were signed with Italy, Japan, and Germany in order to provide around 30 million tons of iron for their steel industries (Treece 1987: 9). The Grande Carajás project was going to be the miracle solution to Brazil's staggering foreign debt (Treece 1987: 13). The railway cut the rainforest in two, separated indigenous communities, and facilitated the arrival of peasants and illegal loggers en masse, whereas the production of iron required the rapid clearing of the forests to produce coal (Cormier 2003a: 125). This left the Indians without their traditional resources and many were compelled to hunt horses and

4   The railway sponsored by the World Bank near the town of Alto Alegre. The town was created ex novo in the 1970s in what were primeval tropical forests inhabited by the Awá. *Photograph courtesy of the author.*

other domesticates in the ranches that had invaded their lands—and the ranchers killed the Indians.

The sad history of the Awá does not end here. They are now the owners of large forest reserves where nobody can enter without a permit issued by the FUNAI. The reality, however, is much different. During August 2006 we had the occasion to go with the police and the FUNAI in an operation to chase illegal loggers in one of the Awá reservations. The loggers had devastated the forest, besieging the Awá in less than one-tenth of their legal territory. Roads, bridges, and campsites crisscross the jungle. The rivers have been dammed up and the oldest and most valuable trees have been cut and sold. Many peasants have invaded the reserve and a large ranch owned by an absentee landlord occupies part of the Indian lands and part of a biological reserve. The Awá complain that game—their staple food—escapes from the sound of the chainsaws and tractors. However, the Companhia da Vale do

Rio Doce, from the Grande Carajás project, has been paying royalties to the FUNAI for the damage caused to the Indians. The money has been used in turning the Awá into agriculturalists and in giving them clothes and other goods that push them a little bit away from savagery and closer to civilization.

What has archaeology and anthropology to do with this situation? Since the nineteenth century, both disciplines have contributed directly or indirectly to the portrayal of Indians in a way that legitimized development policies and the role of the state at the expense of the peoples that live in its margins.

As it has been proven, archaeology played a fundamental role in supporting the enterprise of the expanding Euro-American bourgeoisie (Trigger 1989). By constructing a unilinear tale of order and progress, archaeology helped to give intellectual grounding to colonialism, racism, and Western hegemony in general. In so doing, archaeology was not behaving differently from other sciences (Said 2003). Lubbock's work (1865), which is just the most remarkable of a series of books comparing savages and prehistoric peoples, justified the expropriation of the premoderns by situating modern "primitives" in the lowest step of the ladder of progress and by displacing them to another time (Fabian 1983). In the model of universalistic reason defended by nineteenth-century archaeology and anthropology, the savage was a *homo sacer*, an incomplete human, an "embryo of us" (Hernando Gonzalo 2006: 228).

The case of Brazilian archaeology has been studied by Ferreira (2005). He argues that the archaeology of Brazil during the imperial period (1840–99), with its evolutionist criteria, was a convenient tool in the work of "sieving" the indigenous "races" that would feature in the national image of the country to be transmitted to the imperial elites and to the civilized nations of the world. Thus, with data from archaeological excavations in shell mounds and tumuli, two different groups of Indians were produced by the archaeological imagination of the period: a civilized one and a savage one. The man-eating, indolent, and nomad hunter who lived amid rubbish heaps and produced no monument, art, or craft was ruled out, while the clean, hierarchical, and industrious mound-builder and skilled potter was incorporated into the myths of the national project (Ferreira 2005: 144). The practical effects of this kind of research were noticeable at that time: military colonies were built in which indolent natives, "surveilled and educated by soldiers and missionaries, could learn Portuguese, and the craft of the black-smith, carpenter, shepherd and agriculturalist" (Ferreira 2005: 145). The nomad savage was transformed into the industrious one. These colonies hosted indigenous populations that would later mix with European immigrants thereby whitening the national race.

As I have pointed out above, this sort of unilinear archaeological thought is still pervasive in many Western minds, and it is certainly not restricted to the less enlightened citizens. In places like Brazil, a dangerous universalistic reasoning—a myth of progress—is still stronger and its practical outcomes are quite sinister. Thus, the Serviço de Proteção ao Índio (SPI, 1910–67) and the Fundação Nacional do Índio (FUNAI, 1968 to the present), the national Indian agencies, inherited the imperial perspectives on the indigenous groups that were informed by anthropologists and archaeologists during the nineteenth century. The state posts that were theoretically conceived to protect native populations were in practice locales for the rapid assimilation of the Other into Brazilian culture through improvised strategies of social engineering (cf. Oliveira 1960). These usually involved the supply of Western material culture in the form of technical and moral knowledge. The final goal was to transform the native into a citizen, even if a low-class one (a *camponês*: a peasant). Although the staff of the FUNAI had very few anthropologists on the payroll, that is not the case of private companies, such as the Companhia da Vale do Rio Doce, one of the most important ventures involved in the Grande Carajás project, which contracted anthropologists during the 1980s to assist "in identifying and attracting isolated groups of indigenous peoples to ease the stressful transition of contact through settlement" (Forline 1997: 17). Thence, if archaeology supported evolution from a theoretical standpoint, anthropologists played a major practical role in reordering the wild along progressive lines.

This modernist way of reasoning has also been incorporated, in a sense, by the World Heritage Organization. Brazil has seventeen places included on the World Heritage list (http://whc.unesco.org/en/statesparties/br). The distribution is as follows: seven colonial cities (including Brasília), two Catholic monuments, seven natural reserves, and only one prehistoric site: Serra da Capivara, which has evidence of the earliest occupation of America (ca. 25,000 years old). The other seventeen sites on the tentative list have a similar bias, with several forests and colonial monuments. The conclusion is obvious: Brazil was a *terra nullius* when the Portuguese arrived there in 1500. Today, there is nature and there are the colonizers' monuments. What about "those who have invented nothing"? What about the indigenous cultures that were populating—and still populate—Amazonia when the Europeans disembarked? Their existence is symbolically denied or they are romantically equated with nature. Like the indolent, nomadic hunter-gatherers in the imperial imagination, the Brazilian Aborigines are crossed out from the cultural heritage that deserves conservation and global respect.

That is the case with the Awá themselves. In a coffee-table book produced by the local government of Maranhão with images by a German photographer, the Awá feature along with dunes, monkeys, palm-trees, rivers, and even a few picturesque peasants (Knepper 2002). The title of the book is telling: *The Natural World of Maranhão*. Awá history, then, is at best natural history. The notion is shared by development agencies. Thus, for the Brazilian company Eletrobrás, "Indigenous communities represent one of the most complex environmental problems in the planning and implementation of hydroelectric plants and transmission lines" (quoted in Viveiros de Castro and Andrade 1990: 1). Hunter-gatherers elsewhere are regarded in a similar way—the San, for example, are conceived as an extension of the fauna and flora in South Africa (Meskell and Weiss 2006: 94–95). This view of non-modern societies, and especially foragers, is not surprising, since it is espoused, more or less consciously, by many ethnoarchaeologists working within the sociobiology paradigm.

Ethnoarchaeology, once one of the cornerstones of processual archaeology (Binford 1983), and particularly the ethnoarchaeology of hunter-gatherers, is now largely dominated by bioarchaeologists or biological anthropologists who use their knowledge to understand early hominid behavior and the evolution of humankind (for example, Hawkes et al. 1997). As a matter of fact, they compare the behavior of living hunters with that of pre-sapiens hominids (such as *Homo habilis*). Palaeoanthropologists talk about human ecology with disregard to cultural practices, beliefs, and experiences, and although they assert that they are just interested in the biological side of humanity in general and not in culture, the reality is that when they compare the ecology of humans and primates or talk about adaptation and evolution (Brockman and van Shaik 2005), they do not study lawyers or executives in Manhattan or Tokyo, but "primitives" living in the wild, those who have invented nothing and are, therefore, closer to nature than to culture: half-humans, half-monkeys. If we excavate the genealogy of this approach we will arrive at Lubbock's works and that of many colonial minds of the late nineteenth century and the early twentieth: *Among Pygmies and Gorillas*, for example, is the eloquent title of a book published by William, the prince of Sweden, with the results of a *zoological* expedition to the Congo (William 1926). After the strong reflexive critique of cultural anthropology (Fabian 1983), the prolongation of nature into the "primitive man" established in the nineteenth century survives uninterrupted in some modern studies of ethnoarchaeology and human evolution. A symmetrical approach is needed to dissolve the divide between nature and culture: not only for non-moderns, but for all nature cultures—ours included (Latour 1993, 1999).

Archaeology, therefore, in the work of some of its practitioners, fails to recognize the achievements of those societies that do not create monuments (World Heritage Organization) and keeps producing an image of non-modern peoples as closer to nature than to humankind (ethnoarchaeology), eliminating their cultural peculiarities and the sociopolitical context in favor of understanding the remote origins of *all* humankind. Should we be puzzled by the treatment given by development agencies to those same communities? Unwittingly, archaeology helps to reinforce counter-cosmopolitan, universalistic attitudes that restrict our obligations to others. Our obligations are to full human beings only.

Conclusion: Digging the Present

According to Appiah (2006a: 153), the real challenge for cosmopolitanism today is not "the belief that other people don't matter at all; it's the belief that they don't matter very much." In this chapter, I have dealt with two "non-modern" societies, the Awá in Brazil and the Gumuz in Ethiopia, that do not matter very much for the counter-cosmopolitans—international development agencies, multinationals, the state officials from the countries where they live, and some scholars. Smith and Wobst (2005: 393) have pointed out that an archaeology guided by indigenous peoples' agendas has to engage with the present as much as with the past and has to focus on issues of importance to the survival of indigenous cultures (see also Meskell 2005b). This sort of archaeology, then, has to be vernacular cosmopolitan in spirit. This is why my work is less related to ethnoarchaeology or prehistoric archaeology than it used to be and more engaged with the archaeology of the present. I am not postulating the abandonment of prehistory—on the contrary, it is essential to the long-term understanding of situations as those described in this chapter. I am not for the end of ethnoarchaeology, either, although it needs to be refashioned in a much more postcolonial and cosmopolitan way (González-Ruibal 2006a).

Nonetheless, we must start digging the present as archaeologists and not just in a metaphorical way: we should excavate the devastation brought by a modernism that marginalizes, betrays, and in the worst case annihilates the communities with which we work. In doing that, we should frame the problems of the people whom we study in a long-term perspective—a task for which archaeology is especially well suited. This does not imply any primitivist or romanticized vision of the "native." It is a purely cosmopolitan engagement that arises from a visceral concern for the lives of others. By excavating literally or metaphorically the present, we will be acting as witnesses, bearing testimony to what has happened and is happening—an uncomfortable yet necessary activity. A thick cosmopolitanism, says Byrne (see the chapter by Byrne, this volume), requires history: archaeology can provide (deep) history to any cosmopolitan enterprise.

Finally, as has been advocated many times, we have to carry out a more reflexive practice, but in cosmopolitan not egotistic terms: what are the implications of our work as archaeologists for the communities with which we work? How does our intellectual construction of the locals—needy "little guys" (Graeber 2002) or undeveloped primitives—help to reinforce and shape all-powerful Western identities (Hernando Gonzalo 2006)? How can an archaeological discourse serve to perpetuate inequalities and justify neoliberal policies by portraying "locals" or "natives" in a certain way (Hodder 2003: 63–64; also the Benavides chapter in this volume)? And, on the contrary, how can archaeology challenge accepted visions of native communities as undeveloped, criticize concepts of cooperation and progress, and counterattack ideas of globalizing processes as something inherently creative and positive? The answers will be given through the application of our archaeological sensibilities to the problems of a troubling present.

Note

Data used in this chapter come from projects coordinated by Víctor M. Fernández (Ethiopia) and Almudena Hernando (Brazil), from the Complutense University of Madrid. I am grateful for their invitation to take part in their projects and for the ideas that they have contributed to this work. They are not responsible, however, for the interpretations offered here. I also want to thank Lynn Meskell for inviting me to participate in this book.

Chip Colwell-Chanthaphonh

6 ✺ THE ARCHAEOLOGIST

AS A WORLD CITIZEN

On the Morals of Heritage Preservation

and Destruction

"All We Are Breaking Are Stones"

In March of 2001, the world's major transnational media centers turned their collective gaze toward the Bamiyan Valley in Afghanistan, awaiting the obliteration of two giant and ancient statues of the Buddha (figure 1). In the now infamous global crisis—flames fanned by protests in India and China, pleas from the United Nations, encouragement from Muslim quarters in Chechnya and Sarajevo, and vociferous Internet chatter—Afghanistan's ruling Taliban elected to destroy the Bamiyan Buddhas, as well as many of the country's other statuary relics, purportedly because the icons were an affront to their version of Islam. "These idols have been gods of the infidels, who worshipped them and these are respected even now and perhaps may be turned into gods again. The real God is only Allah and all other false gods should be removed," the Taliban's Mulla Mohammad Omar explained in a decree, supported by a fatwa and a ruling by the Afghan Supreme Court (Colwell-Chanthaphonh 2003b: 76). "If people say these are not our beliefs but only part of the history of Afghanistan, then all we are breaking are stones."

Little doubt remains that the Taliban used the threat of harming the Bamiyan Buddhas as a political ploy—to assert their authority in the global public sphere, to demonstrate their commitment to the most austere interpretation of Islam, and to reveal the West's hypocrisy of a putative humanitarianism moved more swiftly by inert objects than by the daily suffering of Afghanistan's poor and hungry. The destruction of the giant statues, however, is not without precedent, as previous moments of iconoclasm can be found in Islamic history (Martin 1978).

1   Taliban fighters destroyed this colossal statue of the Buddha in
Afghanistan's Bamiyan Valley in 2001. *Photograph by John C. Huntington,
courtesy of the Huntington Archive.*

These previous episodes too, undeniably, were suffused with political machinations, and yet it is not easy to deny the consistent Islamic religious and moral justifications used to support such iconoclasm; Islam clearly does not make iconoclasm requisite, but within certain strands, it is reasoned. The Bamiyan Buddhas did seem to constitute a site of "negative heritage" for fundamentalist believers and the Taliban, "a site of negative memory, one that necessitated jettisoning from the nation's construction of contemporary identity" (Meskell 2002: 561). Thus, as we reflect on the crisis of 2001, we can at least take seriously the Taliban's general claim—if not for this particular event—that the physical destruction of godly icons may have been a religious imperative, necessary for the spiritual well-being of Afghanistan's citizens, a populace made up almost entirely of practicing Muslims. Suppose if it were true that nearly every citizen of Afghanistan genuinely believed that "the real God is only Allah and all other false gods should be removed," then could the destruction of these "false gods" by the nation-state's government be justified? Can the destruction of heritage ever be ethically justified? If so, by what principle, why, and under what conditions?

Framed in these terms, the debate over the fate of the Bamiyan Buddhas is not entirely atypical from others surrounding the preservation of cultural heritage. The debate I am pointing to is not so much the one commonly argued about "right"—whether a government, de facto or otherwise, has the right to ownership, to decide how to care for the cultural property within its borders. Instead, I am pointing to a predicament that might be called the "preservation paradox" because at its core is the way in which one group's preservation of heritage is another group's destruction of heritage. The underlying argument to the Taliban's iconoclasm is that the preservation of Afghanistan's living Muslim heritage required the destruction of Afghanistan's historical heritage, its corporeal heritage of Buddhism. The preservation paradox is not uncommon elsewhere, and indeed I want to argue that it may lie at the heart of multiple conflicts between archaeologists and Native Americans, and even between different Native American communities.

In this chapter, my aim is to explore the preservation paradox, especially as it has effected conflicts over heritage in Native North America. In particular, I highlight two case studies. The first concerns the Zuni Ahayu:da to illustrate how anthropological modes of preservation result in destruction from the perspective of Zuni religious practitioners. The second case study addresses rock art in the American Southwest, which Hopis seek to protect physically as monuments to their ancestors, but that some Navajo medicine men physically damage during curing ceremonies. Following these cases, I argue that resolution to the preservation paradox may lie in notions of cosmopolitanism, a way to express global concerns for heritage while at the same time orienting resolutions toward local actors. Although some scholars might posit that cosmopolitanism is largely descriptive, my reading of it—principally following from Martha C. Nussbaum and Kwame Anthony Appiah—is prescriptive, a political philosophy with profound normative implications. Cosmopolitanism makes claims about our moral and ethical lives.

The Preservation Paradox

In a world without conflict or contradiction, everyone's notion of "preservation" would be identical. Native communities, museums, governments, and international organizations alike could then cooperate in sync to ensure that heritage objects were preserved for the good of communities, nations, humanity. But in actuality preservation is neither a universal concept nor unanimously defined. From the contemporary Australian Aborigines who repaint over ancient images on stone, to the Haisla who leave sacred memorial totem poles to decay, to members of the Six Nations who choose not to relocate burials that are naturally eroding from riverbanks, numerous examples illustrate that the concept of preservation is itself culturally conceived (Groarke and Warrick 2006: 173). These differences profoundly challenge the aims and methods of the modern cultural heritage preservation movement, provoking archaeologists to articulate more clearly what preservation means when its meanings are contested (see the chapters by Byrne, Lydon, and Meskell, this volume). Such cases ultimately evoke what we may term the preservation paradox, because they point to how one group's notion of cultural preservation can be another group's notion of cultural destruction.

The Zuni Ahayu:da   In recent years scholars have chronicled the colonialist threads interwoven into the histories of museums around the globe (for example, Barringer and Flynn 1998; D. Cole 1985). The modern anthropology museum began as part and parcel of colonialist projects of the late nineteenth century and involved a desire to collect and control the material manifestations of newly dominated peoples. Even where such culpable motives were not so evident, seemingly few early museum professionals paused to reflect on how the collection of cultural objects for museum making adversely effected local (usually indigenous) communities, already yoked by colonial rule. Most museum curators and collectors of the late nineteenth century and the early twentieth genuinely believed in opposite terms that their work was an ethical duty. As Amalia Rosenblum (1996: 61) has written, the collection of anthropological specimens from cultures on the brink of destruction became "a moral obligation, wholly consistent with the discipline's concern for its subject peoples. And with the rhetorical circle now complete, it was supposed that future generations of Native peoples themselves stood to benefit from anthropological far-sightedness." And yet during this age in which colonial expansion transformed societies around the world, anthropology museums did in fact obtain countless cultural objects that otherwise would have been lost to time. In the immediate aftermath of colonialism, it very well did seem that the physical preservation of material heritages functioned as a surrogate for the preservation of vanishing cultures.

These strains of the salvaging principle were certainly at work when anthropologists began collecting objects from the Pueblo of Zuni in northwestern New Mexico in the late 1800s (Hinsley 1992: 18–19). In a five-year period alone, between 1879 and 1884, cultural artifacts were taken at a rate of five objects for every occupant of the Pueblo, many under the cover of dark (Parezo 1985, 1987). One object in particular caught the attention of collectors, the Ahayu:da or War Gods, and over the years scores were stolen from the Zuni (figure 2). All Ahayu:da in the possession of museums or collectors were stolen because these sacred objects are owned by the community and are inalienable: they cannot be bought, sold, or traded by any individual for any purpose (Merrill et al. 1993: 532, 536). The Ahayu:da are twin deities first "created in time immemorial by the Sun Father, the ultimate giver of life, to lead the Zunis and help them overcome obstacles in their migration to the Middle Place at Zuni Pueblo" (Merrill et al. 1993: 524). The deities protect the Zuni people and look after their welfare, intervene

2 A stylized representation of a Zuni man making offerings at a War God shrine, likely on Dowa Yalanne, a sacrosanct mesa and ancestral site for the Zuni people. Note the retired Ahayu:da to the right. Image from *Reports of Explorations and Surveys, to Ascertain the Most Practicable and Economical Route for a Railroad from the Mississippi River to the Pacific Ocean*, United States War Department, 1855.

to bring rain and good crops, give courage during war, and cure individual ailments and illnesses that infect the whole tribe (T. J. Ferguson 1990: 8–9; Ferguson and Hart 1985: 57). The Ahayu:da are thus not only associated with war as their English name would suggest, but have a complex role in Zuni society. Sculptural images of the Ahayu:da are made during the winter solstice and other ceremonies connected with the Bow Priesthood, which makes Uyuyemi, the elder brother War God, with the cooperation of the Deer Clan, and Ma'a'sewi, the younger brother War God, with the help of the Bear Clan; Bow Priests are delegated to install the two cylindrical wood sculptures in shrines that surround the Pueblo of Zuni (Ferguson et al. 1996: 251–52; Stevenson 1898). When the newly fashioned Ahayu:da are placed in a shrine, the previous ones are "retired," reverently laid on a nearby pile with other Ahayu:da. "These retired *Ahayu:da* retain an important role in

Zuni ritual," Ferguson and his co-authors (1996: 252) emphasize. "All *Ahayu:da* are to remain at their shrines exposed to natural elements until they disintegrate and return to the earth."

Although some early collectors certainly understood the Zuni esti-mation of the Ahayu:da (Parezo 1985: 771)—for it was in large part their great value to the Zunis that made such objects of great value to anthropologists—it is not necessarily a contradiction to recognize that collectors were also troubled by witnessing these precious objects dete-riorating from sun, wind, and rain. This is the core of the salvage ethic, the urge to "preserve" objects by physically protecting them. But for the Zunis, such acts that aspired to cultural preservation were in fact acts of cultural destruction. As cultural objects, the Ahayu:da are vital to the Zuni people's ongoing traditions, physical health, and spiritual well-being. The deities are sanctified in the complex of Zuni customs and cultural practices; they must be left in place to serve their purposes.

During the efforts of the Zuni tribe to have stolen deities returned, some museum professionals were concerned that repatriated Ahayu:da would be returned to shrines and left in the open to deteriorate (Ferguson et al. 1996: 264). Aside from pointing out that the museums illegally held the Ahayu:da, the Zunis involved emphasized that muse-ums cannot really "preserve" these cultural objects, because for them to be cultural objects—for them to be Ahayu:da—they must be allowed to wear away naturally (Merrill et al. 1993: 546). "That is the natural course of things and the Zunis do not think humans should intervene in the process," Ferguson and his co-authors (1996: 264) wrote. "As the Zunis say, 'All things will eat themselves up.'" In other words, from the Zuni view, when Ahayu:da are put into museums, taken from their sacred shrines, and indefinitely protected from natural decay, they are in part destroyed and injure the Zuni people. It is when the Ahayu:da are allowed to deteriorate physically in their sacred places that they are preserved as meaningful heritage and as religious objects.

Ancestral Pueblo Glyphs   The Diné, the Navajo people, are deeply rooted to the Diné Bikéyah, the country of their ancestors, in the four corners region of the American Southwest (Valkenburgh 1999). The towering mountains, spectacular rock formations, rare rivers and springs, unique plants and animals, and open desert sky form the cultural landscape of the Navajo people's lived experience (Kelley and Francis 1994). An essential feature of this sacred landscape is the many ruins that testify to the lives of the ancients (Kelley and Francis 1993: 155). Navajos call those people that made and left the fallen pueblos the *anaasazi*, or ancient enemy (H. Holt 1983: 595). The Navajo express a deep affinity for these places and ancient people.

Most scholars maintain that Navajos entered northern New Mexico around 1500 AD, generations after the major Ancestral Puebloan villages, like those in Chaco Canyon, were occupied (Towner and Dean 1996: 8). And yet as Robert S. McPherson (1992: 81–85) has detailed in his singular book *Sacred Land, Sacred View*, Navajos believe that their relationship with the ancient Puebloans stretches back to when humans lived in the underworld. Traditional Navajo stories recount that the ancient pueblo world collapsed in the midst of environmental chaos and social anarchy. McPherson (1992: 3) has written: "The Anasazi serve as a good example of what happens when those roots [of connection to the earth] become weakened. The Anasazi culture shriveled and died because the people transgressed the laws of the holy beings and of nature as they sought ease through power which they abused. Their example and the visible remains left behind serve as a reminder of death and destruction in the midst of life."

Of the various kinds of ancient sites that remain today, among the most visible are those with glyphs—pictographs and petroglyphs. Navajos have long taken these images on stone to be wordless transcripts of the Ancestral Puebloans, descriptions of their trials and tribulations before they were destroyed or moved on (McPherson 1992: 76). As glyphs are born from human evils, they, like ruins more broadly, are dangerous and cause disease, blindness, and confusion. Sites where there has been any ceremonial activity "carry a ritual power that is enduring and not to be violated without potentially threatening the welfare of the families involved" (Doyel 1982: 637). Other Navajos believe that glyphs are associated with witching. Handprints on the walls are those of the dead searching for a person to haunt and placing one's hand in the imprints of like images can cause sickness, pain, and aches in the jaw, head, and arm. Some Navajo believe "a painting left in a ruin was made for a reason, a thought behind it continues to permeate its existence"—the ghost carried by the wind can haunt the living (McPherson 1992: 121). To heal those inflicted, curing ceremonies must be held.

Ruins and glyphs are powerful and consequently dangerous, but power does not always result in evil. The power imbued in ancient places can be harnessed for healing (H. Holt 1983: 596). The Navajo cosmology holds the universe to be ordered by natural laws—this order in part comes from the animation of everything, even fixed objects, which may be appealed to for aid. When a Navajo is ill, it is presumed that "the natural order of things has been disrupted, in some cases by patients' improper conduct or contact with impure things" (Schneider and DeHaven 2003: 422). In this view, evil and good are indivisible: "A site or prayer that is used for positive effect can also be used for negative results by just reversing that which is good" (McPherson 1992: 73). The power in ancient sites can thus be used for healing when shrines are placed in ruins, ceremonies conducted there, or artifacts collected for ritual use.

Although most of these uses would seem to have little impact on archaeological sites, one ceremony does not leave the ancient detritus unscathed. The ceremony is little reported in the anthropological literature, but McPherson (1992: 118) briefly describes the ritual, which requires the intentional defacement of ancient glyphs. In some cases, it is believed that glyphs inflict harm and thus must be ritually "killed" by destroying the image, a scattering of the evil contained within it and that is causing some impairment. Thus, at times glyphs are intentionally destroyed, but to ensure the physical and spiritual well-being of those who have fallen ill. But the ritual destruction of rock art is not done for the sake of destruction. For Navajos preserving the material past is not a foreign concept (Begay 2001; Spain 1982). These ceremonies, it would seem, are performed in the genuine belief that they will exorcise evil, and thus "allow for the restoration of harmony on both an individual and a community-wide level" (Schneider and DeHaven 2003: 420).

The Navajo ritual destruction of glyphs is thus no simple case of iconoclasm. Yet, as troubling as this case might be for archaeologists, it remains even more so for the contemporary ancestors of the people who made these ancient images in stone. The Hopi in particular believe that ancient ruins survive into our modern age not by chance but through the designs of their ancestors. Hopi traditions recount that the people of long ago, the Hisatsinom, emerged onto this world and made a covenant with the spirit-being Màasaw to act as stewards of the land. Seeking the Earth Center, the Hopi Mesas, the Hisatsinom sojourned across the land for generations, establishing one village and then another—a migration over centuries that is well attested to in the archaeological record (Bernardini 2005a). Along their migration routes, Màasaw instructed the clans to leave *kuktota*, their "footprints" on the earth, by setting down ritual springs, trails, shrines, and glyphs (Kuwanwisiwma and Ferguson 2004).

Traditional Hopi knowledge holds that petroglyphs were etched to record myriad events, social practices, and topographic features, including plants, animals, migration routes, clan membership, religious societies, ceremonies, astronomical observances, and landforms (Colwell-Chanthaphonh 2005). But Hopis believe that underlying all of these representations is the fact that glyphs made by the Hisatsinom are monuments to Hopi history, proof of ancestral homelands and clan migrations. The importance and sacredness of *tutuveni*, as rock art is known to the Hopi, is signified by glyphs being etched directly onto the bedrock of the Hopi Mesas (Fewkes 1892). Hopis use glyphs adjacent to shrines, and petroglyphs in part demarcate boundaries of Hopi lands (Eggan 1994: 15; Fewkes 1906: 362–64). The creation of glyphs is not long past: into the twentieth century Hopis have been recorded leaving clan symbols on cliffs during pilgrimages (figure 3) (Bernardini 2007; Michaelis 1981).

For the Hopis, then, glyphs not only chronicle Hopi history but also buttress Hopi identity; glyphs confirm the traditions related by Hopi elders and affirm their enduring commitment to land stewardship. Sites with glyphs, as is the case with all ancestral sites, are living monuments that connect Hopis today to their ancestors of long ago (Dongoske et al. 1993; Ferguson et al. 2001). Glyphs are unquestionably sacred for the Hopi. They believe the physical integrity of glyphs is vital to remembering the past and ensuring the survival of the Hopi people into the future.

Thus, the Navajo practice of ritually destroying some glyphs to ensure the well-being of ailing Navajos threatens the well-being of the Hopi people. Navajos may see the ritual destruction as a form of preservation—preserving the health of the Navajo people, Navajo medicine, and traditional ties to the land. But from the Hopi viewpoint, such ritual destruction, as thoughtless vandalism, is not only a physical destruction but a cultural one as well because it is their history that is being erased. With each clan symbol that is wiped out, another Hopi monument is gone.

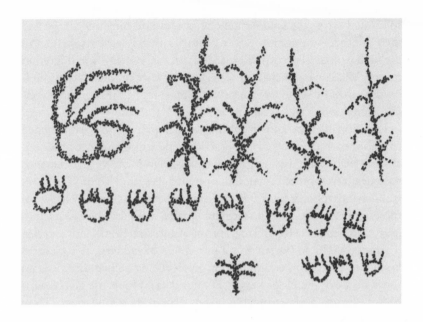

3 This panel of clan symbols is one of scores Hopis have etched during ritual pilgrimages to the Tutuveni Petroglyph Site, which is today located on the Navajo Nation's reservation. In recent years, unknown parties have inflicted heavy damage to the iconography Hopis believe to be sacred and monuments to their past. *Drawing by Chip Colwell-Chanthaphonh.*

Heritage and the *Kosmou Polités*

How ought these conflicts be resolved? The preservation paradox illuminates a core contradiction for archaeologists who are rightly concerned for the objects that constitute the focus of their labors, but who are also rightly concerned about the well-being of communities who give these objects their cultural meanings. In the cases of the Bamiyan Buddhas and Zuni Ahayu:da, the conflict is between broader "universal" norms of the physical preservation of heritage objects and the more localized norms of communities that declare that the physical destruction of heritage objects is needed for preserving the vitality of the community itself. In the case of the Ancestral Pueblo glyphs, the basic conflict is not between putative international and national norms, or between the nation and a local community, but between two local communities that differentially interpret the history, social value, and spiritual function of ancient glyphs.

Undeniably, concrete resolution to such conflicts will entail legal and political considerations that may supercede moral ones. Because any Ahayu:da collectors hold are unavoidably stolen property, they should be returned to the Zuni tribe on these grounds alone, irrespective of how the Zunis care for the deities. Navajos, if caught destroying archaeological sites on federal land, may very well face the consequences of prosecution under the Archaeological Resources Protection Act. The Taliban may not have comprised the legitimate government of Afghanistan. However, while political and legal solutions are needed to fully address these conflicts, ethical questions remain. Setting aside whether museums possess stolen property, or Navajos are violating ARPA, or the Taliban was a legal government, I am trying to clarify the archaeological position on such conflicts. Quite simply, I am asking, from the perspective of archaeological ethics: what is the right thing to do?

More than twenty years ago, John H. Merryman (1986) argued that there are two ways of thinking about cultural property, that objects of cultural patrimony rightfully belong to nations or that they exist independently of national borders and so belong to humanity. More recently, Joe Watkins (2005) has emphasized how enclaves within nations, particularly indigenous communities, provide a third pole, that of the intranationalists. Although these positions are indispensable to clarify legal and political arguments of right and ownership, they contribute far less to discussions about cultural property in terms of lived experiences and moral obligations. Consider: the ancient ruins of Chaco Canyon in New Mexico are at once a Hopi ancestral site, a locus of Navajo spiritual power, a ritual space for New Agers, an archaeological and scientific resource, a National Historical Park of the United States, and a UNESCO World Heritage Site (Finn 1997; Noble 2004). Clearly, in anthropological as much as ethical terms, such a complex convergence of people, communities, and institutions cannot be reduced to just intra-nationalist, nationalist, or internationalist claims. The key ethical problem, then, is not so much categorizing rights but trying to illuminate their interrelationships.

This in essence will mean finding equitable solutions to conflicts over heritage that do not unjustly encumber one group to the advantage of another. But how can stewardship be realized when one place is valued in such different ways? As shown above, there is no "universal" preservation ethic, because preservation is itself a cultural construct. (International organizations and treaties that aver to preserve heritage for the "good of humankind" do not claim that this is a universal ethic, but that this ethic should be universalized.) Nevertheless, this is not to say that preservation is nonsensical, injurious, or necessarily imperialist, but that instead we must develop a sophisticated understanding of how heritage works from the individual level, to the community, to the nation, and beyond it. Because this is the social reality we find ourselves in, a just solution cannot simply pick out the rights of one group but must instead interweave these multiple values. It is this need for a more complex approach to heritage stewardship that leads us to cosmopolitanism.

The Argument of Proximity   When thinking about possible resolutions to these problems, we may intuitively think about various claims to heritage objects as a set of nested relationships. This framework would situate, for example, a range of individuals and communities in relation to each other and the object in question. Following Amartya Sen (2002: 115), broadly stated, we can think of these nested relationships consisting of four sets of identity: kinship, locality, nationality, and humanity. Such a nested, multi-scale structure is akin to what has been codified in the Native American Graves Protection and Repatriation Act (NAGPRA), which orders priority of ownership along a key alignment of affiliation, beginning with lineal descendants and then moving outward to tribal cultural affiliations (Echo-Hawk 2000: 268). The issues of affiliation in NAGPRA are heated not only because the law can turn on how it is determined (T. J. Ferguson 2004), but also because in a moral sense we feel claims of right are proportional to the degree of cultural affinity.

This ordering of right can be termed the "argument of proximity" because it is based on the notion that those individuals and communities most socially or culturally proximate to the cultural object and its creator(s) have the greatest rights to it. Indeed, ample anecdotal and sociological evidence makes clear that often people *do* have more intense emotional experiences with heritage objects that are perceived to be culturally proximate. A Zuni elder seeing an Ahayu:da on display in a museum feels great sadness and senses the deity's own sentiments—clearly a different experience from, say, an Anglo museum visitor who is encountering the Zuni Indians for the first time (T. J. Ferguson 1990: 10). But that same Anglo, say, whose great-grandfather died fighting for the Union Army, will likely have a more evocative experience than the Zuni elder at Gettysburg National Park (Gatewood and Cameron 2004). The argument of proximity is compelling because it captures the essence of cultural heritage—the things we feel deeply connected to, that give us a sense of history, our future, and ourselves. This argument is powerful because it is not abstract and it respects the autonomy of individuals. It recognizes that those who feel closest to heritage objects are perhaps in the best position to determine how the integrity of those objects can be maintained and honored.

However, a generalizable principle of stewardship derived from the argument of proximity—roughly stated, preservation should be decided by those closest to the heritage object in question—is not without problems. One shortcoming with the argument of proximity is that it confuses an *is* with an *ought*. A hierarchy of relations may accurately describe how individuals *feel*—assuredly based on social structures or cultural worldview—more connected to cultural objects, but this social reality does not necessarily imply that they *ought* to have more rights to it. The bare fact of social proximity does not make a moral imperative, in other words.

We can think of many cases in which someone may feel particularly proximate to an object but not have particular claims to it based only on these feelings of affinity. I would argue that descendants of Betsy Ross could not legitimately claim ownership of the first American flag only because of these descendants' social proximity. The descendants may feel closer to the object—perhaps more pride and adoration for the flag than the average American, recognizing as they might that one of their very kin made it—but that fact alone does not give them more *right* to it. In not dissimilar terms, Zunis would say that the carver who made an Ahayu:da does not own it by virtue of his proximity; no one individual can alienate the wooden image because the entire community owns it as an inalienable cultural object. The carver and the carver's family might feel honored that one of their own made the idol, but these feelings alone do not bestow upon them any special rights of control.

The Argument of Inclusivity   Another problem with using a set of nested identities to order a set of moral rights is that the lines between each category can be strangely arbitrary. Few, if any, anthropologists today think of "culture" as a neatly bounded bundle of customs and practices, but instead they emphasize the ways in which culture and the social identities born from it are fluid and flexible phenomena (see the chapter by Hodder, this volume). A Zuni tribal member, after all, not only has kin and religious affiliations but is also a citizen of the United States. So, can cultural identities be so easily parsed and ordered? Can we presume that one identity takes moral precedence over another, particularly if we admit that myriad identities are constituted in the individual? Given that each person has multiple—intersecting and over-lapping—identities why begin with the most particular identity before proceeding outward (if concentric circles) or upward (if a hierarchy)?

Indeed, some political philosophers recommend that we must begin such deliberations not at the most particular and local, but at the most general and universal. Martha C. Nussbaum (2002a), in a forum with twenty-nine scholars, argued for just this view as a critique of unfettered patriotism. Rather than a first loyalty to the nation, Nussbaum argued that our first duty should be to humanity. "Whatever else we are bound by and pursue," Nussbaum (2002b: 133) asserts, "we should recognize, at whatever personal or social cost, that each human being is human and counts as the moral equal of every other." The Stoics of ancient Greece were perhaps the first in Western philosophy to suggest that every individual is a kosmou politês, a world citizen who "dwells, in effect in two communities—the local community of the birth and the community of human argument and aspiration" (Nussbaum 2002a: 7). As Marcus Aurelius, a firm Stoic, wrote, "My city and country, so far as I am Antonius, is Rome, but so far as I am a man, it is the world" (Russell 1979: 272). The Stoics, it is clear then, were not arguing to merely espy humans beyond our horizons or to abolish state governments. "Their point was even more radical," Nussbaum (2002a: 7) writes, "that we should give our first allegiance to no mere form of government, no temporal power, but to the moral community made up by the humanity of all human beings."

The kosmou politês is committed to a moral sphere that begins with humanity rather than ends with it for three basic reasons, according to Nussbaum. The first is egocentric in that the more one understands of the world the more one understands oneself: the study of humanity is thus not only a mirror but also a lens for self-contemplation. The second is that with a genuinely cosmopolitan view, communities can better solve their problems. Factionalism and partisan politics are avoidable if one's commitments are wholly inclusive. The third is that this view is inherently gainful because it "recognizes in people what is especially fundamental about them, most worthy of respect and acknowledgment: their aspirations to justice and goodness and their capacities for reasoning in this connection" (Nussbaum 2002a: 8).

This philosophy of cosmopolitanism is not far from the view of "internationalism," codified in multiple charters and laws, which define cultural property as "components of a common human culture, whatever their places of origin or present location, independent of property rights or national jurisdiction" (Merryman 1986: 831). Excepting the common gendered language in these charters of *man*kind, this view is compelling precisely because it aspires to be so inclusive and non-discriminatory. A cosmopolitan perspective affirms that some cultural objects transcend state boundaries and national imaginings. It addresses the realities of contemporary and historical globalization, that people today as for centuries are fundamentally connected—traveling, exchanging, communicating. The kosmou polités seeks to recognize our common humanity, even as the differences that render possible unique contributions to world heritage are honored.

A cosmopolitan principle of stewardship would therefore state that we should maximize the preservation of cultural heritage objects for the good of the greatest number of people. Here "preservation" would entail the physical conservation of objects so far as possible because if objects were physically destroyed then they could not be appreciated by all of humanity—or at least the portion of humanity that could visit or view the objects in question. The physical preservation of cherished heritage objects might infract the creed of a few, but is justified by their wider appreciation.

However, a principle so formulated is problematical chiefly because it disregards the very reasons that we value heritage objects in such broad terms. We value heritage objects not for their abstract qualities per se, but for the particular experiences they evoke. The cosmopolitan cherishes an Uyuyemi sculptural image not merely because it was made by humans, but because it was made by members of the Bow Priesthood and Deer Clan living at the Pueblo of Zuni in the belief that the deity secures their community's physical and spiritual well-being. Thus, while the principle of preservation from the argument of proximity fails because it is not universal enough, the principle of preservation from the argument of inclusivity fails because it is not particular enough. What is needed is an approach that locates the middle ground where the local and the global meet.

An Argument for Rooted Cosmopolitanism   Some critics have disparaged Nussbaum for missing what is right in front of her when looking so far beyond the horizon—the social connections and ethical duties humans feel toward their family, friends, and intimates. "Above all," Gertrude Himmelfarb (2002: 77) has passionately written, "what cosmopolitanism obscures, even denies, are the givens of life: parents, ancestors, family, race, religion, heritage, history, culture, tradition, community—and nationality. These are not 'accidental' attributes of the individual. They are essential attributes." Sissela Bok (2002: 39) similarly believes that cosmopolitanism unreasonably requires us to ignore our social ties. Suppose, she writes, two people are drowning and one is your intimate while the other is a stranger. Does it really make no difference to you which person is saved first?

But even the Stoics emphasized that the obligations of world citizenship should not replace local affinities, which are distinguished as "a source of great richness in life" (Nussbaum 2002a: 9). As Sen (2002: 112) has written in Nussbaum's defense, "The demands of *fundamental* allegiance need not be identical to those of *exclusive* allegiance." A cosmopolitan ethic hardly requires that we surrender our identities of family, religion, or community, but in fact can easily accommodate special attention to those in our most immediate social circle. Nussbaum believes that this is the most practical way of ensuring human flourishing. As an example, Nussbaum explains that she gives her own daughter exceptional attention because it is better to give one child her full care than only a little care to the world's children. "But," Nussbaum (2002b: 136) ends, "that should not mean that we believe our own country or family is really worth more than the children or families of other people—all are still equally human, of equal moral worth."

The political philosopher Kwame Anthony Appiah (2005, 2006a) has led a spirited defense of cosmopolitanism, but has argued that our commitments to our intimates and kin are not merely practical, but also deeply ethical. Firmly grounded in the tradition of liberalism, Appiah claims that we need to cultivate ethical systems that are simultaneously cosmopolitan and *rooted*. Appiah's justification for this view is extended and complex, and so cannot be related in toto. Nonetheless, as Appiah's reasoning ultimately buttresses my own, it is important here to examine at length some of Appiah's central arguments for a rooted cosmopolitanism, most persuasively articulated in his book *The Ethics of Identity* (2005).

Appiah begins his story with his own father, Joseph Appiah. He is described as a cosmopolitan patriot, a man who deeply loved his family and his Asante roots, was willing to die for his nation of Ghana, and yet admonished his children, "Remember that you are citizens of the world" (Appiah 2005: 213). Joseph loved Ghana. He risked his life for it and was imprisoned for it because he opposed the country's tyrannical government. To explain Joseph's outlook, it is important to consider that while he was born and reared in the Asante region of Ghana, Joseph was also a subject of the British Empire, married a British woman, and had children who came to live in America, Namibia, Nigeria, and Ghana. Indeed, Appiah reminds us that throughout human history, throughout the world—from Alexander the Great's reach in India, to the spread of Bantu ironworks over Africa, to Islam connecting Mecca to Jakarta, to Chinese silk shaping European fashions, and on and on— human communities have journeyed and interacted.

Even as the nature, form, and frequency of our interconnectedness may be shifting in the twenty-first century, Appiah argues that the world has never been nor will ever be a "global village." A village implies a close relationship, but it is impossible to be intimate with the billions of people that populate the earth. But this is a limitation not only of a global outlook. Can a citizen of the United States really know 300 million fellow Americans? Whether speaking of humanity, the nation, or the *ethnie*, we are therefore often speaking of "political strangers." Cosmopolitanism nonetheless acknowledges that not everyone is a stranger; it is not a philosophy that advocates, in Susan Wolf's (1992: 244) term, an "extreme impartialism" in which one is morally required to treat a stranger exactly as one treats a friend. "A tenable cosmopolitanism," Appiah (2005: 223) consequently argues, "in the first instance, must take seriously the value of human life, and the value of particular human lives, the lives people have made for themselves, with the communities that help lend significance to those lives. This prescription captures the challenge. A cosmopolitanism with prospects must reconcile a kind of universalism with the legitimacy of at least some forms of partiality."

A cosmopolitan philosophy must justify the nature and limits of ethical partiality. The concern with "special obligations" is that they seem to undermine three core liberal values, which cosmopolitanism also seeks to uphold: "those of autonomy (that is, some core concern for liberty), loyalty (that is, associational life, in all its richness and responsibility), and moral equality (that is, the notion that persons are of equal worth, or anyway, due equal respect)" (Appiah 2005: 224). Appiah's response is twofold. He first argues that obligations can be both special and universal. The general idea here is that ethical partiality involves "particularist goods." Consider for example, friends and wealth, which can both be intrinsically good, but goods of different kinds: "You may not mind whether you have this million dollars or that million dollars; but you value your friend not as a token of the type *friend* but as this particular person with whom you have a highly particularized relationship" (Appiah 2005: 227). His second argument comes down to the point that we do not demand the same sense of equality from states and individuals. Although we want state governments to be impartial when selecting their policies and running their programs (so as not to unfairly disadvantage, say, women or African Americans or the poor) we deem that partiality at the individual level is not only fair but also often expected. In this way, Appiah (2005: 230) asserts, "Impartiality is a strictly position-dependent obligation. What is a virtue in a referee is not a virtue in a prize-fighter's wife."

Appiah goes on to say that our sense of ethics unfolds from the personal paths each of us seeks in our lives, our "ground projects." These pursuits are shaped by two kinds of relationships, "thick relations" (interactions among those with a shared worldview and a rich collective history) and "thin relations" (the associations we have with political strangers). These relations in turn correspond with two kinds of obligations. The first are "ethical obligations," which involve leading a life that is good or bad, while the second, "moral obligations," are narrower and concern the principles of how to treat others. Thus, thick relations involve ethical obligations and thin relations involve moral obligations. "Ethical concerns and constraints arise from my individuality; moral ones arise from my personhood," Appiah (2005: 232) writes. From this framework, we can begin to see how Appiah's rooted cosmopolitanism uniquely negotiates between the tasks of partiality and impartiality. We are bound by both thick and thin relations, by both ethical and moral obligations.

And so, unlike Nussbaum, Appiah (2005: 241) is arguing that the cosmopolitan's commitment to the local should not just be instrumental, not just "a coolly cerebral decision, an impartial calculation as to how one would best make the world a better place." Indeed, the imaginings of a nation are real to those who imagine them. The happenstance of one's sex does not somehow make one's gender inauthentic. In the end, nationalities matter ethically "for the same reason that football and opera matter: as things cared about by autonomous agents, whose autonomous desires we ought to acknowledge and take account of even if we cannot always accede to them" (Appiah 2005: 245). Thus, rooted cosmopolitanism is not a contradiction in terms, but instead goes to the heart of a life committed to one's kin and community as much as the dignity of every human being.

Appiah presents a kind of universalism that appreciates that human practices and behaviors are historically and socially contingent. But we do not need to obtain perfect theoretical harmony to discover shared practices. Appiah argues that we can and often do agree on moments of moral and ethical judgment. We cannot always agree on the universal, but we can often agree on the particular. The missionary nurse and mother who come to the aid of a sick child come for different reasons, but both come to help *this* ailing child. Appiah suggests that such shared moments are clearly realized when we hear stories in which we come to see the world through the eyes of another (see the chapters by Lilley and Scham, this volume). The anti-universalist, Appiah (2005: 257) concludes, "supposes that the rationalist is bound to think that 'we' are right and 'they' are wrong: but if there is one world only, then it is also possible that *they* might be right. We can learn from each other's stories only if we share both human capacity and a single world: relativism about either is a reason not to converse but to fall silent."

The Principle of Complex Stewardship

The principles of stewardship derived from proximity or inclusivity are what we might consider to be notions of "simple stewardship" because they see preservation as either infinitely variable (depending exclusively on local definitions) or wholly fixed (depending exclusively on a single, universal definition). A perspective of rooted cosmopolitanism leads us, in turn, to "complex stewardship" because it stipulates that archaeologists must comprehend the ways in which preservation can be both locally enacted and universally sought. This tenet is offered not as a universal principle, but as a means to universalize a stewardship ethic derived from rooted cosmopolitanism. In other words, it is a way for archaeologists to frame predicaments of stewardship—as so clearly raised in the preservation paradox. This principle could thus be stated: We should maximize the integrity of heritage objects for the good of the greatest number of people, but not absolutely.

Maximize the integrity of heritage objects. In this principle, "integrity" is conceived as the soundness of a cultural object that includes but is not limited to physical welfare. As we saw in the case of the Ahayu:da, a wooden deity's integrity is derived primarily not from its perpetual physical conservation, but rather from its active participation in the life of Zuni community members, which includes the physical deterioration of the object. Concepts of integrity should not be imposed externally, but ought to be derived from the viewpoints of stakeholders. The scientific archaeologist, as one stakeholder, can make the argument for the physical preservation of an object, but this is just one view that must be negotiated given the local context. This concept of integrity provides the archaeologist with a firm foundation to explain why— from a scientific view—ancient Ancestral Pueblo glyphs should not be destroyed, but that other archaeological artifacts can be destroyed (e.g., carbon samples, sherds for petrographic analyses, and so forth). That is, the argument from the archaeological viewpoint is that the *scientific integrity* of some objects entails their physical destruction while in other cases their physical conservation.

For the good. As a notion of integrity, "the good" is not a ready-made object that can be imposed from above. I think that archaeologists need a minimum concept of the good, which can be found in the notion of universal human dignity. From this flow basic values that archaeologists can reasonably defend: equality, justice, liberty. Archaeologists ought to be committed to human flourishing, but this does not give them license to enjoin their own ideas of "the good" upon others, particularly on impoverished or politically weak communities. Indeed, the basic recognition of human dignity would demand that archaeologists respect how individuals and communities conceive of the good, so long as those individuals and communities do not themselves contravene the basic human dignity of others.

Of the greatest number. Following from a view of rooted cosmopolitanism, our first (but not only) allegiance is to humanity. Beginning at the outermost ring of our nested relationships means a first recognition of our shared identity as human beings, of our entwined histories and collective experiences. Specifically in terms of "heritage," it seems empirically true that most communities deeply value the objects that contribute to their identities, and many communities deeply value the objects of *other* communities. Since cultural heritage (although variously defined and expressed) seems to be prized across a spectrum of communities, it is not only right but also a practical matter to err toward humanity. In other words, if multiple communities are likely to esteem the Rosetta Stone, why start discussions of value with Greeks or Egyptians or archaeologists? Does it not make the most sense, *as a beginning point*, to imagine the values it holds for humanity?

But not absolutely. But since we know that cultural objects are valued precisely because they come from particular human communities—and not humanity in general—we must take into account not just the "greatest number" but also individuals who made objects or experience profound affinities because the objects come from *their* ancestors or community. Archaeologists could also argue that the scientific merits of some particularly special object outweigh the benefits of sharing an object with other stakeholders. This stipulation, then, seeks to be sensitive to the local contexts in which heritage objects are created, used, conveyed, and retired. In Appiah's terms, the phrase "not absolutely" sanctions our thick relations and ethical obligations while "maximiz[ing] the integrity" concerns our thin relations and moral obligations.

It should be clear from this discussion that I am not promoting an absolute rule, but rather a frame archaeologists can use to begin deliberations on ethical predicaments. Although I am using the term "stewardship," this discussion moves away from how "stewardship" is typically conceived by archaeologists and their professional societies (e.g., Groarke and Warrick 2006). Even as ethical archaeologists should seek to engage in dialogues with stakeholders, this principle does not require archaeologists to be arbitrators; however, it does require archaeologists to be anthropologists because they must be aware of how different stakeholders conceive of and enact such key concepts as heritage, preservation, integrity, and the good. They must be aware of how and why heritage objects persist in particular communities, including their own archaeological one. While I have sought to clarify a justifiable and reasonable moral stance for archaeologists, this principle by itself does not provide a clear mechanism for negotiation or resolution of conflicts. Real negotiations must involve legal and political considerations, and not just ethical principles.

The principle of complex stewardship can nonetheless clarify how archaeologists qua archaeologists can approach the preservation paradox. In the case of the Zuni Ahayu:da, it is clear that these wooden images are exceedingly rare, even priceless contributions to the record of humanity. However, a general contribution to humanity is not enough. In this case, the key issue revolves around integrity. Museum professionals and Zuni tribal members approach the images in fundamentally different ways, but it is the Zuni perspective that is most compelling since it is from this community that the objects were made and are still used. The museum world after all marvels at these objects *because* of how the Zunis conceptualize the War Gods. Thus, even the museums should acquiesce to the deep particular meanings the images hold for Zunis.

With the case of the Ancestral Pueblo glyphs we again see conflicting ideas of integrity: for Hopis, the integrity of the objects entails their physical conservation as monuments to Hopi history; for Navajos, the integrity of glyphs depends on their use in the healing of ill Navajos and the maintenance of the Navajo cultural landscape. Although most evidence suggests that Navajos did not arrive in the Southwest until after many of these ancient glyphs were made, this consideration must be balanced by the fact that the Navajos do have some traditions that relate connections with the *anaasazi* (Begay 2003). The most persuasive argument of integrity from the Navajo perspective might be if it could be demonstrated that it was ancient Navajos who made the glyphs that were being damaged in Navajo ceremonies. But unless the issue of integrity between the two primary stakeholders can be clarified, we need to consider the broader values of other Pueblo groups, archaeologists, tourists, and residents of the Southwest and the United States. When these glyphs are destroyed, the absent objects potentially affect the well-being of all these communities as well. For these reasons, and unless additional claims are made or information is offered, archaeologists should have serious ethical reservations about the Navajo practice of damaging ancient Ancestral Pueblo glyphs.

Although the Taliban ostensibly destroyed the Bamiyan Buddhas because of political machinations (Meskell 2002: 563), if their claims of destruction for religious preservation were taken seriously, could archaeologists accept (on ethical grounds) the destruction of the statues? The far-reaching estimation of the Bamiyan Buddhas as a record of humanity is indicated by the archaeological expeditions that Italian, French, Indian, Japanese, and Afghan scholars have undertaken since the 1920s, the substantial investments made by UNESCO since 2001, and the inscription of the Bamiyan Buddhas as a World Heritage Site in 2003 (ICOMOS 2003). Nearly two millennia old, and among the largest standing Buddhist sculptures, the Bamiyan Buddhas were rare cultural objects to be sure. At the same time, a close look at the issue shows that the Bamiyan Buddhas had been threatened many times before and the world had hardly taken notice; indeed, the discourses surrounding the crisis suggest that for many people throughout the world, the prestige of the Bamiyan Buddhas as objects of world heritage actually came *after*—not before—their destruction (Colwell-Chanthaphonh 2003b: 76, 93). An argument based exclusively on notions of inclusivity may not be entirely convincing. The integrity of the Bamiyan Buddhas is twofold. First, although few if any practicing Buddhists live in Afghanistan, when the crisis began, protests in Sri Lanka and China would indicate that Buddhists in those places continue to revere the statues for their religious meanings. Second, the Bamiyan Buddhas' integrity involves their status as heritage objects for Afghans, a status upheld by previous Afghan governments and even initially the Taliban in 1999 (Harding 2001). Because the integrity of the Bamiyan Buddhas—as religious objects beyond Afghanistan, and as heritage objects within Afghanistan—would be fundamentally undermined by their destruction, the strongest ethical redoubt for the Taliban would be a convincing argument about "the good." This argument would have to entail a compelling explanation about how people in the Bamiyan Valley, or in Afghanistan, as adherents of one strain of Islamic fundamentalism, needed to remove these sacrilegious objects in order for society to flourish. In addition to the difficulties of making such a case, defenders of the Taliban would have to explain how such destruction would not contravene a baseline standard of human dignity, as it seems that such naked desolation (dynamiting the statues) menaces contemporary Buddhist adherents. It is difficult to see how archaeologists could be ethically neutral or more in this instance of heritage destruction.

Cosmopolitan Education

When children enter this world, do they begin learning of it first from the particular or the general? Sissela Bok (2002) offers the intuitive argument that humans build their identities from "part to whole," naturally assembling their world from one's kin to one's community to one's nation to our world.

Martha C. Nussbaum's provocative response to this question is that these rings of association do shape how we see the world—and that children do naturally move from these rings of identity—but they begin with humanity. Nussbaum (2002b: 142) writes of how all babies begin their lives first as human beings: "Infants respond, innately, to the sight of a human face. A smile from a human being elicits a reactive smile, and there is reason to think this is an innate capacity of recognition." It is only as the child grows that she begins to learn of particularities, that this person is her mother, that this land is her country, that this lexicon is her language. "All circles develop simultaneously, in a complex and interlacing movement," Nussbaum (2002b: 143) posits. "But surely the outer circle is not the last to form. Long before children have any acquaintance with the idea of nation, or even of one specific religion, they know hunger and loneliness. Long before they encounter patriotism, they have probably encountered death. Long before ideology interferes, they know something of humanity."

If it is true that humans know of humanity from their earliest experiences, then the field of archaeology has the potential to expand and deepen these understandings. As David Hansen (2007) suggests, a "cosmopolitan education" is one that inspires people to learn from every human contact they make and to not withdraw from what is merely different. This approach to pedagogy can lead to human solidarity and the understanding of how we are all each other's relations. Critical explorations in human history and the explication of the relationship between material culture and humans in all times and places are ideal means of learning about similarities and difference among human societies. This realization should encourage cosmopolitan educators and philosophers to incorporate archaeological inquiry more fully into their projects. And in turn, it should compel archaeologists to engage with their local communities as well as far beyond them. Archaeologists ought to remember that they are not only members of a profession and inhabitants of cities and countries; they are also citizens of the world.

Note

I undertook the writing of this chapter while I was a visiting scholar at the American Academy of Arts and Sciences in Cambridge, Massachusetts, in 2005–6; I gratefully acknowledge the support of the academy and the Harvard Humanities Center. I am also greatly indebted to Lynn Meskell for the invitation to participate in this volume and her continual encouragement of my research, as well as to several anonymous reviewers and my fellow visiting scholar, Sarah Song.

Sandra Arnold Scham

7 ✸ "TIME'S WHEEL RUNS BACK"

Conversations with the Middle Eastern Past

For a several decades now, those of us who have done our archaeological service in the Middle East have sought to disabuse ourselves of the idea that we were working at the center of it all. As the erstwhile "cradles of civilization" have failed to appeal to new generations of archaeologists, the biblical and ancient Near Eastern pasts are developing a distinct quaint colonialist aura (Steele 2005). Despite this, our persistent, if inflated, sense of our central place in the discipline remains a constant. Thus, many of us have discovered that our feelings over the return of popular attention to our region, while accompanied by the sobering realization that the events that precipitated it are tragic ones, are not entirely unalloyed with satisfaction.

It is a surprising development for an archaeological subspecialty not exactly known for its timely debates that happenings in our field are engaging the interests of journalists and television reporters. Nevertheless, whether it is seen as a thorn in the imperialist side, a cauldron of extremism, or a last stand of tradition in the face of a commodifying modernity, the region now exerts a profound effect on many aspects of our culture. In analyses focusing on the role of religion (Ahmed 2003; Halliday 2000; Jan 2003; Antoun 2001), economic underdevelopment (Silverstein and Makdisi 2006), victimization and the struggle for subaltern status (Lindholm 2002), popular culture and its discontents (Stein and Swedenburg 2005), colonialism and violence (Dawisha 2003; J. Cole 1992), and the internet and globalization (Hill 2002), our colleagues in the social sciences have sought understanding of this effect with admirable zeal.

The notion that Middle Eastern cultures and values are fixed and immutable is a theme in many of these explorations with some scholars who willingly confront the fallacies of this concept (Massad 2001) and others who suggest that a primary concern in the region is the maintenance or invention of traditions that can be embalmed for future generations (Lewis 2001, 2004; Huntingdon 1998). Most of these tomes, having been spawned in the aftermath of September 11, 2001, have a subtext, whether acknowledged or not, of either decrying (Little 2004; Lockman 2004) or supporting (Lewis 2004) the current policy of the United States in the Middle East even though political analysts of all stripes have begun to detect a certain lack of precision on what that policy now is.

What our government excels at, however, is not transparency in its political or strategic aims but clarity in the realm of values. As President Bush famously admonished: "We must never forget that this is a long struggle, that there are evil people in the world who hate America. And we won't relent. The folks who conducted to act on our country on September 11th made a big mistake. They underestimated America. They underestimated our resolve, our determination, our love for freedom. They misunderestimated the fact that we love a neighbor in need. They misunderestimated the compassion of our country."[1] In this famous foray into neologism, the president articulated what he believed to be American objectives for the Middle East. On the one side is a "loving and compassionate" imperialism influenced by Western religious teachings and imperfectly realized as an antidote to Eastern religious extremism (Lockman 2004; Little 2004). On the other side, it is posited, is a violent dismissal of our values as a corrupting zeitgeist aimed at erasing religion and morality from all public life (Jan 2003; Ahmed 2003).

As a major contributor to perceptions formed both there and abroad, the archaeology of the Middle East has clear subtexts relating to almost every aspect of practice in the region (Pollock and Bernbeck 2005) and it is these subtexts that determine what is conveyed about its narrative. In what follows, I will make some exploratory movements toward fashioning a cosmopolitan adaptation of the Middle Eastern archaeological story based upon concepts that have been articulated by Appiah in *Cosmopolitanism: Ethics in a World of Strangers* (2006a). Based upon Appiah's cosmopolitan philosophy and, additionally, that of Habermas (2003), Derrida (1997), and Nussbaum (1994, 2006), I will examine values that are at the heart of Middle Eastern cultures, both ancient and modern, and what they should mean for Western archaeologists practicing in the region today. From there, the sections below move backward in time from typical approaches to knowledge dissemination about the archaeology of the Middle East today to nationalist perceptions that represent a slightly earlier era to, finally, telling our story as archaeologists of the ancient Near East through the eyes of those Victorian cosmopolitans and anti-cosmopolitans (Appiah 2006a: 1) known to some as Orientalists.

The story will, thus, be presented in stratigraphic terms. While I am not as enslaved to chronologies as many of my colleagues, I find the activity of uncovering the conceptual layers that have formulated our discipline, as one would a site, to be as good an approach as any toward revealing how we came to be where we are. As the quote in the title of this article, from Robert Browning's poem *Rabbi Ben Ezra*, suggests, "Time's wheel" does indeed "run back" both in the ways that we continue to conduct archaeology in the Middle East and in the reverberations of "our" past in concert with all of the other pasts that have shaped the region.

Hospitality and the Cosmopolitan Archaeological Project

After having fairly dismissed the idea of "timelessness" in relation to the Middle East it may seem disingenuous to begin our reverse chronology with a discussion of hospitality—one of those presumably unchanging traits of Middle Eastern life. Nonetheless, it is difficult to find a value that has been more misunderstood, taken advantage of, and mischaracterized by Westerners in the Middle East than hospitality. Biblical scholars still see among the Bedouin of the modern Middle East the very model of what they view as Abraham's welcoming demeanor (Vos 1999; Feiler 2001), hardly recognizing that this conflation of millennia and cultures does no more to elucidate the Bible than it does to convey an accurate sense of the modern culture.

Recently, in expressing a hope that Christians who live in Muslim countries "find welcome and respect" there, Pope Benedict sparked a discussion on the topic of hospitality and its attendant concept, reciprocity. Aside from the observation that "reciprocity," in either its positive or negative form, is not a Christian value, quoting a medieval emperor on the inherent evil of Islam, as the pope did in this same speech, did little to assure that his hopes would be fulfilled. By conjuring up one of the worst periods in the history of relations between Christians and Muslims, the pope reduced what ideally should have been a conversation, which Appiah defines as being neither didactic nor consensus seeking (2006a: 58), between religious practitioners to an implied threat. Under the circumstances, this use of the language of hospitality seems remarkably obtuse and his comments appear to ridicule both the cultural and religious values of the Muslim and Arab worlds.

In contrast, cosmopolitanists posit a role for global moral behavior that, it is argued, should be dependent upon an understanding, through conversation, of the values of others as well as co-extensive with global economic influences (Appiah 2006a). The prospect of one world with many perspectives applies to the phenomenon of cosmopolitanism itself—which has numerous adherents with as many different views as to what constitutes universal values. Both Derrida (1997) and Habermas (2003a) support this philosophical project although Habermas's approach is distinctly more rational than Derrida's. He invites his audience to consider a world in which citizens share equally in a sense of freedom to have lives of dignity but, as Derrida (1997) has noted, such a world is founded upon the notion of universal access to the form of reason Habermas espouses. Tolerance is at the heart of Habermas's vision of a cosmopolitan world and certainly tolerance is most clearly the value that Appiah's system is based upon. Derrida adds another dimension to the debate by suggesting that tolerance is more protective of the power of the person and the state expressing it than it is supportive of true equality.

It is hospitality, according to Derrida, that most closely approximates a true cosmopolitan worldview. "Pure and unconditional hospitality, hospitality itself," he writes, "opens or is, in advance, open to someone who is neither expected nor invited, to whomever arrives as an absolutely foreign visitor, as a new arrival, non-identifiable and unforeseeable, in short, wholly other" (Derrida 1997: 128–29). Offered to the foreign other from the very heart of the familiar self, the place of dwelling, true hospitality subsumes the language of tolerance, which, for Derrida, is no more than a parsimonious "scrutinized hospitality" (Derrida 1997: 128). On balance, Derrida's perspective, of the two, seems more "right" for a cosmopolitan understanding of the Middle East where hospitality is neither a quaint religious tradition nor an obligation that is undertaken only with an end in view. It is, instead, an entire network of dependent and overlapping factors—reciprocal relations that allow for a smoothly functioning social order.

In practicing our own version of hospitality and reciprocity, the consideration of adding to the economic welfare of the communities we work among should not be a secondary one. Discussing this topic on several occasions with archaeologists whom I knew to be working in the same region as I was, I asked if they had ever employed anyone locally to work on their projects. The answers ranged from doubts as to whether their government licenses would permit them to do so to implications that the people in the area were unreliable, untrained, and untrustworthy. Apparently those who held the latter view had not reflected that sites are entrusted to the people living near them whether archaeologists are there or not. In this instance, the hospitable solution is also the practical one.

This not too startling revelation came to me while I was working in the Dead Sea region in Jordan. During the winter months, in preparation for a project, I arrived to find that the local small complex of mud brick houses, which were uninhabited the previous summer, now had people living in them. From the beginning of my work there, young people from those houses would attempt to converse with me, bring tea to me while I was working in the field, and even send me back to Amman with produce and cheese—all of which I attempted to refuse with no success. I had become a regular, but still reluctant, luncheon guest by the time I was joined on the project by Mohammed Balowneh, an archaeological inspector from the Jordanian Antiquities Authority.

The dimension of understanding that the latter's presence began to add to the proceedings was one for which I remain grateful. With limited Arabic skills on my side and little to no English skills on the other, I had found my seemingly pleasant encounters with the local people uncomfortable and burdened with guilt, as I had determined that these were not people who could afford to entertain me on a daily basis. My colleague said to me one day as we were eating, "You know these people are very poor?" I said that I did and had tried very hard to refuse their generous invitations. Dismissing that as the reason for his comment he continued by saying that it would be good to hire people from among my hosts for my project. As far as the hospitality was concerned, he told me later, "It's important—it has to be done," indicating that the obligation falls on both the host and the guest.

The idea that, in choosing people to work with, one might do so on a personal basis is not entirely foreign to our culture. The element of the relationship added by hospitality is intended to operate as an affirmation that one's host is correct in fulfilling social obligations as, hopefully, one's guests will be correct in fulfilling theirs. We may recognize this necessity yet, all too often, we will continually take advantage of the obligation on one side, as I did, without attempting to assume it on the other. Archaeologists working in these countries are no less guests there than tourists—and, one might well argue, they should be more aware of their obligations in that respect by virtue of having spent much more time in the country.

A colleague of mine, a Palestinian archaeologist working in the West Bank, maintains that the employment of local people on archaeological sites can demonstrably reduce the amount of looting that goes on there (Yahya 2005: 75–76). There are model archaeological excavations, some of them mentioned elsewhere in this volume, that integrate a system of sharing, both in economic and in educational terms, with surrounding communities. Çatalhöyük (Hodder 2000), the Kruger National Park Project (Meskell 2005a), and the Rahmatabad Project in Iran (Bernbeck et al. 2005) are good examples. Most archaeology in Israel and Jordan has not incorporated these ideas and research remains firmly under the control of "professionals" and their students. In this sense, we might say that the "Orientalist" scholars of the past assessed this situation more correctly than we—dependent as they were upon a local work force, rather than a host of wealthy Western students. It seems that, in evaluating the theoretical harm done by their views on Middle Eastern culture and society, some of us have elected to counter it by eliminating any economic relationship between ourselves and the local people entirely. To deconstruct the Middle Eastern past in terms of the perspectives that have sustained us for so long may require an acknowledgment that the lineage of our discipline is not a noble one. This does not, however, preclude salvaging something of validity from the idealistic fabrications of our forebears.

Misunderestimating the Middle Eastern Past

Rejecting our past history piecemeal, rather than as a whole, is a seriously complex proposition. It requires a consideration of all of the legacies of the discipline, including a perennial favorite that few wish to disregard—the idea that enlightened and scientific concepts can be subsumed into archaeological practice without doing damage to postmodern concerns about serving the public. Science, so Appiah (2006a: 39) tells us, runs interference with attempts to understand through true conversation. How many archaeologists working in non-Western countries have heard their colleagues expound upon the "unscientific" methods of locally trained scholars? I would venture to say that most of us, at one time or another, have had this experience. Science is still the last bastion of the colonialist defense.

Misunderestimate, everyone's favorite presidential blog word as expressed in the speech concerning the attacks of September 11 cited above, seems to be a particularly apt term for these kinds of mistakes in judgment. It might be defined (if it existed) as "to misunderstand and underestimate simultaneously." The context in which the president uses this word also should have some resonance for us. Even though it is clear that he does, in fact, know the word "underestimate," as he uses it in conjunction with "resolve," "determination," and "freedom," "misunderestimate" is, peculiarly, reserved for "love," "compassion," and, on numerous other occasions, his own abilities. One has to assume that Bush is well aware that whatever love or compassion is displayed by citizens of the United States toward each other is of virtually no concern to its enemies. The suggestion is, rather, that these are "hidden" qualities—ones that are not readily discernible. It is this gnostic aspect of our Middle East policy that has been assiduously relied upon in numerous follow-up discussions as to the direction of our interventions in Middle Eastern political processes (R. Marshall 2005).

Just as the president has no problem conveying meaning through nonexistent words, we attempt to paint our pictures of the Middle Eastern past through the medium of the nonexistent, but nonetheless meaningful, "collective memories" of our listeners. The "biblical" versus "Near Eastern" versus "Middle Eastern" past are radically different versions of the same archaeological record adjusted for different audiences. In exploring how far some of our notions about the past in the Middle East may have moved us toward the untenable present, one need only look at the ways in which the archaeology of this region is taught and its artifacts interpreted. The idea that "important" material culture is that which reflects religious rather than secular ideology is axiomatic for archaeologists who traditionally assign "ritual" functions to enigmatic objects. This both continually re-creates and reinforces the view that the East is more religious (read "irrational") than the West (Said 1978; JanMohamed 1985). In this light, it is understandable why seals are given major significance among archaeological finds in the region. In fact, the meaning invested in them has inspired many famous forgeries of these items (Vaughn and Rollston 2005) and the discovery of different forms of seals generates archaeological excitement far in excess of their value in providing information about ancient cultures. The "loaded symbolism" of these objects can be directly traced to religious perspectives (that is, seals or bullae with biblical names on them) or indirectly, in terms of the sense of both the finality and the approbation they represent. For example, on the holiest day of the Jewish calendar, Yom Kippur, religious Jews express the wish to be happily sealed in the Book of Life while for Christians the breaking of seven seals heralds the end of the world and for Muslims Mohammed is the "Seal of the Prophets."

A long-range perspective that incorporates outdated origins of the state models (Service 1964; Carneiro 1977; Wittfogel 1967) is still popular both in and out of the classroom. A preoccupation with towers and walls in Middle Eastern archaeology, as symbols of boundaries, borders, and landscapes of control, of nationalism and militarism, suggests more than a mere superimposition of the present on the past. Such preoccupation reflects a continuing classificatory mindset that requires either a hierarchical or unconnected relationship between cultures and societies. Most archaeological data suggest that this is likely to be a complete mischaracterization of past realities. Nonetheless, when it comes to the ancient Near East, the choice of relationships between sites traditionally comes down to conquered, conqueror, or disaffected.

To the extent that the region's archaeological record demonstrates a secular ideology it is always assumed to be as a result of that mysterious force in the ancient world known as "hellenization" (Mazar 2000). This is not to say that an interest in establishing a synthesis between Eastern and Western civilizations is not, also, an obsession. A theory that has long fascinated scholars of the ancient Near East—"The Axial Age" (Jaspers 1953)—juxtaposes the so-called universalizing philosophies of Europe and Asia. This simplistic construct can literally be placed into the service of any view on religion and politics. The familiar unctuous rhetoric of politicians who speak of values shared by all of the world's great religions, values that curiously sound quite particularistic, implies that the appeal of this concept lives on.

In recent decades, critical historical perceptions of the consequences of religious intolerance, from martyred Christians to the Holocaust, have become a common thread in our education, so much so that it has created a distrust of religion in public life that fundamentalists are now finding so deplorable (Antoun 2001). While we are wont to abrogate the role of religion in politics, education in the Middle East focuses on economic and political factors as the most insidious historical forces (Zubaida 1999; Ahmed 2003). While our historical education represents the Crusades as a period of religious activism, heroic to some but alarming to many others (Scham 2002), Arab education emphasizes that Crusaders were impelled by a feudal system that economically disenfranchised younger sons (Maalouf 1984).

These kinds of differences, though they seem only to extend to interpretations of certain historical episodes, can result in some bizarrely mismatched perspectives in the field between archaeologists and the communities in which they work. Our concern with delineating space and material culture as either sacred or secular, ritual or functional can suggest to others that we are bent upon viewing religion as a force apart from all other aspects of society and culture (Zedeno 2000). Our categories tend to be mutually exclusive rather than overlapping. Thus, in a sense, Western scholars might be considered as extreme in our thought as we have deemed others to be in their deeds (Appiah 2005: 138–41). We can excuse this tendency as a "reasoned approach," but is a dedication to reason inherently superior to a zeal for god and country? We assume so, yet in the end there is little incontrovertible evidence that we can summon to support this proposition.

Nationalism and Patrimonial Archaeology

One might expect that cosmopolitanism and nationalism are mutually exclusive. Indeed, given the kind of damage that is possible, cosmopolitan perceptions of both religion and patriotism might be assumed to be fraught with misgivings. Curiously, neither Appiah nor Nussbaum (1994, 2006), who has written extensively on this subject, are dismissive of these as emotional attachments. Suggesting that cosmopolitanism, rather than being an alternative to these feelings, might be viewed as the imagined community writ large, Appiah seems to declare that his own brand of "rooted" cosmopolitanism encompasses the soul of patriotism and religious feeling if not all of their outward expressions (2005: 155–210).

The cosmopolitan patriot can in fact maintain local attachments alongside of an appreciation of difference not only through tourism but also as a result of migration, nomadism, and diaspora. "In the past, these processes have too often been the result of forces we should deplore; the old migrants were often refugees, and older diasporas often began in an involuntary exile," Appiah writes. "But what can be hateful, if coerced can be celebrated when it flows from the free decisions of individuals or of groups" (Appiah 1997a: 618). The conundrum of cosmopolitan patriotism arises with the realization that the "roots" of cosmopolitanism are firmly planted in this coercive past. Appiah's own family history might be said to have resulted from multiple migrations, forced as well as chosen.

To be a cosmopolitan patriot is to be unique in one's understanding of the relationship of individuals to places and from a contemplation of what makes us different rather than like our nationalist neighbors. "Becoming a citizen of the world is often a lonely business," Nussbaum (1994: 6) tells us. "It is, in effect, as Diogenes said, a kind of exile—from the comfort of local truths, from the warm nestling feeling of patriotism, from the absorbing drama of pride in oneself and one's own." Nussbaum's argument that "cosmopolitanism seems to have a hard time gripping the imagination" in comparison to a patriotism "full of color and intensity and passion" (Nussbaum 1994: 5) reminds us, as archaeologists, of the difficulty in getting people to care about places that they don't view as their patrimony.

The postmodern dilemma is how much of a dichotomy between cultures one can embrace fully while, at the same time, attempting to comprehend the cosmopolitan society. The unspoken assumption of many postmodernists, that there is a "bad" nationalism that has incited nations to seize power and a "good" nationalism that empowers formerly colonized people to control their own past, needs to be examined carefully. This problem might best be approached by a further examination of whether there might be a distinction between nationalism and patriotism. Nationalist archaeology, which we have all come to condemn, may be distinct from patrimonial archaeology, although the latter concept is not one that should make us entirely comfortable. Nevertheless, just as there are a host of factors beyond simple intellectual curiosity that motivate scholars, both as individuals and as members of groups, what other people make of places is neither predictable nor controllable.

Rather than an argument for universalism, multiculturalism, or globalization, Appiah's cosmopolitanism (2005: 222) has, at its heart, a message for anthropologists and archaeologists (see also the chapter by

Breglia, this volume). People, that is, individuals, in all of their unregulated glory and resplendent with a sense of choice, trump cultures. Take heed any one of us who would preserve aspects of cultures that their practitioners are no longer interested in, for in a cosmopolitan world there is a right to select those affiliations that one would remember—and those that one would rather forget (see the Benavides chapter in this volume). In the Middle East, it is unfortunately the most politically and socially engaged archaeologists who have discovered this hard lesson. Several of my colleagues in Palestine and Jordan have become involved in movements toward reviving original crafts—looking upon it as an authentic way in which to stimulate the interests of communities in their pasts. These activists are not people who lack understanding about the region—many of them, in fact, were born there. They were, however, educated in the West and, as Appiah notes, therefore are wont to seek an uncontaminated and pristine version of their own cultures (Appiah 2005: 136). All of these endeavors, well intentioned as they are, have had virtually no impact, economically or otherwise.

What this means for archaeologists elsewhere is also a rather daunting prospect. Our visions of pickling the past must fall aside in the face of such a perspective. What is left is a sense that the past was formed not so much by those anonymous automatons that constituted past "cultures" but by individuals. We have known this for some time, electing to couch this realization in the term "agency" in order to maintain a safe distance from it (Dobres and Robb 2000; Dobres 2000; Pauketat 2001). Coming back to seeking the "Indian behind the artifact," in reality rather than just symbolically, we find that our views about preservation and authenticity are based upon a concept of cultural difference that is bounded and that fails to admit difference on its own terms.

There is no real prescription for making either heritage or archaeology value neutral, and such a project would eventually be destructive of the entire enterprise of understanding past cultures (see the chapter by Colwell-Chanthaphonh, this volume). We cannot simply leave the question at that, however, because to do so would reinforce the kinds of categorizations that we have been so comfortable in making in the past. In Near Eastern archaeology in particular, we find it difficult to resist the typological temptation. The traditional "pottery reading" that takes place at most sites in the Near East, ostensibly done in order to educate students, is really a performance intended to gratify archaeologists. This is perhaps where the expression "non-diagnostic" entered our vocabulary as a substitute for "I don't know." This kind of thinking is not conducive to the conduct of real conversations with the people we work among.

Naturally, the resurgence of religious nationalism in the Middle East has further complicated all of these questions because of our propensity to want to work at or near "sacred" sites. Jerusalem, which most of us know to be a frustrating and virtually impossible archaeological venue, still draws scores of volunteers to work on dull salvage digs in advance of construction projects. Notably, archaeologists of Muslim heritage favor survey work over excavation projects in places like Jerusalem while archaeologists of Jewish heritage want to dig up the city (Scham 2001). The religious nationalist constituencies of both support these views although the archaeologists themselves are not religious. Contested sites like Jerusalem engage their proponents in an essential war of wills over control and access to them and each side realizes that, ultimately, the fate of such places will be decided more by perseverance than by power (Scham 2003b).

While I was conducting a survey near a Chalcolithic (ca. 6500 BP) site in Jordan, a local man asked me, "What Arab peoples are you studying here?" He was with his young son and had asked the question presumably for the child's benefit. In response to his ready classification, which I didn't like, I was on the verge of countering with my own when it occurred to me that, since I had only the most imprecise idea of what constituted an Arab past identity, I was not in a position to comment on the question. Such an identity could easily encompass any trace of past or present cultures found on Arab soil. Just as religious Jews view all skeletal remains found in the land of Israel from the Paleolithic era forward as Jewish it would not be unusual for a Muslim in Jordan, which this man seemed to be, to make the same case about archaeological remains there.

That this was in fact the beginning of a real conversation that I failed to pursue now occurs to me. As products of our education, we archaeologists strive for certainty in determining the categories to which our data belong and we don't invite questions that take us outside of our study boundaries. As products of a discipline that incorporates theological foundations of the nineteenth century and philosophy of the post-Enlightenment (Silberman 1998; Ostigard 2001), we archaeologists working in the Near East in particular remain as confused as anyone else about the ways in which religious and secular ideology operate within our own culture and that of both the ancient and modern Middle East.

The Ancient Near East and the West:
A Fallibilist Love Story

Spurred by a national identity developing from a fragmented base, requiring the desperate sacrifice of thousands and lasting, by some accounts, over fifty years, the Risorgimento eventually resulted in the extrication of Italy from the twin grip of imperial Austria and the papacy. It is difficult *not* to see in this historical episode comparisons to the situation in the Middle East today even to the extent of finding modern echoes of the redoubtable Metternich, whose famous pronouncements include "Error has never approached my spirit" and "Italy is only a geographical expression" (Reinerman 1971). Robert Browning was a cynical observer of the Italian resurgence as he was of most of the nationalist enterprises of his day (Poston 1973). He was not, like his wife Elizabeth Barrett Browning, an engaged and emotional observer of the Italian revolution, even though he spent much of his adult life in Italy in self-imposed exile and many of his most famous monologues were composed there (Ryals 1996). His detachment and seeming alienation from his surroundings have caused some critics to accuse him of manifesting an "Italianism" in his perspectives on Italy that differs little, in their view, from Orientalism (Russo 1994).

Browning's natural candor and political skepticism distinguishes him from the more impetuous poets of a previous generation. As a willing exile, he stood, perhaps, as a force between the jingoistic imperialism of his age and the fraught foreign emotional attachments of the Romantic poets. Upon his return to England a few years after his wife of almost twenty years died, he wrote "Rabbi Ben Ezra." Like many of his dramatic poems, this one reads like an internal cosmopolitan conversation between the poet and his protagonist:

> For thence—a paradox,
> Which comforts while it mocks—
> Shall life succeed in that it seems to fail?
> What I aspired to be,

And was not, comforts me:
A brute I might have been,
but would not sink i' the scale.

His conversations typically disclose without resolving and often present startling revelations. "Rabbi Ben Ezra" is a would-be lament of the aging philosopher. A lesser poet might have written a litany of regrets in such a work for thoughts and feelings not acted upon. This poem rather presents the paradox that the protagonist's failure to achieve his aspirations was, in fact, his salvation. To subordinate all emotion to reason, it suggests, is to not live life. To do the reverse is to submit to brutality.

A cosmopolitan understanding of conflict and its devastating effects necessitates a similar stand between the claims of reason and emotion (Appiah 2006a). To converse in an atmosphere of contention it is necessary to approach the project with a belief in paradox. In a subsequent stanza of Browning's poem, Rabbi Ben Ezra asks, "Was I, the world arraigned, were they, my soul disdained, Right?" An admission of uncertainty is not, as much of our Western education has taught us, a poor basis upon which to begin a discussion nor is it necessary to make each exchange a negotiation. This is rather the process of acknowledging *fallibilism* (Appiah 2005: 188; 2006: 144)—the imperfections in knowledge that we have persisted in protecting and passing on to future generations.

In a remarkably concise summation of all of the attendant prejudices that have accompanied the exploration of the ancient Near East, the archaeologist William Dever has said that the Bible is "not 'history,' but 'His' story—the dramatic account of God's miraculous dealings with a particular people designated to become his chosen" (Dever 1997: 20). Less traditional practitioners would be reluctant to buy into this particular view as the basis for the discipline but, even with its essentialist faults, today's biblical and Near Eastern archaeologists still believe in "our" story. Our story is uniquely our own, distinct from other archaeologists' stories and, more significantly, distinct from the stories of the people we encounter. It is the conversation we have with ourselves and it admits of no distractions or diversions.

Near Eastern archaeologists are fond of beginning our story with Nabonidus, the last Babylonian emperor, who supposedly conducted the first archaeological excavation (Bahn 1999: 1–2). Most of us see symmetry in this, rather than the irony that it actually represents, reasoning that even if Nabonidus appeared inept, or worse, deranged, to his own countrymen, at least he had the redeeming trait of intellectual curiosity. Perhaps it is well that we begin with Nabonidus as he may have established a precedent for the ways in which we have regarded the contributions of Orientalists to our discipline. No better illustration can be found for this than the reverence that both specialists in the Bible and in the Near East have for Flinders Petrie, the pioneering excavator of sites in Egypt and the Levant during the early part of the twentieth century.

Archaeological raconteurs make much of the peculiar, if not apocryphal, stories of Petrie having climbed the Great Pyramid in a tutu as well as his having willed his head to University College London so that his estimable intellectual capabilities might one day be fully explored by scientists (http://www.pobonline.com). The leading textbook used for the teaching of biblical archaeology to undergraduates informs us that it was Petrie's methodology for excavating tells and subsequent pottery typology that constituted "a major breakthrough" (Mazar 2000: 7) for Near Eastern archaeology. General archaeological textbooks (Fagan 2005: 108; 2001: 236; Bahn 1999: 148–49; Price and Feinman 2001: 226) are no less laudatory concerning Petrie's achievements with the exception of Wenke's (1999: 469–470), which refers to Petrie's "dynastic race" theories in a polite and noncommittal discussion of Afro-centric views on Egyptology.

While the standard narrative on Petrie's contributions appear to suggest that, once again, an inquisitive spirit cancels out a seemingly harmless derangement, the correlation between Petrie's classification theories and his overbearing racism are obvious to many in the field. University College London, perhaps feeling a particular sense of responsibility on this issue given its association with Petrie, has undertaken to ameliorate this situation on its "digitalegypt" website, which tells us that, "[Petrie's] classification rests on assumptions concerning the evolution of human societies over time. . . . Such assumptions may be symptomatic of the social Darwinism and associated racism of late nineteenth and early twentieth century Western science" (http://www .digitalegypt.ucl.ac.uk).

The question of connections between "our story" as archaeologists and "the story" that now seems to be informing most of the developing views and policies on the Middle Eastern past can be understood more easily by examining the rhetoric of all of these purveyors of the East in the West. The problem with dismissing such views as merely racist or colonialist returns us again to the old enemy of understanding—classification. On reading the letters of the early explorers of the Palestine Exploration Fund (Moscrop 2000) and the pronouncements of Flinders Petrie (Drower 1996) it is impossible to imagine that even the most insensitive encounters between these individuals and the "natives" whose aid they so attentively sought in their endeavors were burdened with an ongoing racist rhetoric. The overt racism of Western archaeologists was more likely reserved for communications with their perceived peers. Mortimer Wheeler is, therefore, famously touted for both his good relations with his Indian co-workers and his blanket dismissals of the intellectual capabilities of his Indian students (Hawkes 1982).

It is more likely that methodology was the ground upon which most of the clashes between East and West were fought. Any attempt to introduce cosmopolitanism into archaeology will likely fail in the realm of practice as much post-processual theory has before. Positivism is a privileged form of communication, no less so in the social sciences, and science remains our model for all modes of discourse (Appiah 2005: 57–58; 2006a: 13–15). No doubt our forbears in the field were positivists as well as racists—both of them traits that caused them to express frustration and hostility toward the slovenly habits of their workers.

If science and reason cannot be appealed to as a basis for achieving a cosmopolitan understanding of the Middle Eastern past, what is left? Though the danger of suggesting such a possibility is apparent, I believe that sentiment holds more promise. The emotional ties that early explorers and archaeologists genuinely seem to have felt toward the region are understandably dismissed by many of us as the "Lawrence of Arabia" phenomenon—an anomalous product of imperialist intervention. Said, in his typically pragmatic way, views these ties as an idealization of the East based upon fantasies and miscalculations (Said 1978). This is true to the extent that it describes the effects of such emotions on the objectified "beloved Orient," but the question of whether this emotion in any way transforms those who have it may be more complex than we have supposed.

William Foxwell Albright, the putative originator of biblical archaeology, wrote to his mother in 1921 that "there is not a spot in the whole world which suits me like Jerusalem, not only for its associations, but also because of the opportunities for research at the fountain head, and because of the cultivated cosmopolitan atmosphere which I love" (Long 1996). This admiration of the East may be at the heart of the problem, but it might also prefigure the resolution. There is no doubt that Petrie, Wheeler, and Albright cherished deep feelings for the East. Emotion, particularly emotion that informs the entire adult life of an individual, is not something that I am wont to dismiss lightly. Certainly, it is not to be trusted and, in the case of the Middle East, it has seldom conveyed to the benefit of real people living there. Yet, it may contain within it an uncultivated seed of understanding for difference (Appiah 2005; Nussbaum 1994).

Conclusion

The depiction of the "cosmopolitan" past is an adjustment that has yet to be made. Perhaps we have never truly believed that there is a market for this version. Cosmopolitan archaeology is not heritage studies nor is it the public archaeology of preservation and protection that is the specialty of UNESCO and the World Monuments Fund. Archaeological projects designed to incorporate notions of true conversation will address more than a concern with the examination and preservation of the site for future generations. Appiah points out that "there are two strands that intertwine in the notion of cosmopolitanism. One is the idea that we have obligations that stretch beyond those to whom we are related by the ties of kith and kin, or even the more formal ties of a shared citizenship. The other is that we take seriously the value, not just of human life but of particular human lives, which means taking an interest in the practices and beliefs that lend them significance" (2006a: 19).

Appiah begins *Cosmopolitanism* with the story of Richard Francis Burton, whom he views as both exemplary and anti-exemplary of the mode of thought he espouses in the book. Though he was not an archaeological explorer, Burton, nonetheless, is very much a part of the ancient Near Eastern story. His attempts to embed himself within the culture of the Middle East and his linguistic abilities are looked upon even today with both envy and outrage. Burton, so Appiah tells us, was the "least Victorian of men—and the most" (2006a: 7). Where one might consider that Browning's detachment made him largely non-participatory (and non-critical) in the grandiose political and cultural program of the Victorian Age, we must place Burton squarely in the middle of it. By combining the passion of the dedicated Orientalist with a brutality of character that seemed preternaturally suited to the military, Burton represents the quintessence of the Western assault on the Middle East. We have newly assessed Burton as an arrogant expropriator of culture but, in doing so, we still fail to acknowledge that his views remain entrenched in Near Eastern studies. What continues to bring archaeologists to the Middle East is that Burtonian sense of confronting an exotic culture that, nevertheless, belongs to us. In our acceptance of this we perpetuate and support the attempts of Western politicians and religious leaders to affix the region and its people to a moment in time when we believed ourselves to be in more control over them.

"Time's wheel runs back or stops: Potter and clay endure," as Browning, in the persona of an eleventh-century Jewish philosopher, admonishes in order to convey to his audience the futility of the active but unexamined life, of the sort that Burton might be said to personify. Although the poem indicates that Browning also was an expropriator of Middle Eastern culture, the poet never presents his vision as authentic nor does he purport to have translated the works of those in whose guise he speaks. Representing two aspects of a complex age, these Victorian cosmopolitans are as much the roots of our discipline as theology, ideology, and imperialism. We need not, however, continue to conduct our dialogue with the Middle East from either the alienated stance of a Browning or the involved but destructive stance of a Burton. The rules of engagement of Western scholars with the Middle Eastern past can still be rewritten.

Note

1 "President Thanks CIA: Remarks by the President to Employees of the Central Intelligence Agency at CIA Headquarters, Langley, Virginia," White House Press Release, September 26, 2001.

8 ✺ MAVILI'S VOICE

In this chapter the load that I wish to give to the term "cosmopolitan" is the complex blending of the global and the particular in ways that do not replicate Western perspectives and that do not construct the local as a product of the global. In the same way that Appiah (2006a: xiii) moves away from "globalization" and "multiculturalism," both problematic terms that have become very extended in meaning, I wish to use the term "cosmopolitan" as part of an attempt to move away from global/local dichotomies. So in this chapter I will use the term to refer to the complex alliances that are set up between groups and individuals that crosscut the global, national, and local categories.

Several writers have discussed the principles, ethical and otherwise, on which cosmopolitan dialogue should be based. Appiah (2006a: 78) talks of "taking an interest in" other peoples and places, even if agreement cannot be reached. Benhabib (2002) describes a deliberative democratic process. Both Appiah and Benhabib, in different ways, are concerned with individual rights. Both therefore minimize the rights of individuals with respect to their membership of cultural groups. Appiah (2006a: 131) argues that "the mere fact that something you own is important to the descendants of people who gave it away does not generally give them an entitlement to it."

Benhabib (2002: 33) rightly makes the point that cultures are fluid and constructed. She notes that most people today "are members of more than one community, one linguistic group, one ethnos." She thus promotes perspectives on public policy regarding cultural preservation that empower "the members of cultural groups to appropriate, enrich, and even subvert the terms of their own cultures as they may decide" (2002: 66). She prefers a deliberative democratic process based on respect and egalitarian reciprocity (2002: 37), but she admits that her approach does not address the cultural heritages of indigenous peoples (2002: 185). These groups often cling to their cultural identities in the face of long histories of exploitation, conquest, policing, and subjugation. For such groups, an open dialogue and an egalitarian reciprocity that do not acknowledge preferential restitution seem inadequate and disempowering. Respect for pluralism and diversity seems inadequate as the sole basis for ensuring group rights.

In contrast to these perspectives, the processes that led to NAGPRA in the United States, to the Burra Charter in Australia, and to the code of ethics of the World Archaeological Congress firmly link indigenous rights to the recognition of cultural affiliation. Certainly in some instances cultural affiliation is the basis for claims of recognition and restitution. I agree that international human rights issues should not assume a Western tone, and in particular we should not assume a priori that individual rights should trump group rights. Group rights are key in heritage contexts and in claims to restitution by historically savaged groups.

But the problem with both NAGPRA and with writers such as Appiah and Benhabib is that they assume a priori positions about whether rights to cultural heritage are primary. In practice, in different contexts, sometimes cultural heritage rights are the basis for claims to other rights (recognition, economic welfare, freedom of expression, and so forth), while in other contexts, cultural categorization may in fact subvert or deny individual rights (when, for example, cultural groups exclude those who claim membership).

It seems important, therefore, to recognize that in a cosmopolitan world of complex and shifting alliances, cultural heritage claims should be linked strategically to the specifics of the cosmopolitan mix. While accepting and championing group rights we should not also deny individual rights. Rather than imposing overall strictures (group or individual rights, for example) we should trust to a *process* of deliberation and negotiation. There seems wide recognition that claims to heritage should as far as possible be resolved through processes of dialogue, respect, recognition, and restitution in an open democratic process. Rather than starting these processes on the basis of a priori strictures about whether human and cultural heritage rights should be based on the individual or the group, we should focus on dealing with the conditions that make a democratic dialogue possible. In such a process, I argue, it will often be necessary to empower local groups or individual voices through complex cosmopolitan alliances that cut across individual, local group, regional and national group, and global scales. In this chapter I wish to explore some examples that purport to show how individual and local group rights can be enhanced through complex cosmopolitan interactions, alliances, and dialogues.

The Right to One's Past? Introducing Three Examples from the Cultural Heritage of Turkey

During the summer of 2006, an exhibit about Çatalhöyük, a Neolithic site in central Turkey, was opened in Istanbul. It lasted for four months and was funded by the major Turkish bank Yapı Kredi. Held in the Yapı Kredi Gallery on one of the busiest streets in Istanbul—Istiklal Caddesi—the exhibit was prepared and mounted by a culture and arts section within Yapı Kredi, in close liaison with the public relations department of the bank.

The Çatalhöyük Research Project, which I direct, is multinational, involving teams from the United States, the United Kingdom, and Poland, as well as three teams from Turkey (Hodder 2000). The project was closely involved in the planning and implementation of the exhibit, and some of the video material developed by the project was chosen for use in the exhibit, including a video used in the on-site visitor center where people are introduced to the site. Since the project aims to have close links with the local communities close to the site, Mavili Tokyağsun, a woman from the local village, provided the voice for the Turkish version of the video. Mavili has worked for the project in the dig house, in the kitchen, and in some collaborative research. She has two children and has been divorced, about which there is some stigma in the village, but she is now remarried. The video using her voice is played daily to visitors to the site, most of whom are Turkish speakers, and it has been received very well.

A few days before the exhibit opened I was told that the public relations department at the bank had decided to replace Mavili's voice on the version of the video to be used in the exhibit in Istanbul. It was explained to me that her accent made understanding her words difficult, although we had not encountered this problem at the site. The new voice-over was made by someone from Istanbul. Despite protestations from me about how this erasing of Mavili's voice would harm our relationships with the village and would set back our attempts to build close ties and "ownership" of the site in the village, the exhibit went ahead with a nonlocal voice on the introductory video. While I was initially assured that there would be a section in the exhibit that described the involvement of the local community in the project, this too disappeared in the final version of the exhibit displays.

In this case a regional dialect and a local contribution were silenced. It would be possible to read the reaction of the educated Istanbul Turks as being about class. Indeed, there may have been some snobbery about lower-class uneducated provincials in the decision to remove Mavili's voice. But if there were any reasons beyond the desire to have the words easily understandable, a wider context is provided by the debate within Turkey between secularists and Islamists. In 1928, five years after the founding of the Turkish republic, a clause retaining Islam as the state religion was removed from the constitution. Secularism was a central strut of the republicanism envisaged by Kemal Atatürk, the founder of modern Turkey. Mavili's voice came from the Konya region, that part of the country associated most clearly with a newly powerful Islamist perspective in Turkey, one feared by the urban elites that had benefited the most from the Kemalist position, which had been dominant since the early days of the republic.

The long interaction between secularists and Islamists in Turkey and the social context of the debate have been chronicled by many authors (Abu-Rabi 2006; Zubaida 1996). The Islamist movement emerged soon after the founding of the secular republic in 1923 (Narli 1999). It failed to gain wide support in the 1920s to the 1940s. From the 1950s onward, there was a major expansion of Turkey's modernization. Many felt excluded from the new wealth and higher levels of education, and it was particularly in the provincial areas and among upwardly mobile classes that the environment was created for the growth of Islamic parties. Islamist groups provided social welfare for the new aspiring university students, professionals, shopkeepers, merchants, or workers. Financial assistance was provided by a newly formed Islamist business elite. The newly educated and financed groups moved increasingly into urban contexts, including Ankara and Istanbul.

Narli (1999) argues that several types of relationships were embroiled in the Islamist-secularist conflict: center-periphery, class, regional cleavages, and sectarian antagonism (such as Sunnis versus Alevis). Thus, through time, a series of socioeconomic and regional groups in the periphery have backed a succession of Islamist parties in order to voice their grievances: the National Order, National Salvation, Welfare, and Virtue parties. More recent pro-Islamist parties include Saadet or Happiness Party and the present governing AK (Justice and Development) Party. The current AK Party, led by Recep Tayyip Erdoğan, is a complex and ever shifting attempt to attract support from across the divide. While undoubtedly rooted in the Turkish Islamist tradition, it has sought to pursue Turkey's membership in the Europe Union and supports some liberal reforms (for example, in 2004 the state-run TV broadcast the first Kurdish-language program). Konya, one of the heartlands of its provincial success, is a complex mix of restraints on alcohol but burgeoning capitalist and internationalist economic programs.

Thus, there is a lot going on when the urban elites in Istanbul say that it is inappropriate to air Mavili's voice in the exhibit in Istiklal Caddesi. At one level, there may be simply a desire to make the words easily understandable. But at other levels, the use of a local Konya voice is tied up in the debates within Turkey that deal with tensions between urban and provincial, upper and lower classes, old and new money, center and periphery, secularists and Islamists, West and East.

My second example also refers to the secularist-Islamist tensions in Turkey, though more directly. In the summer of 2007, the Çatalhöyük project received the results of some radiocarbon determinations on human bone that had been excavated from graves across the site. We had thought the graves were late Byzantine in date, but the radiocarbon results in the thirteenth to fifteenth centuries AD suggested that the burials could, after all, be early Islamic. Team members identified parallels in the grave construction techniques and in the layout of the skeletons that confirmed an Islamic attribution. During the Selcuk period in the Konya region there was a very mixed multiculturalism, and many religious affiliations, but it seemed clear that around sixty-four of the graves that we had excavated over the previous fifteen years at Çatalhöyük were in fact Islamic.

We immediately consulted with the Ministry of Culture and Tourism and with local officials such as the regional governor or *kaymakam*. We also had meetings with the village head or *muhtar*. As a result of these and broader discussions in the community and among project members, it was decided to rebury the skeletons in a designated part of the local village cemetery. The requisite letters for permission were written to the local, regional, and national authorities, including the village imams. As well as the request to rebury, the letters stated that the project would try to avoid uncovering Islamic burials wherever possible in future excavation strategy. The letters also asked for permission to study the skeletal remains of any Islamic burials that were uncovered before the remains were reburied.

Again, there is a lot going on in these consultations and discussions. The events took place in the run-up to the national elections in Turkey on July 22, 2007. These elections were dominated by the debates between secularists and Islamists in Turkey. The reburial issue at the site played out these larger issues in microcosm. Many of the Turks consulted felt that the bones should be reburied in the village cemetery. This was the immediate and clear view of the village *muhtar* and elders, and of the local community. But many on the project felt it was wrong to accede to the interests of the local community. It was felt that such a move would play into the hands of the Islamists.

My third example derives from the fact that the Çatalhöyük project is now a close institutional partner of Selcuk University in Konya, in central Turkey. Konya is one of the largest cities in Turkey and is usually seen as very traditional. Its university has over eighty thousand students. Within the highly centralized education system in Turkey, the administration of the university follows the Kemalist and government policy that none of its students should wear the "turban" head scarf, worn to fit closely over the hair and forehead, on campus. This policy is particularly stark in the Konya region, where religious strictures are followed in many areas of life (for example, alcohol is not available in most restaurants). The female students from Selcuk University who participate in the Çatalhöyük project are not allowed to wear the turban, even though most female visitors to the site, including their friends and families, are covered. The project is thus complicit in the ban on an expression of religious diversity.

Should the project allow the students from Selcuk to wear the turban? In practice local and national state officials turn a blind eye to the fact that the local female workers on the project do wear turbans. The turban is even worn in local government offices in the Çatalhöyük area. But what should the project do about the students from Selcuk University? The wider debate about wearing the turban in Turkey (Kilicbay and Binark 2002) should not be seen simply as an example of the divide between secularists and Islamists. There are many religious, political, social, and personal layers of meaning that are involved and a great diversity of perspectives and opinions (Göçek 1999). The established meanings of veiling include adherence to the Islamic notion of concealing the female body from the male gaze, and the veil as a sign of "political Islam." But today the articulation of Islamic faith into consumption culture has opened up a greater diversity of shifting meanings. While many in Turkey today see the turban as Islamist, anti-secular, and political, for many others wearing the turban is about personal choice and individual rights in a global consumer market.

Atatürk banned religious dress in public places and argued against veiling women, but it was left to a government in 1979 to make wearing the turban illegal. For many women, the injunction against wearing the turban or head scarf in universities, government offices, and many professions is against their values, against human rights, and an insult. For others, wearing the turban is a threat to secularism and freedom of thought and expression. In rural Konya, women may have little choice but to wear the turban if they are to remain within village society and culture. And yet a young woman from the village who has started working on the project and who wishes to go to university and become an athlete is uncovered, unlike her age-mates. Should the project actively encourage such employees, in line with university and government policy? Or, in its links with Selcuk University, does the project undermine the rights of those who wish to wear the turban, and in so doing does it restrain a multicultural heritage?

Global Heritage and Multiculturalism

Most discourse on heritage deriving from the United States, and increasingly from the United Kingdom, takes for granted the rights of indigenous groups to have a say in controlling their own past, even if that means that those groups rebury their heritage or secrete it away in traditional locales (e.g., Swidler et al. 1997). "We," as archaeologists and heritage managers in Western developed countries have come to celebrate identity difference and cultural diversity in relation to heritage. There has been a massive increase in international charters for the management of archaeological sites over recent decades, and many of these have turned their attention to the processes of collaboration with local communities around sites and monuments. For example, in 1987, the General Assembly of ICOMOS adopted the Charter for the Conservation of Historic Towns and Urban Areas, which includes guidelines for the participation of residents. The Charter for Sustainable Tourism that emerged from the World Conference on Sustainable Tourism in 1995 stated that tourism must be "ethically and socially equitable for local communities." The Australian chapter of ICOMOS (the International Council on Monuments and Sites) has produced the Burra

Charter, which moves away from defining sites and monuments in objectivist terms and toward the description of cultural landscapes as understood and perceived by indigenous peoples (Australia ICOMOS 1981). The Corinth Workshop on Archaeological Site Management in May 2000, organized by the Getty Conservation Institute, refers to the importance of collaboration with local community members. Indeed, the Getty Conservation Institute has modified and developed the planning framework outlined in the Burra Charter (Avrami et al. 2000; see also de la Torre 1997). Specific examples of collaborative work include that at the Nevada test site (Stoffle et al. 2001) and at the Barunga rock art site in Australia (Smith et al. 1995; see also Smith and Ward 2000). The Code of Ethics of the World Archaeological Congress (WAC) seeks to ensure the primacy of indigenous perspectives in relation to ethical principles.

At times this type of focus on heritage rights suggests a multiculturalism in which a diversity of perspectives is celebrated and in which multiple stakeholders are identified as having a voice around the heritage management table. Much heritage management embraces this focus on multiple voices around the table. But many of the authors in this volume would decry this position as politically weak, and would in fact join the larger critique of multiculturalism and pluralism as a whole. The critique aims to replace multiculturalism with a more grounded concern with diversity and with historical inequalities and exploitation. In many contexts it argues that those who have suffered the most should gain the most at the heritage stakeholder table (Meskell and Pels 2005). It argues that complex alliances other than those centered on the West can be formed in the protection of individual and local heritage rights. Rather than a global approach centered in the West we can identify complex decentered global and local heritage alliances and "multiple cosmopolitanisms partly rooted in local cultures, partly positioned in global networks" (Anderson 1998: 273; see also Appiah 2006a).

This focus on cosmopolitan heritage rights reacts against the general assumption made worldwide that cultural heritage is the property of the nation-state. The rise of archaeology, antiquities management, and museums is closely tied to the rise of the nation-state (Kohl and Fawcett 1995), and the ultimate rights of the nation-state in relation to heritage are enshrined in UNESCO's documents regarding World Heritage Sites. It should be noted, however, that the protection of Native American rights under NAGPRA was obtained through state intervention and the provision of a legal apparatus by central government (Watkins 2000). Within the nation-state it seems that a focus on multiculturalism and diversity does not of itself produce the protection of heritage rights. Rather, public coalitions and activism allied with state intervention are at times needed to create and enforce individual and local rights of cultural difference.

The sovereignty of the nation-state in its relation to heritage is being eroded by perspectives that would enforce some form of "universal" access over and above diverse and minority interests. In the developed world this view is associated with the several UNESCO charters that refer to the universal outstanding value of World Heritage Sites and that see a value of heritage sites and antiquities for all humanity (Cleere 1989). Such global prescriptions are typically the result of a Western sensitivity (Byrne 1991). A universalist position is also associated with the scientific claim for unrestricted access to knowledge. Thus many archaeologists and biological anthropologists in the United States and Europe argue that human remains should be available for all to study, and not reburied (for an insight into the debate, see Kane 2003; Zimmerman 1989). A universalist position is also argued by those that seek a deregulated trade in licit antiquities (Merryman 2005).

International agencies, from UNESCO to NGOs such as the Global Heritage Fund, increasingly work with, between, and across national governments in their desire to protect sites, develop tourism through heritage, build museums, and restore the monuments of displaced peoples. Their international and global character is often accompanied by a Western perspective (see the chapter by Lydon, this volume). Cosmopolitan alliances of local groups and national and international agencies can work to further the interests of minority groups and revive local economies. "What the new archives, geographies, and practices of different historical cosmopolitanisms might reveal is precisely a cultural illogic for modernity that makes perfectly good nonmodern sense. They might help us see that cosmopolitanism is not a circle created by culture diffused from a center, but instead, that centers are everywhere and circumferences nowhere. This ultimately suggests that we already are and have always been cosmopolitan, though we may not always have known it" (Breckenridge et al. 2002: 12). These cosmopolitan alliances are not just decentered open networks. In order effectively to champion and protect individual and local rights, there is the need to create partnerships that are practical and effective. When decisions are made about competing claims, and when the historical rights of indigenous groups are decided upon, there is a need to move beyond an ethical multiculturalism and embrace a grounded cosmopolitanism.

It could be argued that "we were there first" or "we were always there" are the arguments that should underpin all heritage rights issues. According to this view, archaeology and cultural heritage should be used in origins debates to demonstrate the rights of displaced minorities and indigenous groups. But archaeologists have long been critical of origins debates (e.g., Conkey with Williams 1991), and given the lack of congruence between material culture, language, genes, and aspects of identity it is difficult for archaeologists to adjudicate on questions of origins. Origins debates have typically led to claim and counterclaim in an escalating cycle that can lead to extreme conflict. Most local groups are mixed, and they are as capable as national and colonial states, or as any group of people, of mistreatment of those around and within them.

The notion that contemporary identities are complex, fluid, and hybrid threatens the ability of local and displaced groups to make claims asserting rights. In many instances national or international bodies need to be involved in dealing with cultural heritage and cultural difference in order to protect the rights of others. A focus on open and unfettered dialogue around the heritage management table, whether the dialogue be local, regional, national, or international, or some complex mixture, does not of itself protect individual or local heritage rights. "A metropolitan cultural politics that espouses a hands off approach to a museumized cultural other leaves the neocolonial staging of that other—fundamentalism, ethnicism, patriarchal nationalism— untouched" (Cheah 1998: 290). At the level of the nation state, deregulation does not seem to guarantee basic rights to heritage. At the international level too, neither open access nor universalist strictures can protect individual, indigenous, or local rights to heritage in and of themselves.

I would like now to return to the three cases in Turkey with which I began to explore them more closely in relation to this general discussion. Can we see here evidence of what is needed to guarantee individual and local rights to heritage? Are there dangers in an open deregulated negotiation of rights?

In the case of whether Mavili's voice should be retained on the video in Istanbul, multiculturalist intellectuals in elite academic circles in Istanbul argued that the project should support the retention of her voice and should resist the attempts by a large private bank to silence the local contribution to the exhibit.

In Mavili's local village, Küçükköy, about one kilometer from Çatalhöyük, the villagers are suffering as a result of changes in agricultural policy, which are themselves part of the attempt by Turkey to gain membership in the European Union and to comply with the EU's agricultural policies. Some government subsidies have been withdrawn. Life in the village is also hard because large state irrigation schemes have made it difficult for villagers to get access to water for their homes and fields. Mavili's particular life is difficult in a traditional society that limits the roles of women. In such a context of long-term marginalization of women I have thought it right that the project insists on employing and paying women (initially against the wishes of some elders in the village). The project has also attempted to contribute to local economic growth, through attracting tourists to the site and through providing direct employment.

In this case it seemed correct to argue against the silencing of the local voice, but it is important to point out that here "the local" is thoroughly divided between an Islamist perspective and those parts of the village that seek change and greater choice. As we have seen, the nation of Turkey too is divided between those who wish a greater Islamic presence in public life and those (such as in the judiciary) who adhere to a strong secular agenda and a Kemalist perspective. There are also intellectual elites calling for a form of multiculturalism and a degree of toleration of religious and cultural difference in public life.

So it is not a matter of supporting the local against the national or global. The situation is too complex and multi-stranded for that. The situation may quickly change, but at this particular historical moment the project's support of those in the village such as Mavili, and the attempt to empower the villagers through identification with "their own" cultural heritage, with employment, and with a voice in exhibits, offers a concrete opportunity, in a real sense, to transcend the situation in which they find themselves. The project has been involved in educational schemes in the villages, and has supported the quest by the villagers and local town to change their names to Çatalhöyük. It has provided space in the visitor center for exhibits by the local community and has involved them in the interpretation and publication of the site. The villagers are by no means passive in this process, but it has to be recognized that the whole project of local engagement is born out of an interventionist agenda. The international archaeological project has embedded itself close to the village, with international funding and with the support of the Turkish state. There is an undoubted paternalist intervention in the attempts made to educate and involve and engage the local community in the cultural heritage schemes. As already noted, the villagers are not passive in this process, but as well meaning as the attempts at engagement are, this multiculturalism has been partly promoted by global and national processes.

As a result of James Mellaart's excavations in the 1960s (Mellaart 1967), for both the nation and the world Çatalhöyük means something. Initially it meant very little to the local community. Today the village and the local town vie with each other to take on the name of Çatalhöyük. That Mavili's voice has the potential to be heard is the result of the intersection of local, national, and global interests in many dimensions. The local senses of cultural heritage and identity have here been constructed through interventionist policies. Neoliberal market economies have played their role. It is through them that the bank is able to achieve economic gain through marketing sponsorship and its exhibit. It is through private and corporate sponsorship that the project can function. But Mavili's voice is weakly heard. It is all too easily quashed, as this example shows. Any hope of freedom or equality for Mavili and other villagers through heritage depends on a cosmopolitan fraternity—her voice in relation to "her" heritage depends on being promoted and pursued by international bodies and by national interests over the long term.

In fact few such interests exist to assist Mavili. There is no requirement by most of the numerous institutional funders and sponsors of Çatalhöyük for support of Mavili and other educational and empowerment programs. It still seems to me remarkable and unethical that bodies such as the National Science Foundation in the United States do not make consideration of local impact a requirement for funding. There are shifts occurring. For example, the project has been able to apply to the U.S. State Department's Ambassadors Fund and to the British Academy (British Institute of Archaeology at Ankara) for outreach funding. But many governmental, research, and scientific foundations remain uninterested in outreach issues. Most funds for such activities at Çatalhöyük have come from NGOs and private and corporate sponsors wishing to make charitable donations. We have wonderful educational programs funded by Shell, Thames Water, Boeing, and Yapı Kredi. But we have seen how these interests may by themselves allow the erasure of regional, local, and minority interests. Neoliberal economics may provide a mechanism for Mavili's voice to be heard, but some regulation and intervention by the state or by global communities acting through or across the state seem also to be needed.

I wish to add a further example with a superficially different outcome. This is the case of Sadrettin's voice. Sadrettin also lives in Küçükköy. He left school at the age of twelve and after a series of jobs became one of the guards at Çatalhöyük during the early years of the project in the 1990s. Since as a guard his job was also to show people around the site, I and others on the project taught him as much as we could about the site and about the Neolithic in the region. One day he announced that he wanted to write a book about the site and the project. Because I had seen so many pictures of the huge "local workforces" that had excavated the great archaeological sites in the Middle East and elsewhere in the world, and yet had never read a word written by these people who made archaeology possible, it seemed to me important to encourage and help him in his venture. Members of the project helped him in the translation and editing of his text (translated by Duygu Camurcuoğlu Cleere), and finally the book was published in English by Left Coast Press in the United States, thanks to the vision and support of Mitch Allen (Dural 2007). It talks of his social encounters, his economic deals, his memories of his childhood, and of his response to the archaeologists. "Once tourists came here and asked me what I thought about foreigners and Turks working together, and in the past I felt that they would not be able to work together. But now I do not feel it matters who does the digging" (Dural 2007: 145–46).

Sadrettin's book is not a success story. It does not chart the successful education and empowerment of one of those many who have for so long been overlooked at the edges, but are actually at the center, of archaeology. His story is tragic and unending. "I realize how tired I am. The tiredness has nothing to do with writing this book, but with seeing my life not going the way I wanted" (Dural 2007: 130). But those reading his book can hardly fail to be moved by Sadrettin's point of view, and archaeologists can hardly avoid the implications of his words and his plight, hardly remain unimpressed by the silences that we have created round him. There is much to learn from his book about how Çatalhöyük might be managed and interpreted, and about how archaeologists might work with local communities.

In an interview with Sadrettin published at the end of the book, I asked him several times how and why he felt empowered to write a book. I asked him why he, rather than any one of the countless number of site workers and guards who had remained silent on archaeological sites, should feel able to write, and why he thought anyone would listen. What made him feel able to write and interpret in the face of so much specialism and high-level science? Given all that, and all the teaching he had been given, did he think he could have an independent voice? His answer was clear. "It is possible for me to have opinions independently from what I learned from the archaeologists. I still produce ideas" (Dural 2007: 147). But yet his book is a very cosmopolitan hybrid, infused with the education he has been given and made possible by a postcolonial sensitivity to difference and otherness that is more at home in a Californian publisher's office than it is in central Turkey. For Sadrettin himself, as he makes clear in his book, his story is a sad one that has not ended well. His time as a guard at Çatalhöyük and in writing the book has not produced the life that he would have liked. He has been able to "write back," but this privilege has been hard won and it has not benefited him materially or in his life's dreams. Multiculturalism and diversity, even economic empowerment through cosmopolitan alliances, have not made life better for Sadrettin. There are many reasons for this, but at least part of the answer is that "finding a voice" does not necessarily lead to real and sustained partnerships, with economic and social benefit. In the West we may be fascinated by otherness, but it is difficult to turn such "play" into long-term change (see also the chapter by González-Ruibal, this volume).

A similar conclusion about multiculturalism and cosmopolitan alliances can be made in relation to the issue of the reburial of Islamic remains from Çatalhöyük in the village cemetery. Many of the local government officials accepted the view that the remains should be reburied. As noted elsewhere in this chapter, the Konya region is generally seen as a center for Islamist perspectives. The wealth in the region is new, and it is built from small, medium, and large businesses. The region is seen as a strong base of support for the AK Party and Tayyip Erdoğan.

Several members of the project, especially the more educated Turks from Istanbul, argued against the reburial. For them, to rebury the remains was to play into the hands of the Islamists. A secularist position for them involved treating the remains as scientific instruments of study. The skeletons should be kept in the laboratory for long-term analysis, for future generations of researchers. After all, they argued, if the Islamic skeletons were reburied, surely we should rebury all the Byzantine burials in a Christian cemetery, and so on. Maybe it was even wrong to excavate the Neolithic burials at Çatalhöyük.

There were other cross-cutting concerns. It seemed that on many sites in Turkey and the Middle East, scant attention had at times been paid to later burials. Some authorities raised the specter of possible "chaos" if the Çatalhöyük project raised awareness of this issue. Perhaps excavation on many sites would become difficult. It was agreed that in any reburial ceremony in Küçükköy the press coverage should be kept at a minimum.

Indeed, the debate about the Çatalhöyük skeletal remains, while apparently local, regional, and national, also seemed inflected by a wider, more global set of concerns. Most of the foreign members of the project were of the clear view that the bones should be reburied. This view was informed by the way that even early Christian burials have to be treated in Britain (informing the police and reburial in sanctified ground). But it was also very much inflected by the reburial debate in the United States and Australia (for example), where it has come to be accepted that the remains of indigenous people should be returned by museums to affiliated groups for appropriate burial.

In fact it was the project itself that raised the issue of the Islamic burials on the site and put forward the solution of reburial. The initial sensitivities derived from a global and postcolonial experience. Certainly the issue then became taken up within the domains of local, regional, and national politics, but the desire and decision to rebury were inflected by complex and very cosmopolitan intersections. At the core of these concerns were the villagers who felt most closely affiliated with the remains. In fact, in discussions with the villagers they immediately referred to the belief that present-day Küçükköy had migrated from an earlier village located immediately by Çatalhöyük. Indeed, they argued that the skeletons recovered were perhaps the remains of those who had lived in the old village and who had used the mound as a graveyard. This local concern resonated with national politics and the debate between secularists and Islamists, but it also resonated with global sensitivities about indigenous rights and the reburial of ancestral remains. In this strange cosmopolitan mix of alliances, the small local voice was made louder, and was heard, because of its intersection with larger scales of influence.

But the foreign members of the project remained slightly surprised and disappointed at the relative lack of interest shown by the various Turkish groups—local, regional, and national—in the whole topic. It did not seem to be a major area of concern after all. A global discourse about reburial and indigenous rights just did not seem to have the same impact in this context where the term "indigenous" has little clear meaning. So here a global discourse of rights meets a set of local concerns (about secularism and Islam) that resonate with but do not duplicate the international perspective. The different perspectives make use of each other, but they do not coincide. The end result is a cosmopolitan mélange that has little ability to transform lives.

In the third case, it would perhaps be thought ethical for the Çatal-höyük project to refuse to collaborate with a university that does not allow its female students to wear the turban. After all, the project does not seek to ban the many women wearing the turban who visit and work at the site. The decision to collaborate with the university is not here a matter of supporting the local against the global. The predominant local practice is for the turban to be worn. Rather, the project has to position itself in relation to the larger debate within Turkey as a whole regarding the secular state established by Kemal Atatürk.

As an example of this debate and how it impinges on archaeology, the *Turkish Daily News* for October 20, 2006, described the plight of a ninety-two-year-old Turkish archaeologist who was to go on trial for inciting religious hatred. She had written a paper saying that the use of head scarves by women dated back to pre-Islamic sexual rites. Muazzez Ilmiye Çig is a specialist in the Sumerians and she argued that head scarves had been worn by Sumerian priestesses initiating young people into sex, although they did not prostitute themselves. The prosecutor charged both her and her publisher with "inciting hatred based on religious differences." Çig's aim was to argue against the wearing of head scarves, at least in the arena of the state.

The high-level administration at Selcuk University is very liberal. One of the vice rectors plays Van Morrison and Pink Floyd as we drive around in his chauffeur-driven BMW. The administration believes strongly in using international collaboration as a mechanism for raising standards. The rectors are receptive to Western ideals and values. Yet the administration's leaders argue forcefully for the need to ban the turban, which is seen as a threat to the secular world they have inherited and wish to reproduce. They fear Islamic fundamentalism and they decry as naïve the Istanbul multiculturalist intellectuals who think that loosening the secular ideal does not lead to a full move to Sharia law.

In America and Britain there is much acceptance of a multiculturalist agenda and thus much criticism of the decision by the French government to ban the head scarf in its schools. But in the Konya region it is understandable that the state, in however paternalistic a way, protects the common good of access to knowledge. The implications of a shift to fundamentalist religious teaching in the Konya region are clear. The Çatalhöyük project was the lead partner in a TEMPER Project funded by the European Union that developed heritage educational schemes for primary and middle schools in Turkey. In preparing and producing educational books about prehistory for local schools in the Konya region, members of the project were told that the teachers would not use the books if they told of evolution rather than following the Koran. Some archaeology students from Selcuk University working on the Çatalhöyük project have said they were surprised to be told about prehistory. There is a real fear, then, that some versions of a religious fundamentalist agenda would restrict access to knowledge about prehistory and might restrict the rights of people to engage in the distant human past. In the Konya region the common good is served by understanding and respecting the decisions by the Selcuk University rectors to ban the turban. It seems that in this specific context, openness, transparency, and multiple engagement are best achieved by taking a restrictive, statist, course. It remains possible, at the same time however, to argue against the terms of the opposition between secularists and Islamists. It remains possible to argue that wearing the turban might not, of itself, imply a wholesale adoption of religious beliefs in all areas of life. One might wear the turban and also teach or be taught evolution.

Conclusions

In 2006 Elif Shafak went on trial in Turkey, having been accused of affronting Turkishness in her novel *The Bastard of Istanbul*. In the novel there is a description of the mass deaths of Ottoman Armenians in 1915 as genocide. Her trial recalls the attempt by the nationalist lawyer Kemal Kerinçsiz to prosecute Orhan Pamuk. In 2005 Turkish state prosecutors dropped the charge that the Nobel Prize-winning author had "insulted Turkishness" by referring to the mass killings of Kurds and Armenians in the Ottoman Empire. Authors such as Elif Shafak refuse to accept that one has to be either a Muslim fundamentalist or a secular European. As she says, "My ideal is cosmopolitanism, refusing to belong to either side in this polarized world. Ambiguity, synthesis: these are the things that compose Turkish society, and that is not something to be ashamed of" (interview with the *Guardian*, September 21, 2006). As discussed earlier, the rights of groups in relation to heritage cannot be based on fixed categories and boundaries.

The various forms of multiculturalism that have increasingly held sway in discussions about heritage rights seem closely linked to an agenda that minimizes state and international regulation and intervention. There are those on "the left" in global cultural heritage in the Anglo-American world who would go so far as to argue that local customs should always be accepted and not interfered with, however repugnant they might seem to outsiders. This view seems to me an abrogation of our responsibilities to each other—of fraternity. There are many problems with this liberal view, not least of which is the point that cultural difference is always generated within global interactions and dependencies. Like it or not we are co-dependent at the global scale, and our "localness" is produced in relation to and within global processes. It seems difficult to stand by and watch injustice under the banner of "respecting cultural difference," if we have been complicit in producing difference and inequality as a result of processes of colonialism and globalization (see also the discussion by González-Ruibal of the Žižek critique, this volume).

In practice, access by minorities and the disadvantaged to economic and social benefits through heritage often hinges on the membership of historically and culturally defined groups. It is through recognition of past injustices to identified groups that reconciliation and restitution are often sought. Like it or not, archaeology is embroiled in claims of origins and can in the process contribute to an amelioration of access to economic and social goods. But it is inadequate to leave decisions about group membership, histories, reconciliation, and restitution to an open set of negotiations. Certainly debate around the cultural heritage table should involve multiple stakeholders, but in this chapter I have been critical of the links between a notion of open and equal dialogue and a pluralistic multiculturalism.

In the three examples I have explored in relation to the cultural heritage of Turkey, the rights of disadvantaged minorities can only be promoted by cosmopolitan alliances between local groups and individuals and state or global interventions. At present, there is little in the way of an international legal framework that protects minority rights in relation to cultural heritage. There are many charters and ethical guidelines at the global scale (UNESCO, ICOMOS, WAC), but historically these have largely abrogated responsibility to the nation-state, and more recently increasingly to stakeholder negotiations at the local scale.

It seems that a sea change is needed at all levels—legal, financial, ethical—to promote a stronger global framework that protects rights at whatever scale they may be threatened. Pluralistic multiculturalism often seems to celebrate diversity, the local, and the indigenous without providing a framework that can in practice protect rights. There is a need for an agenda that is concerned with historical inequalities and includes a commitment to global and interventionist principles that can protect the rights of individuals, minorities, and the disadvantaged. What is needed is careful discussion between national and global structures leading to a viable set of legal frameworks, even an international court, that protects minority rights in relation to heritage. A related position has been put forward by Jürgen Habermas (2000), who "advocates a model of *cosmopolitan* law which would supersede international law, confer actionable legal rights *directly* on individuals, and mandate the creation of supranational political agencies and institutions to ensure the implementation of human rights on a global scale. While nation-states would retain limited sovereignty, their citizens would be able to appeal to the coercive legal authority of regional or global agencies, against their own governments if necessary" (Cronin and De Greiff 1998: xx–xxi).

It seems to me that what is *not* needed is archaeologists deciding alone on the moral, social, and political issues surrounding cultural heritage rights. It should not, for example, be for archaeologists to determine whether universal rights to heritage should trump local, national rights in general or particular. There is often a complex mix of stakeholder interests and multiple scales of formal and informal cosmopolitan alliances into which the archaeologist or heritage manager is inserted. "The neologism *cosmopolitics* is also intended to underline the need to introduce intellectual order and accountability into this newly dynamic space of gushingly unrestrained sentiments, pieties, and urgencies for which no adequately discriminating lexicon has had time to develop" (Robbins 1998: 9). Archaeologists should certainly be part of the debate and raise awareness of the complex claims and rights that are involved. But in the end the right to cultural heritage needs to be ordered intellectually, ethically, and legally. Perhaps the best way forward is to situate heritage rights within a larger cosmopolitan framework of human rights legislation. The process that leads us there needs to be decentered and cosmopolitan, while at the same time providing a structured framework of protective rights for the individual or minority voice.

I have tried to leave open the question of whether heritage rights should be conferred on individuals or groups. Rather than a universalist answer to this question, I would prefer to avoid absolute strictures and trust in the processes of heritage dialogue themselves. My focus on the need for a framework to protect minority rights is aimed at the process of heritage itself. The important point seems to be that both minority and individual rights need to be protected through cosmopolitan alliances that recognize the historical contexts of heritage claims. These alliances may need to draw on structures of power and authority at national and international levels. Whether it is best to protect Mavili's or Sadrettin's rights to heritage through links to human rights concerning the individual, or whether it is best to refer to the heritage of the group depends very much on the specific historical context.

But what does seem clear from the examples given here is that minority rights to heritage depend on cosmopolitan alliances that also work within and between states or other institutions. It is the institutional frameworks that can provide the long-term commitment to change that is needed when voices are weakly heard. Hearing Mavili's voice depends to some degree on regulation and intervention by the state or by global communities acting through or across the state. Sadrettin's voice has been more widely heard in that he has published a book.

And yet this success has yet to be translated into personal betterment and fulfillment. We may in the West buy his book and be fascinated by the otherness and the empowerment that it might appear to exude. But we do not take long-term responsibility for his life or for those of his children. Our Western sensitivities too may encourage reburial of skeletal remains at Çatalhöyük, but "giving this heritage back" may do little to alleviate the social and economic problems within which the local communities exist. Alleviating such problems would involve longer and more institutionalized engagements of the type that can be provided by states and international agencies. In the example of the restriction on wearing the turban or head scarf by students at Selcuk University, the dissemination of knowledge about heritage seems to depend on taking a statist, interventionist line. It is by working with the university's and the government's secularist position that an open dialogue about prehistory remains possible. One might argue against the institutions of the state and say that a woman wearing the turban might also teach or be taught evolution. This is the sort of cosmopolitan compromise that is sought by Elif Shafak. But the fact remains that for a hybrid cosmopolitanism to be a successful basis for open teaching about prehistory in the Konya region, some intervention and protection by state institutions seem necessary. In all these examples from Turkey, cosmopolitan heritage needs grounding in political, legal, economic, and social institutions at national and global scales.

Lisa Breglia

9 ✳ "WALKING AROUND LIKE THEY OWN THE PLACE"

Quotidian Cosmopolitanism at a Maya and

World Heritage Archaeological Site

Indigenous Maya guards and custodians at Chichén Itzá, a premier archaeological heritage site located in Mexico's Yucatán Peninsula, say that *nacionales*—Mexican nationals—are the most troublesome visitors to the site. In this chapter, I examine the ideological and historical conditions that feed a tension between "Maya" and "Mexican" at this World Heritage Site, finding that neither group holds a premium on claiming the site as theirs, given a long history of transnational and private sector intervention. I suggest that the circumstance of hailing "Mexicans" as disruptive to the archaeological site reveals the national as a marked and troubled—rather than unmarked, stable, or default—category. As *nacionales* "walk around like they own the place" (according to the charges of Maya site workers), these citizen-visitors perform their relationship with the Mexican state, testing the boundaries of the constitutional guarantees that Chichén Itzá, like all of the archaeological heritage within the national territory, is the patrimony of the nation and, it would seem, of its people. At the same time, as indigenous Maya site workers criticize what they view as the inappropriate behavior of Mexicans, they call into sharp relief the artifice of archaeology's relationship with nationalism at the site. This chapter demonstrates that these simultaneous assertions and effacements—both of which bypass a firm and proper place of the national at Chichén Itzá—are expressions of what I call a quotidian cosmopolitanism. I find that the quotidian cosmopolitan sensibility at Chichén Itzá is a participatory collaboration between both workers and visitors to the site as they negotiate the meaning and significance of the site in its multiple and often contradictory historical and contemporary social, political, and economic contexts.

Mexico-in-Chichén Itzá: A Multilayered Problematic

In recent years I have spent a great deal of time inside the archaeological zone of Chichén Itzá conducting ethnographic research into the social relations that constitute the history and everyday life of the site (Breglia 2005, 2006). My primary interlocutors have been neither the "experts" on Chichén Itzá (such as archaeologists) nor the site's most vociferous interpreters (for example, tour guides). Instead, I have spent many a steamy morning and long afternoon with guards and groundskeepers at Chichén Itzá, watching throngs of tourists climb up and down the Piramide of Kulkulkan (or Castillo), taking tickets and stamping hands at the entrance gates, and even pulling stubborn weeds from between the cracks of ancient hewn stone. The guards are federal employees of the National Institute of Anthropology and History (INAH), the state agency responsible for the identification, investigation, and protection of the nation's archaeological, historic, and artistic heritage. I am still learning about what Chichén Itzá means to them, though the depth and complexity of its significance is obvious as they claim that this archaeological heritage is "in [their] blood." I have come to understand the bold and perhaps counterintuitive ways in which these site workers define their own stakes in Chichén Itzá. These "heritage workers" don't confine themselves within the parameters of indigenous identity politics—a discourse that requires these contemporary Maya to align themselves with the ancient Maya, as construed by archaeology. Instead, they position their attitudes, perspectives, and claims within a cosmopolitan discourse on global culture, internationalism, and supranational constructions of rights and duties typically associated with citizenship. This cosmopolitan sensibility among Chichén Itzá's guards and groundskeepers is—rather than newly formulated alongside the policies and discourse of world heritage—historicized within the archaeological development of the site as an international tourism destination, on the one hand, and a rejection of the limitations of a highly localized identity politics, on the other. What's more, theirs is a cosmopolitan orientation to Maya, Mexican, and world heritage that profoundly troubles the spatial and ideological hegemony of the Mexican state—the constitutionally mandated patrimonial custodian of all historic, artistic, and archaeological heritage within the nation's territory.

This latter assertion is unexpectedly crystallized in the guards' oft-reproduced commentary on the comportment and attitudes of certain visitors to the site, especially the *nacionales*. Perhaps feeling a little too at home, Mexican tourists at Chichén Itzá have been known to purposefully ignore the many restrictions on climbing delicate or crumbling structures. Mexicans, the guards charge, boldly enter cordoned-off areas and even engage in flagrant littering. As one frustrated guard put it, "They walk around like they own the place" (alternatively, "They make themselves right at home"). According to the guards, Mexicans display a high (and, it is perceived, unwarranted) degree of entitlement to the site, stepping around protective (however precarious) rail fencing, climbing where prohibitions are clearly posted, and, in perhaps the most notorious case of the past few years, attempting to slide down the balustrade of the pyramid of Kulkulkan. Site workers' narratives of the behavior of Mexican tourists at Chichén Itzá are intriguing in the ironies, contradictions, and subtextual meanings they mobilize. Indeed, it would seem that as *nacionales*, as Mexican citizens, they do "own" the patrimonial site. However, as I'll explore in this piece, the Maya workers feel or exhibit an ownership claim over the site and its symbols. Yet Chichén Itzá—as a site of national patrimony—simultaneously belongs to the whole of the nation.

Troubling the Nation

The charge of "walking around like they own the place" leveled by local Yucatec Maya distinguishes and marks Mexicans from outside of Yucatán as Other. I find this alterizing act a provocative point of entry into the problematic of representing or performing "Mexico" and "Mexicanness" in Chichén Itzá, a site of national patrimony, international tourism, and global heritage. As one might expect, ownership of and custodianship of cultural patrimony are contentious issues not only at Chichén Itzá but at heritage sites across the globe. Increasingly the terms for struggles over the fate of monumental heritage have shifted to the lexicon of neoliberal globalization. Whereas the old-style welfare state carefully guarded archaeological materials as inalienable national patrimony (protected by constitutional mandate in Mexico) for the common good of all citizens (the general assumption made about heritage worldwide according to Hodder's discussion in his contribution to this volume), the oft-touted decline of the nation-state under conditions of neoliberalization—most significantly, privatization agendas—has, perhaps put cultural patrimony into peril. What's more, some evidence suggests that some archaeological heritage was never quite safely sequestered in the commons at all (Breglia 2006).

Thus, my interest in the charge of "walking around like they own the place" leveled by Maya guards against Mexican visitors to Chichén Itzá is multifold. I suggest that in a supposedly unambiguous national space, "Mexicans" can exist as a marked category as opposed to an unmarked or default category among the hundreds of thousands of visitors to Chichén Itzá. Further, it seems that this problematic of Mexico-in-Chichén Itzá or Chichén Itzá-in-Mexico represents a crisis of "nationality," so to speak, at the intersection of territory and identity. Is this problem emergent with or exacerbated by the intensification of neoliberal agendas threatening national sovereignty over traditional venues of national patrimonial control, such as archaeological heritage sites?

I contend that as Maya workers at Chichén Itzá think and feel beyond the national, the points of reference upon which site meaning is constructed and patrimonial claims are made are neither wholly local nor entirely conjoined with the "internationalization" of Chichén Itzá through the discourse on world heritage and the flow of tourism. I consider that, by calling out "Mexicanness" at the site, Maya heritage workers are actively engaging in a cosmopolitan, postnational politics of location that highlights the tenuousness of the modern apparatus that grafts together archaeology, heritage, tourism, and nationalism, hiding the diverse interests of each in order to create the illusion of a supposedly transparent site of Mexicanness. I use "cosmopolitanism" here not so much to emphasize how workers at Chichén Itzá articulate a specific agenda aimed at an emancipatory political practice. Rather, I am more concerned with using cosmopolitanism to highlight a quotidian sensibility that has percolated within the site and its environs over the course of several decades, the genealogy of which begins to coalesce with the presence of transnational discovery and development ideologies at the beginning of the twentieth century.

There are several ways to approach the multiply-layered problematic of Mexico-in-Chichén Itzá, none more tried and true than the approach that takes as a given baseline unit of analysis a stable and coherent nation-state. Such studies, even as they propose to investigate the foundations of nationalist ideologies and the complicities of archaeology and the scientific and governmentalistic discourse of the patrimonial nation, often solidify rather than destabilize the nation as an unmarked, hidden in plain sight, category. In this discussion I work the problematic of Mexico-in-Chichén Itzá and Chichén Itzá-in-Mexico by drawing on two decidedly distinct literatures. On the one hand, I look to Yucatec historiography, which allows us to address empirically the issue of the multifaceted "apartness" or disjunction between Yucatán, the Maya, and the Mexican nation-state that social actors ranging from politicians to archaeologists and ethnographers to Maya *campesinos* have asserted and negotiated for decades. On the other hand, I bring to the problematic of Chichén Itzá a series of compelling (and sometimes confounding) ideas drawn from recent literature on cosmopolitanism. Together, these two strands creatively indicate why it should not be surprising that making space for Mexicans at Chichén Itzá is a tricky task, one that was assumed to have been handily accomplished in Mexico's twentieth-century nation-building projects but is—in the contemporary moment—undone.

Nationalism Out-of-Joint

Chichén Itzá is Mexico's third most heavily visited archaeological site and one of only a select few that holds both UNESCO World Heritage status and special status by presidential decree. Known by Europeans since the earliest incursions of the Spanish conquistadors into the Yucatán Peninsula, it began to attract proto-archaeological amateur explorers in the mid-nineteenth century, most notably the English traveler John Lloyd Stephens and his artist companion Frederick Catherwood. The appearance (especially the integrity of many architectural features) of the site today is largely due to the extensive reconstruction efforts carried out by Mexican archaeologists and the Carnegie Institution of Washington beginning in the late 1920s. As Wren and Schmidt (1991) point out, though under almost continuous investigation since the mid-nineteenth century, the archaeological distinctiveness of the site has been poorly understood and thus an issue of much debate. At the core of this debate for the practice of archaeology lay the problem of untangling the hybrid mix of Chichén Itzá's architectural styles (clearly representing occupations by different cultural groups), clashing archaeological and ethnohistorical records, and what is now a bungled and jumbled stratigraphic record. At stake is determining the critical role of Chichén Itzá in the contact between Maya and others with strong ties to central Mexico and during the Late Classic and Early Postclassic

Periods (AD 968–87). Particularly crucial here became the question of cultural dominance: did the barbarian foreign invaders completely wipe out the culture of the peaceful Maya at Chichén Itzá? (L. Jones 1997; Wren and Schmidt 1991). We'll return to this debate shortly.

Though the archaeological narrative of Chichén Itzá is compelling, it is fair to say that the site is less significant today for the reliability of its archaeological record than for its popular attractiveness and economic significance for local and regional tourism. Its appeal to the touristic imagination lies in its multiplicity. As with many a heritage site, Chichén Itzá is a space of mixed temporality—what Foucault would call a heterotopia. Not only is Chichén Itzá at once both ancient and modern, both of the past and of the present, but it also evokes a mixed sense of place. It is a dizzying amalgamation of Mexican national territory, pre-Hispanic Maya sovereign space, a workplace, a stop on a whirlwind guided tour, what have you.

Even as a nation aligns (or disciplines) a heritage site into purview, this multiplicity cannot be tamed. For Mexico, Chichén Itzá is both a space of intensification and dilution of the nation, conditioned by both history and the contemporary everyday practices of producing the site for international tourism. When foreign visitors tour Chichén Itzá, it is a perfect, intensely packed synecdoche for "Mexico." For Mexican nationals, the site extends the reach of what is *nuestro patrimonio* (a term that conveys the sense of "our heritage" in both tangible and intangible aspects) from pre-Hispanic times to the age of digital photos on the top of the Piramide of Kulkulkan. Yet at the same time Chichén Itzá figures, in narratives of both its ancient and modern past, as a disorderly space, a site of invasions, takeovers, simultaneous occupations, and multiple possible interpretations. Thus, as intensely as the site of Chichén Itzá indeed both signifies and stands in for "Mexico," woven through are a wealth of counternarratives continuously diluting, or deterritorializing, if you like, this seeming univocality. In other words, lots of the rich stuff of everyday life at Chichén Itzá, both historical and contemporary, happens outside of and, in some cases despite, existing within the auspices of "Mexico"—as national custodian, as purveyor of national identity, as staker of national territory, and as embracer of "subnational" indigenous ethnicities.

In part, the dilution of "Mexico" at Chichén Itzá sustains rather than tames a tension between Mexican and Maya at Chichén Itzá. This tension, with roots traceable to pre-Conquest times, has alternately been exacerbated and quelled by disciplinary analyses of the site. One illustration can be found in UNESCO's site description for Chichén Itzá, inscribed on the organization's World Heritage List in 1988.

> This sacred site [Chichén Itzá] was one of the greatest Mayan centres of the Yucatán peninsula. Throughout its nearly 1,000-year history, different peoples have left their mark on the city. The Maya, Toltec and Aztec vision of the world and the universe is revealed in their stone monuments and artistic works. The fusion of Mayan construction techniques with new elements from central Mexico make Chichen-Itza one of the most important examples of the Mayan-Toltec civilization in Yucatán.[1]

Multiplicity, wrought harmonious by "fusion," is the neutralized discourse presented by UNESCO. Academic archaeologists and historians, on the other hand, present ancient Chichén Itzá as a Maya space impinged upon by foreigners, or "Mexicans." For example, Michael Coe, in his primer *The Maya* (2005), describes the Post-Classic Toltec occupation of Chichén Itzá as part of the "Mexican" invasion of the Maya lowlands.[2] Coe's (and others') identification of a pre-Conquest, pre-colonization, and pre-independence (in other words pre-nation) "Mexican" identity works to support and consolidate the Otherness of Mexico at Chichén Itzá and at the same time reveals the historical relations of power in contemporary tensions between Maya and Mexican.

Translated into the popular, touristic imagination, Chichén Itzá is an authentic, richly resonant site of "pure" ancient Maya culture. For the Mexican state, in contrast, Chichén Itzá is a spectacular example of the ancient cultural diversity of the nation. For yet another group of social actors—in this case archaeologists, epigraphers, art historians, museologists, and other specialists—Chichén Itzá is, as UNESCO's site description notes and quite contrary to the popular or nationalist sentiments, an example of "Mayan-Toltec civilization." This third iteration comes to UNESCO's description through an especially thick genealogy crafted within archaeological discourse, at the center of which we find the story of the Toltec conquest or invasion of Chichén Itzá—an event created not in the course of history, but in the course of modern interpretation of Chichén Itzá's past. This third "expert" interpretation of Chichén Itzá is far from a dry, scientific exposition on the pre-Hispanic goings-on at the site. Instead, Lindsay Jones (1997) finds within archaeological narrative produced by some of the seminal figures of Maya archaeology (Tozzer, Morley, J. E. S. Thompson, among others) the construction of an ancient drama pitting the civilized (Maya) against the savage (central Mexicans). The meeting of two kinds of Indians—noble savages and bloodthirsty warriors—sets into motion a powerful stereotype with political resonance. According to Jones, "The fascination with the infamous Toltec conquest of the Maya, which seems now not to have been an historical circumstance at all, is actually the manifestation of imaginative (and colonialist) processes that began with the initial encounters between Europeans and Indigenous Americans" (1997: 278). Through the device of polarization, Chichén Itzá is a scene of arrested proto-pre-Conquest invasion. In other words, the site becomes a scene of ancient struggle between native Maya and foreign Mexican invader.

This "Mexicanization of the Maya" narrative seems to be built right into the twentieth-century reconstruction of Chichén Itzá. Thus, the Toltec conquest or invasion of Chichén Itzá and the characterization layered upon and folded within are supposedly neutralized through empirical evidence presented by the site's architecture—a clear juxtaposition between the "pure Maya" and Mexicanized/Toltec architectural styles in the modern representations of the southern and northern portions of the tourist site, respectively. Castañeda (2000) uses the occasion of reflecting on an aerial photograph of the Temple of the Warriors and the Castillo taken by Charles Lindbergh in 1929 to discuss the ideology of Mexican dominance over the Maya and Yucatán. The story of the ancient roots of Mexican hegemony at Chichén Itzá "no matter how weakly based on evidence, serves too well twentieth century nation building and nationalist ideology" (Castañeda 2000: 47). Certainly, the Toltec "Mexicanization," if it were to serve any modern agenda would be freely available for mobilization by the Mexican state as "Toltec," is not an ethnic marker currently in play in the field of Mexican indigenous identity politics. As a noncontested category, it easily slips into "modern Mexican."

However, the evidence for Chichén Itzá's two heritages—one Maya and one Mexican—is not only physically manifest in obvious architectural differences that characterize the Maya and Toltec portions of the archaeological site as we know it today. Rather, raced, ethnicized, and gendered differences are woven into the archaeological and historical narratives that use Chichén Itzá to create an image of both the Maya and the peninsula (their geographical culture area) that feeds the notion that Yucatán is a world apart from Mexico. To what extent, then, is this notion of Maya-Mexican polarity relevant in describing Maya-Mexican discursive tensions performed within the contemporary contours of Chichén Itzá? At the outset of my ethnographic research at archaeological sites and their neighboring communities in Yucatán, I quickly learned that both indigenous Maya and white Yucatecos use the term "Mexican" to distinguish non-Yucatec people or things usually associated with the central Mexican mainland.[3] This distinction is more than a quirk of colloquial nomenclature. The distinction hints at the social, cultural, and geographic disjunctures between the Yucatán Peninsula and (mainland) central Mexico from the time of Spanish conquest and colonization (beginning in 1517) and exacerbated rather than resolved by independence (1821). Thus, over and against the modernist drive to align identity and territory unambiguously, we find that "Mexican" at Chichén Itzá has become a category increasingly "out of joint." Far from a very recent phenomenon, this disjuncture has taken shape by different causes in varying degrees of intensity over the course of more than a century.

While asserting that Mexican is a category out of joint at Chichén Itzá (and before detailing the precise reasons why), it is important to note that it should *not* be. A preponderance of laws, ideologies, boundaries, and representational practices should guarantee that Chichén Itzá is wholly and securely within "Mexico": a constitutional guarantee protects all archaeological heritage under the custodianship of the nation. It follows equally that "Mexican" should be an unmarked rather than marked category or identity. Indeed, the contemporary and historical ambiguity and insecurity of these categories and identities stands contrary to the major thrust of the project of Mexican nationalism, which found particularly fertile resources in ancient ruins—not unlike the role of pre-Hispanic ruins in the project of founding Ecuadorian national modernity described by Benavides (in his chapter, this volume).

Throughout the twentieth century, the development of archaeological sites went hand in hand with efforts to develop a national consciousness that would blend and supercede ethnic or subnational difference. The historian Paul Eiss (2004: 125) describes the prevailing attitude among Yucatec officials at the time of the nascent nationalist ideology:

"The diminished conditions of Yucatán's Indians derived not only from an imputed lack of 'civilization,' but also from a continuing process of racial 'degeneration.'" But, perhaps, one hope for incorporating the Maya into Mexico lay in the fertile possibilities already being mobilized by both foreign and Mexican archaeologists within Yucatán's rich material cultural heritage. Chichén Itzá, which by the late nineteenth century had already aroused worldwide curiosity of amateur, pseudo-, and proto-scientific ilk over its magnificent ruins, was a perfect meeting ground where the roots of *mestizaje* could cross-fertilize. Alonso (2004: 467) describes, on the one hand, the European element, a holdover of the *científico*, Enlightenment rationality that prevailed during the pre-revolutionary dictatorship of Porfirio Díaz and, on the other hand, the Indian element, which "grounds the nation's claim to territory, provides a continuity of blood, and roots the nation's history in that of ancient, pre-Columbian civilizations whose art and mythology is integral to the 'national soul.'"

During the reorganization of the Mexican state following the revolution of 1910, concerns for securing both national identity and national property were twin efforts. Not only did the post-revolutionary, reinvented nation secure its geographical territory and its natural resource contents, but the new, modern Mexico wished to pinion down its cultural resources as well. Premier among these were archaeological and historical vestiges. Ruins, facades, and artifacts visible and buried were, along with waters, minerals, and, later, oil deposits, transformed into Mexican national patrimony. Meanwhile, social scientists set to the task of dealing with the nation's other heritage: its new citizens. Figuring prominently in this history is the anthropologist Manuel Gamio's "nationalist-indigenist" (Zermeño 2002: 318) project of "Forjando Patria" (1916). Gamio sought to incorporate multiple, diverse, and, for the most part, disenfranchised populations into one nation, a task that as de la Pena (2005: 724) describes, "required careful state-sponsored research to distinguish 'positive' from 'negative' aspects in vernacular cultures and to find the best strategies for their gradual transformation." Gamio specifically identified anthropology (including archaeology) as a tool of governance. The otherness of the Maya as an Indian race was particularly acute within the Mexican national landscape, evidenced by Gamio's belief that the Maya world was a crucial arena for pursuing the ideological work of integration. Castañeda (2003: 244) speculates that this led Gamio to support the work of the Carnegie Institution of Washington at Chichén Itzá as the CIW, in addition to archaeological excavation and restoration projects, used the site as a home base for multidisciplinary projects including ethnography, linguistics, nutrition, and natural sciences. Though Mexican archaeologists carried out research and reconstruction in the early years at Chichén Itzá as well, all of the bells and whistles are attributed to the Sylvanus G. Morley, the director of the CIW's Project Chichén Itzá, and his team.

By the early decades of the twentieth century, Chichén Itzá had been Mexicanized twice, once by archaeologists' imaginings of a pre-Hispanic contaminating conquest on Maya culture seated at Chichén Itzá and once by the modern Mexican state, which sought to pull material culture as well as diverse populations into the nation's patrimonial fold. What would the place for the Maya be in the now doubly Mexicanized site? In the case of the first Mexicanization, a distinct place for celebrating the artistic genius of the ancient Maya is carved out. Set as it is wholly within the distant past, no address is made in this narrative to contemporary Maya populations. This is not, however, at all what we see in the second case. The modern Mexican state that claimed Chichén Itzá for its national patrimony would eventually need to promote it by celebrating the genius of the ancient Maya while erasing the otherness of the contemporary Maya. In order to create and preserve a Mexican Chichén Itzá, the contemporary descendants of the ancient Maya would need to be effaced.

Yucatán as Apart from Mexico: Historical Narrative

Let us step back again to examine further yet another thread in the deep historical roots of the tension between Maya and Mexican at Chichén Itzá—in other words, let us go back to why Maya site workers are calling fellow citizens "Mexicans" and accusing them of impropriety. Obviously, the archaeological narrative on the "Toltec conquest" by itself cannot explain why these tensions would play out in the everyday practice of operating a premier archaeological tourism destination. The conflict between Maya and Mexican is thus one not only construed by archaeological narrations of ancient invasions, occupations, and proto-Mexican nationality. Indeed, one could argue that pre-Hispanic activities at Chichén Itzá have read the past through the lens of the region's decidedly non-ancient political history—in other words, in the region's modern experiences as part of the Spanish colonial empire in the Americas, and following this period as an ambivalent constituent of independent Mexico. I turn to how Yucatán imagined itself as a geo-political entity vis-à-vis Mexico after its independence from Spanish colonial rule because these circumstances are critical constituents of the complex genealogy of the problematic of appropriateness of "Mexico" and "Mexicanness" at Chichén Itzá.

Gilbert Joseph (1988: 15), in his comprehensive study of relations between Yucatán, Mexico, and the United States during the late nine-teenth century and the early twentieth, reads the history of the isolation and marginalization of Yucatán from Mexico as first and foremost a problem of geography: separated from central Mexico by mountains and swamps, and served by inadequate sea, rail, and road transporta-tion through the middle of the twentieth century. Moseley and Terry (1980: 1) concur: "Cut off from the rest of Mexico by sea, great dis-tance, and harsh terrain, the peninsula has been a virtual 'island' during most of its history. This isolation has given the people a sense of cultural and psychological separatism. They consider their land to be 'un otro mundo'—a world apart." Cultural differences—especially those based in pre-Hispanic indigenous heritage—as well as physical obstacles were exacerbated by political ideology from the time of independence through the Mexican Revolution. According to Joseph (1988: 15), "The entire course of Yucatecan history suggests that rather early the federal gov-ernment resigned itself to the inevitability of Yucatán's geographical isolation and then formulated political and economic policies that fur-ther marginalized the region within the national political structure." In terms of fiscal policy, Mexico treated Yucatán as more distant, so to speak, than a foreign country (Joseph 1988: 16). Even today, Maya migrant workers are likely to mean mainland Mexico when using the phrase "el otro lado" (the other side)—whereas the same phrase would be used by central Mexicans to refer to the United States.

Given these circumstances of geography and culture, Yucatán has long regarded itself as distinct from the rest of Mexico. Both the region's indigenous Maya population as well as its white Yucatec elite landown-ing class have historically resisted integration into the Mexican pol-ity. These resistances have periodically taken place since independence (1821), and include several declared secessions and calls for autonomy from the Mexican state. That Yucatán declared independence from Spain separately from Mexico in 1821 was a powerful foreshadowing of the demonstrated "apartness" that the region demonstrated throughout the nineteenth century and even into the twentieth.[4] Though it is indeed true that "the rise of the modern nation-state and nationalist movements altered the landscape of political identity" (Held 2003: 49), the attempt to suture Yucatán and its populations of white elites and Maya has left an incision as yet unhealed. However, this contentious history of disjuncture between Mexico and Yucatán is seemingly effaced within contemporary Yucatán. But if not effaced, it is carefully and relatively seamlessly glossed over at Chichén Itzá. That anthropologists and historians have described Yucatán, the regional home to Chichén Itzá, as "a world apart" from Mexico is due to cultural as well as political and economic distinctiveness. In sum, these circumstances work in concert to condition the possibility for one group of Mexican citizens, local Maya of Yucatán, to call a group of fellow citizens "Mexicans."

Excavating a Quotidian Cosmopolitan Sensibility

Chichén Itzá and its practitioners are not cosmopolitan solely by dint of the high degree of transnational flows traversing the site and its history. In other words, cosmopolitan aspects of Chichén Itzá are not limited to the formal global connectedness of this internationally famous archaeological site to either World Heritage or tourism markets. Alongside these extranational conditions is a cosmopolitan sensibility imbued within the site and its environs, which is based not in formal networks (tourism) or designations (World Heritage), but rather in the social relations between and among site workers, local residents, landowners, managers, archaeologists, bureaucrats, tourists, and others. The archaeological heritage at Chichén Itzá is a form of material culture highly resonant within the production and circulation of both local and extra-local meanings, peoples, and things.

My own understanding of the heterogeneity of the local at Chichén Itzá has been developed through long-term ethnographic research within the archaeological site itself, in surrounding communities, and in other regional nodes that serve as points of comparative study. Much of my ethnographic research at Chichén Itzá is focused on the employees of Mexico's National Institute of Anthropology and History (INAH), the federal agency created to carry out the constitutional mandate of protecting the nation's cultural heritage. These thirty-six workers, many of whom were second- and even third-generation presences in the archaeological zone, are as a group distinct from many other local residents around Chichén Itzá due in large part to their steady, salaried employment, their strong unionization, and their entrepreneurial activities inside the archaeological zone. As to the latter, for decades the oldest generation of INAH workers at Chichén Itzá used their de facto presence within the federal archaeological zone as a means by which to garner exclusive economic benefits through the provision of tourist services. Chichén Itzá's guards, those who level the charge of "bad behavior" at Mexicans, see the heritage rights of non-Yucatecos and non-Maya as illegitimate while using a particularly clever argument to assert their own patrimonial claims to the site—which is not about cultural affiliation with the ancient Maya, or within a discourse of indigenous identity politics. In my book *Monumental Ambivalence* (2006), I describe how the site's successive generations of federally employed guards and custodians regard the site as inheritable family patrimony. They claim that caring for the site—literally, their employment in the maintenance and protection of the ruins—as well as the right to benefit from it economically, is "in [their] blood" (Breglia 2005, 2006). Neither being Maya nor being Mexican, in their eyes, makes one a legitimate heir to the patrimony of Chichén Itzá.

Claiming their rights to Chichén Itzá in this fashion troubles an easy understanding of how these Maya cultural workers orient themselves to the site and how they situate themselves within the ever expanding horizons of region, state, nation, and even the world. The apparent deep sense of place that characterizes these workers' articulations of their own genealogies to the ruins would suggest that the Maya root their identity locally. It would follow from this that any cosmopolitan sensibility would be of Appiah's (2005) rooted variety. Yet I find a more amenable fit here with notions of cosmopolitanism that don't depend so strongly on geographical locatedness to secure identity. One of these alternatives is offered by Waldron (1995, 1996), who suggests that cosmopolitan identity is a "melange" of commitments, affiliations, and roles that reflects disparate and disjunctive cultural influences.

Certainly, this would more appropriately describe how contemporary mostly "Maya" employees of a modernized and Mexicanized site of hybrid and contested heritage fashion claims to the patrimony that Chichén Itzá represents.

The confidence to negotiate this "mélange" is very much a part of the workers' quotidian cosmopolitan sensibility. At Chichén Itzá, the quotidian cosmopolitan sensibility is both local and extra-local, drawn into practice by the site's Maya workers, among others (tour guides, administrators, and tourists), whose approach to the ruins connects past to present and local to global without either routing or rooting their identity in the national. This is especially evident in how workers claim rights to the site by virtue of a host of characteristics (membership in the local community or inherited job positions working within the archaeological zone) that do not, significantly, include Mexican citizenship. The cosmopolitanism of the Maya heritage workers at Chichén Itzá is a critical stance, an intervention into the state's attempt to coalesce the territory and identity of the site under the unifying embrace of "Mexico."[5]

The cosmopolitan sensibility practiced at Chichén Itzá is at once both self-conscious and unwitting. I say unwitting because of the way in which cosmopolitanism becomes a worldview compatible with different styles of making identity claims, on the one hand, and forms of economic exploitation, on the other, both of which introduce the danger of rendering cosmopolitanism compatible with (neo)liberal multiculturalism. As the political and social agenda of multiculturalism has consistently failed to live up to its promises of righting social and economic inequalities, social injustices, and colonial legacies of racism and sexism, it is not so much being "Mexican" as being Maya that becomes the problem at Chichén Itzá that is effaced rather than addressed by the cosmopolitan sensibility.

In other words, not only is "Mexican" a problem at Chichén Itzá, as I have discussed here at length, but so too is "Maya." Like many similar cases across the colonized world, the "Maya" of Yucatán did not use this label as a marker of self-identity at the time of the Spanish conquest and subsequent colonization. Restall (2004) argues that the imposition of the identity category represents a "Maya ethnogenesis," instigating a multi-century tug of war of resistance against the imposed ethnic designation. Even today, workers at Chichén Itzá tend to back away from a strong universal notion of asserting or identifying (with) an authentic Maya identity. People are historically wary of indigenist-inflected discourse due to the legacies of the state-sponsored *indigenismo* ideology turned policy of national racialist integration. In more rural parts of Yucatán such as on the outskirts of Chichén Itzá, residents may perceive "indigenous" as a derogatory category. Many associate the term with the work of the Mexican state agency, the Instituto Nacional Indigenista (INI), whose rural development mission included cultural and educational campaigns administered from numerous coordinating centers across the country. The critical response from some recipients of the INI's attentions was their understanding that "indigenous" INI workers really meant "illiterate."

At Chichén Itzá, nearly a century of cultivating sites of valorization of Maya heritage recuperated a sense of "Maya" that came not necessarily to be wholly tied to "indigenous." However, in the contemporary arena of heritage politics, there are rather limited parameters on how local communities, especially relatively disempowered subjects, may articulate claims to archaeological sites, monuments, and materials. The spectrum of possible positions is anchored at one end by law and at the other by identity politics. Indigenous identity may be constructed as a legal necessity (such as for Native American tribes recognized by the U.S. government under the repatriation procedures laid out by NAGPRA) or as a political strategy (such as for First Nations peoples of Canada and the Arctic, Aboriginal peoples of Australia, and many fourth world people across the globe). In the first instance, indigenous identity construction must respond explicitly to the demands of the state. The recognition of indigenous claims and any hopes for restitution of material remains of the past is dependent upon an intricate demonstration of cultural affiliation—a proof, if you will, of identity. In Mexico, no law such as NAGPRA exists, and no vocal demand or visible movement for such a law can be discerned in the public arena in Yucatán. In terms of the second instance, "Maya identity" has been fruitfully used as a political strategy in the Maya cultural activism movement in Guatemala and also in the Zapatista movement within Chiapas, Mexico, and beyond. Indeed, to be Maya, or to be called Maya, in Yucatán resounds much differently than in Guatemala and even Chiapas, so close yet a world away from Yucatán. Maya intellectuals and those who stand on their side have vociferously called for increased access to and recognition regarding Maya cultural heritage sites, becoming highly critical of the work of archaeology in the process.

Neither identity-based political activism nor state-sponsored legal protection find fertile ground in contemporary Chichén Itzá. Both of these options would require the following two conditions: (1) that "indigenous" and "Maya" be rejoined NAGPRA-style in a legal cultural affiliation between the contemporary population and the ancient Maya; and (2) that the state be welcomed as the ultimate mediator or arbiter of identity, conceding once and for all that Chichén Itzá had indeed been Mexicanized. The quotidian cosmopolitanism sensibility demonstrated by workers at Chichén Itzá is not necessarily a politically instrumentalized orientation to the world that seeks to address universal human rights, freedom, and justice in the world. Instead, it is a methodological cosmopolitanism engaged in by everyday users of the site. This cosmopolitan sensibility is one that allows for multiple meanings. Rooted in the anxiety and indeed the insecurity of Mexico, the national does not sit conveniently and comfortably in a safe and guaranteed niche between the local and the global. This notion of national cultural patrimony manifest most boldly in archaeological ruins seeks to trap Maya in a carefully prescriptive identity politics making Chichén Itzá "theirs" primarily by virtue of Mexican citizenship.

Cosmopolitan Territory: Toward a Postnational Space

I centered this discussion upon a deceptively simple question: Is there a place for Mexico at Chichén Itzá? A look at the formal apparatus that governs the geographical and legal terrain of Chichén Itzá (both the physical location along with the laws, policies, and administrative procedures that govern, produce, and reproduce the site) would assume and dictate the unassailable "Mexicanness" of Chichén Itzá. Indeed, all archaeological sites in Mexico are constitutionally claimed and protected as property of the nation. Yet ruins are sites of competing and often contradictory claims of ownership, custodianship, and heritage (Breglia 2006). Perhaps the contestation of ruins is more obvious at Chichén Itzá, a site that has experienced the interventions of archaeology, tourism development, and those of the Mexican state for nearly a century. At the same time, it has experienced the very local patrimonial claims articulated by Chichén Itzá's neighboring indigenous

Maya residents based on a sort of kinship tie to the site, not in terms of a cultural affiliation, but based, rather, on the successive generations of family-based excavation and site maintenance labor carried out at Chichén Itzá. Compounding these other-than-national claims is the status of the actual ownership of land upon which the famous monuments of Chichén Itzá sit: it is an astonishing fact that this site is privately owned and has been so for generations. I argue that these factors work in such orchestration as to render "Mexico" only a bit player, so to speak, in this so-called national space. The tension between the local and the global at Chichén Itzá effaces an appropriate space for the nation, thereby promoting a crisis in grounding citizenship vis-à-vis this site of national patrimony.

In heterotopic space such as the Mexican, Maya, and World Heritage site of Chichén Itzá, "national space" is constantly and continuously undergoing deterritorialization. This process effects an anxiety and ambivalence for both Maya and Mexican as a sure ground for displaying and claiming citizenship within this seemingly national space, which is spatially and discursively undermined. The site's long history of transnational interventions through foreign archaeology, on the one hand, and touristic development, on the other, are two continual tides in the ongoing territorialization of Chichén Itzá. These interventions posit with one hand the appropriate place for Mexico at Chichén Itzá while undermining its signifying power with the other.

This deterritorialization and reterritorialization sleight of hand has been played at Chichén Itzá since the late nineteenth century and continues in various forms through the present time. Notable signposts in the site's genealogy include the purchase of the site by an American diplomat in 1896 for the purpose of excavating and exploring the ruins. The amateur archaeologist Edward H. Thompson, backed by the U.S. government and with funds from the American Antiquarian Society and Harvard's Peabody Museum, among others, purchased the land and ruins comprising Chichén Itzá, ushering in more than a century of private ownership of the site and Chichén Itzá's ruins. The site was subsequently sold off piece by piece to the Yucatec tourism entrepreneur Fernando Barbachano beginning in the 1930s. The site remains in the hands of Barbachano's descendents and associates (Breglia 2005, 2006).

Another discursive and territorial intervention in Chichén Itzá is the granting of World Heritage status to the site. While World Heritage does not make world citizens, it does mark territories in particular ways that gesture toward a pedagogy of global responsibility. At Chichén Itzá, World Heritage works subtly rather than overtly. Rather than protocol, World Heritage offers the subtlest of suggestions as to how to practice a cosmopolitan sensibility. What World Heritage status does is trouble the hegemony and sovereignty of the nation-state as it simultaneously deterritorializes and reterritorializes any given site of national heritage (Breglia 2005, 2006). Sites are deterritorialized from the boundaries and borders of local, regional, and national meanings (and, in some cases, policies) as they become discursively attached to UNESCO's World Heritage program. Sites are reterritorialized as they are brought into accordance with UNESCO's standard of "universal cultural value," over and above particularities of culture area and national boundaries. National agencies, in turn, appeal to and support abstract notions of "cultural good," bolstering these with specifically nationalist ideologies. Living communities surrounding or, in many cases, located within archaeological sites negotiate these ideals and mandates according to the dynamics of the everyday life of the archaeological heritage site.

While it could be argued that these stakeholders negotiate contradictory state versus private interests, perhaps this does not adequately characterize the contemporary situation. While the neoliberal state contemplates the relinquishment of territorial control over national properties through privatization, my ethnographic and archival evidence from Chichén Itzá clearly supports the claim that the state has, for at least a century, merely assumed—through its laws, policies, and institutional management—that sites of monumental cultural patrimony were within its firm grasp all along. While a certain kind of security of monumental heritage sites is assumed by the liberal nation-state by dint of the principle of territorial sovereignty (in other words Mexican heritage is safely bundled within Mexican national space), ethnographic and archival evidence strongly suggests that the stability and coherence of this linkage (space [Chichén Itzá] / ideology [patrimony]) is tenuous at best. It is only referred to in its problematization, such as in the spatio-ideological problem of "Mexicans" walking around like they own Chichén Itzá, misbehaving, and in misreading the stability of the nation in this space of a disjunctive "national," of an anxious "Mexico," and of acting-out "Mexicans."

The consideration of the cosmopolitan sensibility at Chichén Itzá that I offer here is (lamentably, in my opinion) more backward- than forward-looking. It now seems that the cosmpolitanism rooted in Chichén Itzá's ruins that has been emerging over the decades has a circumscribed (limited) political potential whose horizon is presently contracting rather than expanding. In other words, the already existing cosmopolitanism doesn't change the condition and indeed inequalities of labor regimes, land use, tenure, and ownership, and the exercise of local, indigenous politics at Chichén Itzá. What is more, the proto- and postnational space that is Chichén Itzá cannot resist ongoing waves of territorialization vigorously and repeatedly produced by capitalism in a neoliberal mode.

Given this matrix of competing interests in claiming the archaeological heritage site, it would be impossible for us to conceive of Chichén Itzá as a hegemonic national space and, what is more, assert that Chichén Itzá is an open ground, free and clear for the exercise of national identity. Using a concept borrowed from Jonathan Inda (2000: 86), we might understand Chichén Itzá as a "postnational zone . . . a space continually traversed by transnational flows of peoples and things" and, I might add, continually traversed by competing histories, beliefs, and rhetorics of belonging. The use of the "post" prefix here does not chronologically mark a recent decline or "death" of the nation; rather, "post" signifies the renewal of vigor in our analyses of how "the nation" operates in this geographical, discursive, and imagined site. I would like to suggest here that we understand Chichén Itzá as a postnational space in which "Mexicanness" comes to stand for a critical disjunction between local Maya claims to patrimony, the anxiety of national control over this cultural resource, private sector interventions, and the globalizing discourse of World Heritage.

The quotidian cosmopolitan sensibility at Chichén Itzá, as performed by the various users of the archaeological site, informs and is informed by the larger challenge presenting itself at heritage sites across the globe. Specifically, I am speaking of the ability of the public sector, ranging from local communities to national governments, to maintain a controlling interest in heritage. As we contemplate the place of national patrimony in the globalizing world, we are led to ask: Is

Mexico "losing control," as Saskia Sassen (1996) would put it, over its national cultural resources? Does the archaeological heritage field give us yet another example of the floundering, shrinking, or weakening of the sovereign nation-state, as many versions of globalization would have us imagine? We might use this case of the deterritorializing nation at Chichén Itzá as part of a broader critical inquiry at the intersection of local and global, taking neither as univocal or stable, to focus on the points of vulnerability in the supposedly stable mediating discourse and structure: the national. While many theories of globalization assume or somehow require the stability of the nation-state as a mediating "space" between the local and the global, thinking through the performance of quotidian cosmopolitanism throws into question not only the veracity but the ideology of this assumption.

One goal of this volume to which I hope this case study contributes is to distinguish the challenge of cosmopolitanism from the political largesse of multiculturalism. Especially instructive toward this end is the inherent refusal on the part of Chichén Itzá's workers to situate themselves within the limited scope of identity politics. What I have also attempted here in this study of a Mexican national and World Heritage site is a critical intervention into what Beck and Sznaider (2006) call "methodological nationalism." Translated into my own research, this means seeking to understand how "Mexico" signifies in practices, beliefs, and communities outside of the Mexican national territory. For me, the question has a slight (and ironic) twist: my goal is to understand how "Mexico" has a fragile foothold at an archaeological heritage site that is, rather unambiguously, situated within Mexico's national territory. More than a philosophical reflection or semiotic analysis, this critical stance vis-à-vis the nation is an expression of cosmopolitanism that can be practiced equally by visitors and the visited in a site of international tourism.

Afterword

A recent trip to Chichén Itzá provided further pause for thought regarding the place of Mexico at the archaeological site. I arrived at 8:30 AM, opening time on a Sunday—the "free entrance day"—as in all of the state's archaeological zones. But something was different. Already perspiring groups of early arrivals were crowded around the ticket window that should have been closed, purchasing their entrance tickets before approaching the INAH guards who awaited them at the bank of turnstiles with their stamp-pads and hole punchers in hand. Was Sunday no longer free, I asked myself? Then I noticed a steady trickle of people moving through the last turnstile, this one marked with a sign: Sunday is free for Mexican nationals (with proper identification). Mexicans passed through unencumbered, free to enjoy the heritage site. Perhaps there is, after all, a place for Mexico at Chichén Itzá.

Notes

1 UNESCO, Pre-Hispanic City of Chichen-Itza, http://whc.unesco.org/en/list/483 (accessed November 1, 2006).

2 As Lindsay Jones (1997: 288) points out, "The term Mexicanization, when applied to the glamorous confrontational drama between the Toltecs and the Maya at Chichén Itzá, is an obvious and telling misnomer since the Mexica, the preeminent third of the Aztec triple alliance, did not rise to prominence until some three centuries after the presumed Toltec conquest of Yucatán."

3 Residents of Yucatán are not likely to refer to themselves as "Mexicanos" in cultural terms though they might in political terms. By this I refer to specific references to the rights and duties associated with formal citizenship ("somos Mexicanos" when speaking of voting rights), or when speaking of Mexican citizens in relation to other nations, for example, the plight faced by "us Mexicans" when crossing the border into the United States.

4 Yucatán was briefly independent in 1823 upon the fall of the emperor Agustin Iturbide, and the whole of the peninsula (including the present-day states of Yucatán, Campeche, and Quintana Roo) was declared a state within Mexico in 1824. Opposed to centralist authority emanating from Mexico City, Yucatán's non-Maya landowners engineered the peninsula's secession in 1839. The briefly independent Yucatán found its white elite-controlled government severely compromised by a Maya rebellion known as the Caste War. The divided region was defeated by government forces in 1843. Though the Mexican government promised autonomy to the region, Yucatán seceded again in January of 1846 when that promise was broken. During this secession, Yucatán contracted with the then Republic of Texas to provide naval support. Felipe Carillo Puerto's short-lived Socialist Republic of Yucatán was declared in 1915. The political marginalization of the peninsula was complete when Yucatán lost the territory of Quintana Roo (the location of present-day Cancún) in 1902. This represented a "political defeat for the region as well as a severe economic loss," and what's more, "it demonstrated a complete subjugation

of potential regional growth to national interests and priorities" (Joseph 1988: 67).

5   The workers' position is aligned with what Beck and Sznaider (2006) describe in their use of cosmopolitanism as a critical intervention into "methodological nationalism," the use of the nation-state as a referential unit of territorial, societal, and cultural space, encompassing practices and processes therein.

O. *Hugo Benavides*

10 ✳ TRANSLATING

ECUADORIAN MODERNITIES

Pre-Hispanic Archaeology and the Reproduction

of Global Difference

This is something. This has got to be contemporary. He's really going to town. It's very jaunty, very authoritative. His errand might prove to be impossible. He is challenging something—or something has challenged him. He's grounded in immediate reality by the bicycle. . . . He's apparently a very proud and silent man. He's dressed sort of polyglot. Nothing looks like it fits him too well.—JAMES BALDWIN, *Perspectives: Angles on African Art*

Anthony Appiah (1997b: 422) uses Baldwin's particular description of a contemporary African art piece titled "Yoruba Man on a Bicycle" to open his discussion of the place of the modern in defining authentic African culture and identity. According to Appiah (1997b) unlike the other curators who had selected "authentic" pieces meant to emphasize the "primitivism" identity of the African past, Baldwin was interested in a broader understanding of what it meant to be African in today's world. It is this initial insight that Appiah has continued to develop in the last decade, serving in many ways as the central piece of his most recent book, *Cosmopolitanism* (2006a). In this contribution Appiah champions a much more dynamic understanding of identities and cultures, one in which the past and the foreign are essential elements in the reproduction of contemporary and authentic cultural traditions.

As highlighted in the *New York Times* Sunday magazine, cosmopolitanism was proposed as the newest philosophical trend looking to bridge the conservative and progressive divide. In this fashion authentic cultures no longer need to deny foreign elements but are rather defined by modern and postmodern ways of interpreting not only these same foreign elements but also notions of their ancient and recent pasts. This is possible according to Appiah because "cultures are made of continuities and changes, and the identity of society can survive through these changes. Societies without changes aren't authentic; they're just dead" (Appiah 2006b: 34).

The powerful implications of seeing and defining cultures through change and the timing of such emphasis in the current moments of uneven global flows marks the backdrop for this chapter on the relationship between archaeology and Ecuadorian modernities. More specifically I look to assess the power of a "cosmopolitan" ideology, as elaborated by Appiah and others (see Sahlins 1994; Žižek 2002, 2004; see also Baldwin 1984, 1990; and Coetzee 1996), within the context of Ecuadorian archaeological production, examining how the research of the past in the national landscape enters into, and contributes to, the debate of Ecuadorian and global modernities in such ways that it elucidates the definition of the modern signifier itself. I will also address how these same archaeological enterprises contribute to contemporary forms of political and social identities in both subtle and explicit forms that are part of larger parameters and implications within the reproduction of global difference.

Reproducing Global Difference: The Specter of the Other

Two of the most salient characteristics of a cosmopolitan ideology are its timeliness within the current moment of emphatic globalization and the fact that culture as change is an old anthropological motto. One must wonder about the central place of change in this contemporary definition of culture when modern and cyber capital are central forces in the reproduction of transnational economic exchanges. It is vital, in this fashion, to highlight the unequal manner in which global flows are exerted and the varying ways in which they ultimately sustain their ambiguous forces, precisely because they never work only in one direction, or in any type of moral absolute.

In J. M. Coetzee's novel *Foe* is a telling commentary: "Cruso raised his head and cast me a look full of defiance. 'I will leave behind my terraces and walls,' he said. 'They will be enough. They will be more than enough.' And he fell silent again. As for myself, I wondered who would cross the ocean to see terraces and walls, of which we surely had an abundance at home, but I held my peace." As Kincaid (1997) has highlighted, the power to travel to see foreign "terraces and walls" is both an economic and a cultural privilege with its own set of effusive forms of productive effects. Even the fact of who gets deigned to be a native, when we are all natives of sorts, is not without larger symbolic significations in a modern enterprise of globalization that wishes to hide many of the colonial specters hidden within its contemporary figuration. To this degree, who visits whom, what products and services are exchanged, and what cultural markers are reproduced within these exchanges are of enormous political consequences, precisely because these rituals of capitalist exchanges have been singularly prescribed in the last two centuries, and yet there are multiple forms of identification, signification, and reiteration that escape this homogenous form of political categorization (see Sahlins 1994).

As S. Hall (1997a, 1997b) elaborates, the fact that there is always something that escapes the social is a very powerful thing because it is precisely through that flight that new forms of political identities and agencies are enabled. It is in this sense that seeing culture as change has always been a very central ideological construct for the Western anthropological enterprise. Much earlier than other social scientists, anthropologists realized that the exotic and foreign other was far from that isolated native begging to be instructed in the rites of civilization. Perhaps this was because the mere presence of the anthropologists marked the long-standing nature of cultural interaction or even the fact that what had taken the anthropologists to these "supposedly" far away places was the ideological construct of otherness central to the Western sense of self.

The other, or more specifically the specter of the other, plays a particular form of cultural haunting within the modern forms of globalization and its central processes. To a certain degree it is expected that the old and neocolonial forms of exchanges and relationships will be forgotten within the new paradigm of development and globalization. However, the fact that the new development map could be easily fitted into a nineteenth-century grid of colonizing and colonized regions speaks volumes to the persistent nature of exploitative global relations. The specter of the other is central to the imaginary of a modern and postmodern citizenry that continuously attempts to distance itself from the harrowing pictures of widespread ethnological and genocidal practices that contributed (and continue to do so) to the wealth and growth of capital in Europe and the United States.

It is within this double model of both postcolonial politics and also of Lacanian notions of the Real that Žižek understands the modern system of state terrorism and Islamic guerrilla mentality. It is at this particular crux that Žižek (2002) adequately refers to MacJihad, emphasizing the integrated nature of both the Western and Islamic claims to political supremacy. However, it is not only that one necessarily feeds (and needs) the other, but that actually both forms of military intervention are the effects (excesses in Lacanian parlance) of much broader and richer cultural interactions that have determined the manner in which many of these social movements throughout the globe have been able to reify themselves as culturally authentic enterprises.

It is these multiple specters of the other that are central to the paranoid production of a conservative trend in the global sphere (see Appadurai 2006; S. Hall 1997a). These many forms of self-otherizing allow for new forms of cultural production that, as such, are both political and morally ambiguous, enabling multiple projects of political identification. In the Ecuadorian landscape, as in many other nation-states and nationalizing projects (see Fox 1990; Dominguez 1990; and Williams 1990, 1996), it is not only the past but also the present that gets continuously otherized to re-create forms of cultural authenticity that are used to redefine the national sphere in the same xenophobic and racist manner that is globally prevalent. Meanwhile, multiple forms of progressive entities, from the launching of new forms of sustainable development to eco-tourism and the reclaiming of indigenous human rights, are ambiguously invested in the reproduction of global difference. The past, particularly the pre-Hispanic and colonial past, plays a pivotal role in all of these different cultural enterprises, marking, in varied manners, new cultural forms of modernities within the Ecuadorian landscape.

It is these reifications of the other, particularly past others, that I wish to assess in the following analysis. Particularly I am interested in the manner in which these remnants of the pre-Hispanic past are continuously reused to define, reclaim, and legitimize new cultural ventures, both in terms of identification and in political negotiations. The archaeological enterprise becomes an invaluable tool in the hegemonic reproduction, allowing a series of imaginary constructs to participate continuously in the dynamic articulation of multiple forms of Ecuadorian modernities that get reproduced through, and against the backdrop of, global difference.

As a nation-state, Ecuador is continuously struggling to reproduce coherent narratives of self-legitimization that in many ways will cover

up its founding history of genocide and its unremitting racist exploitation and discrimination. The Ecuadorian racial landscape is a complex
one in which class and status markers are charged with meanings to
create hybrid identities (i.e., *cholos*, *montubios*, *mestizos*, and so forth)
and legitimize discriminatory forms of violence and rape. Mythical images of white foreigners (sometimes referred to as *pishtacos*, *Nakaq*, or
sacaojos) accused of removing body parts, including fat, are rampant
throughout the Andes and speak to the complex manner in which biology, history, economics, and politics intermingle in the social production of racial images. (See Weismantel 2001 for a thorough discussion
of some of the main racial mythical images of the Andes.)

The initial decimation of the Native American (i.e., Indian) communities in the national territory is usually placed squarely on the colonizing shoulders of the Spanish Empire and never ascribed to the current
Ecuadorian citizenry. However, this particular historical narrative is
obviously one of fragile constitution, since the consistent forms of racial exploitation of indigenous peoples as indentured servants, maids,
and other forms of exploitative labor have continued unremittingly for
the last two centuries. Even after the defeat of the Spanish Empire in
the early 1800s and the transition to neocolonial forms of domination
at the hands of European entities, that is, France and Great Britain,
and finally the United States, the racist constitution of the Ecuadorian
nation has remained constant.

This particular racial hierarchy has proved precious to the nation's
reproduction of capital, allowing a white and *mestizo* minority to claim
greater ownership of national public life and ultimately to define not
only the political future of the nation but also to limit the historiographical narrative production in the country. This particular racial
legacy has also been inscribed within the country's three national geographical regions: the coast (including the Galapagos archipelago), the
highlands, and the Amazon. The coast includes the most populous port
city of Guayaquil (see below) and the province of Esmeraldas (bordering with Colombia at the north), which presents the highest concentra-
tion of Afro-Ecuadorians in the territory.

Meanwhile, the highlands hold the majority of the surviving Quechua-
speaking Indian communities, with the Amazon representing a mixture
of recent national migrants and traditional tribal communities. It is not
a coincidence that these tribal groups have come to national and international attention through their litigation with oil companies that look

to literally mine their homelands (see Benavides 2004b). It is in these geographical landscapes that not only Indians but Afro-Ecuadorian communities have been continuously reified as the national other even though, or perhaps precisely because, their claim to a national Ecuadorian identity has equal or even greater geographical legitimization than does that of the white elite.

What is particularly telling is how these same nationally reified others—Indians and blacks (along with Arab- and Asian-Ecuadorians who are pejoratively referred to as Turks and Chinese, respectively)—are also identities reproduced within the global landscape. Indians and black diasporic communities have been historically reproduced within the transnational and global distribution of capital, allowing both identities to achieve particular forms of global differentiations translatable in a wider market of symbolic signification. Therefore, it is this local reification of diasporic otherness that is both indebted to and contributes to broader forms of global capital, which become an essential element of cosmopolitan articulation.

In the following three cases, I will examine the archaeological enterprise behind the constitution of Ecuador's largest city, Guayaquil, the current pan-Indian movement, and the ambiguous place of Afro-Ecuadorians within this same dynamic reproduction of the nation's past (and present). My objective is to assess the manners in which these local-global articulating identities, which represent a larger membership in a global market and an authentic rearticulation of vital forms of Ecuadorian modernities, are continuously reproduced in meaningful ways in the varying national landscape.

Guayaquilean Modernity: The Indian Past of a South American Miami

One of the most significant traditional songs of Guayaquilean identification contains the following verse:

Guayaquileño madera de guerrero
más fuerte y más valiente en todo el Ecuador,
no hay nadie que te iguale en fuerza y en coraje
lo digo en mi canción.
(Guayaquilean of warring stock
stronger and braver in all of Ecuador,

nobody equals you in strength and courage
I say so in my song.)

It reflects not only the ambiguous elements of a warring Indian past, but also the essentially competitive patriarchal nature of the city. As part of their enculturation to their city, Guayaquileans are continuously reminded of their brave Indian origins in the shape of the original pre-Hispanic inhabitants of the same geographical landscape, the Manteños-Huancavilcas. These pre-Hispanic Indians are heralded as brave warriors who fought fiercely against Inca domination and were subdued only by the greater technology of the Spaniards and the onslaught of the epidemic diseases disseminated by them. Repeatedly the courage and bravery of this warring tribe is heralded as one of the primary traits inherited by Guayaquileans from the pre-Hispanic past, and it is one that serves to reinscribe the competitive nature of regional identification within the larger national landscape of the country.

The image of fierce resistance and proud heritage is similarly enshrined in the most popular explanation given for the origin of the city's name: Guayaquil is supposed to have come from the names of the leader of the Huancavilcas, Guayas, and his wife, Quil, who resisted the Spanish to their deaths. That is, when Guayas was killed by the Spaniards after he was captured, his wife preferred to jump to her death in the river (which carries her husband's name) rather than "belong" to any Spanish men. This particular origin myth is quite similar to the racial and gender problematics presented in other American settings such as that with the Malinche in Mexico and in Peru. In this instance Quil is hailed as the true heroine, doing what La Malinche is blamed for not doing: dying rather than engaging in sexual intercourse, sleeping with the enemy, and in the process creating a new *mestizo* race (see Anzaldúa 1987; de la Cadena 2000; Mallon 1996).

What both of these Indian references express is the ambiguously fragile nature of the city's Indian past, where multiple forms of historical narratives need to be contained in hegemonic fashion to legitimize the current white and *mestizo* elite's ideological stronghold. The Indian nature of the city cannot be denied: it is visible everywhere, from the physical elements in the bodies of Guayaquileans to the contemporary Indian presence at market places and construction sites to the very origins of many families whose grandparents migrated from highland Indian communities almost a century ago. However, this oversignifica-

tion of an Indian past offers an impossible scenario of obsessive attachments to a reified city identity that also must deny this Indian presence
within the postcolonial mores of a whiter, that is, more "civilized" heritage (see Butler 1997; Butler et al. 2002).

It is this particular schizophrenic divide that has defined the city's
historiographical enterprise from its inception. This historical paranoia
even goes to the extreme of reproducing the ideology of an "ancient
past" (which is less than a century old), locally referred to as *Guayaquil
antiguo*, as a metonymic device to rid the city of its Indian and black
citizens. The images of Guayaquil at the end of the nineteenth century
and the beginning of the twentieth have forever been captured in stencil
representations and photographs. As are all reconstructions of the past,
this one is also an artifice to reconstruct the past we thought or perhaps
more accurately wished might have been (see Abu-el Haj 1995; Alonso
1988; Castañeda 1996; Handler and Gable 1997; Kohl and Fawcett 1995;
Patterson and Schmidt 1995; Trouillot 1995).

The title *Guayaquil antiguo* itself offers antiquity, and through it authority and authenticity to a past that is less than a century old. But
more importantly the black and white representations of grand wooden
houses, lumberyards, and empty central avenues depict a setting devoid
of the class conflict, racial tension, and sexual repression that permeated
the city at that time. These idealized representations of Guayaquil also
provide a romantic fantasy of peace and tranquility for the largely white
and white-*mestizo*, landholding elite. The lack of evidence of urban chaos
in these pictures speaks volumes against the presence of two of the largest social movements in the city (Liberal Revolution and the Worker's
Movement), as well as the massacre of thousands of workers that occurred in Guayaquil during this period.

Archaeology, not surprisingly, has played an essential role in the dynamic reproduction of the city's official past, one in which dangerous racial and sexual specters are eliminated from the social imaginary of what
the city might have been like, and even, more importantly, is like today.
In its most immediate effect the image of the Indian must be simultaneously incorporated (since after all that is the objective of all pre-Hispanic
archaeological excavations in the country) and sanitized to fit within the
preordained cultural mores of appropriate behavior (*buenas costumbres*)
and a troubled postcolonial identity. Most archaeological excavations
have always taken place at a safe (geographically speaking) distance from
the city's current location, particularly on the country's Pacific coast.

Pre-Hispanic archaeological coastal sites such as Real Alto (Marcos 1986, 1988), Salango (Norton 1986), and Agua Blanca (McEwan 1990; McEwan and Hudson 2006) have provided the main reproductive sites where a modern (even postmodern) form of Indian ethnicity is created. All three sites are heralded as important landmarks in Ecuador's glorious Indian past, ones that are consistently denied any continuity of relationship or identification with any of the contemporary self-identified modern Indian communities, most of which are strategically located in the highland (sierra) region of the country (see Benavides 2004a; Crain 1990). The Indian identities reproduced by the archaeological research in these three main sites, as well as several others located closer to Guayaquil itself, can be incorporated into museum displays and contemporary debates of the city's (and coastal) Indian past without questioning the exploitative and hierarchically discriminating practices against Indians today.

What is equally telling is that all three sites have elaborated an integrative approach to their archaeological research, aiming to incorporate the local communities into the research agenda itself. The sites have developed *in situ* museums that weave the archaeological data into a coherent and continuous narrative with the local populations (*comuna*) that currently inhabit the towns closest to these ancient Indian communities. This particular form of historiographical recovery and production of heritage illustrates the telling racial and cultural processes that are both determined by and reflect the changing manner in which the Ecuadorian nation-state produces global difference at a local scale.

At all three sites, the archaeological data have contributed enormous political might to the local population's struggle to be recognized as ethnic "Indians"—an identity that is no longer Indian in the traditional sense. Of course, the pitfall in this current political debate, as highlighted by Appiah's (2006a) contribution, is that even the self-identified Indian communities of the highlands that make up the powerful CONAIE (Confederation of Indian Nationalities of Ecuador) are not traditional or authentic in some sort of past or "primitivist" conventional way. As Baldwin (see the opening epigraph to this chapter) so beautifully highlighted for the African exhibition described by Appiah (1997b), what is truly Indian is not some pristine form of cultural identification but rather a dynamic reworking of elements (and life itself) that makes this form of identity sustainable in both historical and social terms.

It is these same different types of Ecuadorian Indian identities, enabled and legitimized by global processes and sustained by the fluid nature of modern capital, that redefine what it means to be Indian and Ecuadorian, and even what globalization comes to mean in local terms. The identities reproduced in these coastal sites are no longer simply reproducing the "authentic" genre of the CONAIE (see below) but rather use archaeology to assert authenticity in a different fashion. All three sites reproblematize an ethnic identification of *cholos* that is normally used to refer to ex-Indian populations that have lost their ties with their ancestral population but still fail to reclaim authoritative identification within white and *mestizo* racial discourses.

The term *cholos* is almost exclusively used not as a descriptive racial marker but as one inherently embedded with pejorative and demeaning connotations. Therefore it is quite a momentous endeavor to provide these *cholo* communities with an official claim to an ex-Indian identity while looking to offer a form of racial and cultural pride that goes against the very postcolonial structure of Guayaquil's ethos as a non-Indian and modern city. It is these archaeological contributions that allow the *comunas* to reclaim territorial rights to their lands based on the assertion of a pre-Hispanic ancestry and continuous occupation.

It is this same paradoxical identification offered by several decades of archeological research at these three sites that goes directly against the very nature of Guayaquil's moral structure, which as the most modern city of Ecuador consistently thrives to dis-Indianize itself. The last decade has also seen an enormous investment in the city's infrastructure with the remodeling of the central promenade (el Malecón) and also the construction of one of the biggest shopping malls in all of Latin America. It is exactly this particular sign of the Guayaquilean modern—reproducing itself as a South American Miami—that enters into direct conflict with its own Indian past. Yet at the same time it is also this Indian past that is selectively used by archaeologist and coastal (*cholo*) communities to reclaim their authenticity in translatable modern and global terms.

The ultimate historical irony, and even appropriately so, is that the supposed Huancavilca community that so proudly supports Guayaquilean patriarchal authority never seemed to have occupied the current area of the city's location at all. Furthermore, the ethno-historic accounts of the group depict quite explicit engagement of pervasive ritualized homosexuality, which contradicts the official Guayaquilean patriarchal scripts highlighted in the city's museums and official textbooks (see Benavides 2002).

Authentic Indian Identities:
The CONAIE's Reproduction of Global Hegemony

The CONAIE has garnered the most political muscle in the country within the last two decades in terms of projecting an authentic Indian identity. As the largest ethnic coalition, representing approximately twenty mainly highland and Amazonian Indian groups, it has been able to use an oppressed Indian identity as a political weapon that has been successfully wielded within the national and international political scenes. Since the group's initial explosion onto the mainstream political landscape, it has effectively stopped the country weeks at a time through nationally coordinated strikes, toppled two presidents, and formed one of the leading political parties, Pachakutik Nuevo País.

This particular explosion of the Indian into the national spotlight was quite slow in the coming, a direct product of decades (perhaps even centuries) of long-term strategizing and painful historical lessons (CONAIE 1989, 1997, 1998). It is only in this last period that an ethnic Indian identity, historically treated as a social handicap, has actually been transformed into a cultural asset, contributing to a surge in the actual number of self-identified Indians in the country (a numerical increase that cannot be explained purely by birth ratios). However, it is precisely this ambiguous success of the CONAIE (and its political party, Pachakutik Nuevo País) and ultimately of a new form of Indian politics that provides an interesting scenario for exploring the multiple ways in which modern signifiers are reproduced within contested types of global difference, and the dynamic manner in which the pre-Hispanic past is used to legitimize "new old ways" of reinstituting the sign of the local (see S. Hall 1997b).

The pre-Hispanic past plays an ambivalent role within the Indians' reclaiming of territorial rights, a greater participation in the resources of the nation, and their ultimate goal of independent sovereignty (see CONAIE 1998). It is quite telling, and somewhat contradictory, that to date the CONAIE has never officially claimed any rights or direct control over an archaeological site. On the contrary, similar to Native American communities in the United States (see Deloria 1979 for the most explicit example), the Indian communities in Ecuador look at the archaeological establishment as intimately tied to the xenophobic state apparatus. This sentiment is expressed by the group's position that an Indian history has yet to be written because if it is written it will only represent the official lies of the government and its white and *mestizo* representatives (CONAIE 1989).

However, even though official archaeological sites and the practice of archaeology itself have never been a direct object of appropriation by the CONAIE or any of its constitutive communities, the archaeological discourse is far from being considered a neutral enterprise. Many of the official publications of the CONAIE claim that archaeological discourses are strategically used to convey a new alternative version of the Ecuadorian past, one in which the Indian is no longer this inferior and defeated identity but rather is invested with intense racial pride and a reified cultural heritage. This alternative history offers a new narrative of the pre-Hispanic past in which all of the ancient Indian groups, including the conquering Incas, are invested with a new pan-Andean identity, and ultimately it forms one coherent historical entity.

The archaeological narrative serves to inscribe a new Indian identity that glosses over its modern configuration by representing itself as the authentic and traditional one. Not unlike the scenario highlighted by Baldwin and Appiah (1997b), it is the "primitivist" element, that is, a historically pristine context, that is favored in this particular variant of the modern Indian identity. Therefore a new modern (one could argue even for a postmodern) identification is derived from these contesting archaeological narratives to present itself as a valid Indian identity within the new reproduction of global capital. There is no way that Indians in Ecuador could have, so productively on their own, the political power to transform their modern identification as they have been able to do without this archaeological reinforcement in the last couple of decades.

The fact that Indian communities have struggled to reclaim lands and resources that they feel are rightfully theirs is not a new historical reality. Rather, what is new is their modern identity, which is greatly indebted to a global form of enabling capital that allows them to translate their Indian difference in powerfully meaningful ways. It is no longer the Indian communities themselves battling against the oppressive postcolonial structure of the Ecuadorian nation-state. On the contrary, it is these same Indian communities forming coalitions with the Catholic and evangelical churches, the Ecuadorian army, the World Bank, the Inter-American

Development Bank, transnational NGOs (nongovernmental organizations), and human rights and ecological organizations that allow Indians in Ecuador to negotiate their cultural identity favorably.

But it is the nature of the political context of the reproduction of an Indian cultural identity that speaks volumes to the manner in which the local and the global are mutually invested in the articulation of social difference, precisely because the Indians have been so successful in joining with the same forces (or at least their historical descendants) that were central in the genocidal destruction of Indian communities throughout the Americas for the last five centuries. The vital question is why is it that global capital seems more than ever invested in reproducing global differences in a way that seems to contradict the traditional economic exploitation that usually has little regard for the cultural survival of minority communities. Although the sincerity of global capital's commitment to Indian (and native) identity could easily be doubted, it still begs the question of the place and role of global difference within the new market production of local identities, and their ultimate role in the postmodern form of globalization.

If contemporary Ecuadorian Indian communities and a global market are the local and global factors enabling a new definition of the native, the archaeological enterprise is particularly invested in this same identity production. The archaeological agenda carried out in Ecuador since the mid-nineteenth century has both explicitly and implicitly contributed to varying definitions of what the Indian is or means and the role that this racialized identity plays in the larger national imaginary, but it has never directly taken up the larger political implications of the discipline's work. This contradictory presence of global capital has made archaeologists scramble for foreign and government money for their research and today allows the great transnational oil companies to be the most important source of funds for archaeological research in the country.

The fact that the salvage archaeology projects carried out in the Amazon, Ecuador's version of cultural resource management, are funded by these transnational oil companies speaks volumes to the modern forms of cultural production, particularly of the past, and in which archaeological research plays a central role. These transnational funds evidence how Ecuador as a whole cannot be a competitive player in today's global market without a coherent story of a pre-Hispanic historical narrative. Therefore, archaeologists provide in profound ways the means for legitimizing not only contemporary national political struggles but more importantly the way for a hegemonic entry into the contested domains of transnational market concerns (see Silberman 1995).

It is through questioning the greening of the past, the naturalization of native rights, and the politics of transnational exploitation that funds archaeological research that a more realistic picture of the Amazon region and Ecuador can be brought into focus. It is also in this charged environment that national imaginaries, Indian communities, and archaeological research in Ecuador will continue to enact the differing local and global forces at play in the region.

Therefore, this paradoxically modern Indian identity is profoundly effected by the way in which archaeology is funded and carried out in the country. The archaeological discourses are translated in varying manners to meet the political agendas of the state, Indian groups, archaeologists, and the general population at large. This is why constant coverage of the archaeological excavations, visits to *in situ* museums (as those discussed above), and continued reference to a glorious national Indian past are considered as central to the country's national imaginary.

The CONAIE's strategic usage of the pre-Hispanic past belies a powerful hegemonic agenda that actually utilizes many of the same political elements it means to defeat. To a certain degree the growing influence of the CONAIE has allowed it to write its own particular version of the Indian past as the true one, in opposition to the one officially promulgated by the state. Although in this alternative version, it is the Indian and not the white Ecuadorian who can claim the central role in the script, it still fails to break free from many of the same postcolonial concerns of race, class, and gender that limit the playing field on which this new version is being defined. It is certain males from the Quechua communities with professional degrees that control the CONAIE's agenda and in a profound way bring their own imaginations to what this new Indian identity is, or more importantly should look like.

The problem, of course, lies in assessing a manner in which truly liberated forms of cultural identification are possible when the local/global paradox is essential to these new modern (and postmodern) forms of identity. At the same time the use of the pre-Hispanic past in the construction of Indianness in Ecuador speaks to the central concern of Appiah (2006a) and all the other authors (see Baldwin 1984; Butler 1997; Sahlins 1994) with the hybrid manner in which culture is always produced. Indian identity in Ecuador today does not have the traditional, pristine character that is sold to tourists, activists, and the World Bank. Rather, the more normative hegemonic Indian identity put forward by the CONAIE is a powerful and strategic political tool with which to counter the oppression of Indian communities that has continued despite the supposed democratic transformation of the world market. The key of course is not to question the authenticity of this modern Indian identity but rather to question our own limited notions and assumptions about authenticity and cultural purity (see Malkki 1995), just as Appiah (2006a) has done.

The Indian movement is not a representative of some pristine cultural authenticity but rather a "reconversion" of previous social symbols and meanings in contemporary terms (García-Canclini 1992). In this complex reality the Indian movement is the most modern signifier of Ecuador's contemporary political struggle—a struggle that is now fought beyond the country's borders. This particular global context renders the Indian movement's financial support and identity very fragile. If the counter-hegemonic demands of the CONAIE are met, and this could only occur in a global economic reordering, the movement would pretty soon find itself with no more first world NGOs and development projects to fund it, and perhaps more dramatically, it would find itself without a cultural global understanding in which Indians could translate their identity in such a positive manner. After all it is instructive that it has taken Indian groups this long to find a cultural context that would enable their political projects and historical legacy, since Indian uprisings are not new but their current transnational success is.

Making Afro-Ecuadorian Histories: Challenging the Multicultural Past

The most recent success of Ecuador in the World Cup (2006) highlighted yet another of Ecuador's vital racial fractures, the presence of a significant Afro-Ecuadorian population. Most, if not all, Ecuadorians were delighted by the fact that Ecuador's national soccer team was able to pass to the next round of the competition and represent the country with enormous pride and success. However, not all Ecuadorians were equally delighted by the fact that almost two-thirds of the team was made up of black men, and many voiced their worries over what kind of image this would give to the rest of the world. The main preoccupation of course was that people around the globe would believe Ecuador to be a black nation, which for most of Ecuador's citizens is just not true in any regard.

This same concern arose when a black woman was elected Miss Ecuador to represent the country at the Miss Universe pageant twice, in 1995 and again in 1997. The ensuing national debate in newspapers, radio programs, and magazines was consistently defensive about it not being a racist one. On the contrary, most opinions highlighted the beauty and qualities of each contestant (as everybody did about the brilliant athletes that represented Ecuador in the World Cup) while questioning the authenticity of having Afro-Ecuadorians represent the nation as a whole. Of course the underlying racist assumption in such a debate was unconscious for many but served to refocus the debate on Ecuador's national identity, particularly within the new global context of multiculturalism and participation in the democratic respect for minorities and natives central to a transnational human rights agenda (see Benavides 2004b).

What most Ecuadorians failed to assess was the particular position of Afro-Ecuadorians within the Ecuadorian historical landscape, and the specific contradictions in envisioning a multicultural past that is more a present chimera than an archaeological reality. The presence of black communities in Ecuador is indebted to the southern extension in the Americas of the colonial market of African slaves, most of whom were brought through the Caribbean all the way down the South American Pacific coast. As Bryant (2005) elaborates, Quito, Ecuador's capital, is much more instructive as a case study of colonial Afro-American ethonogenesis than has been traditionally accepted. Meanwhile, the northern province of Esmeraldas, which has the highest presence of Afro-Ecuadorian inhabitants, traditionally has been reified as a runaway slave community that succeeded in maintaining its independence from the colonial government of the time.

True or not, the presence of black communities in Ecuador is as recent as that of white and *mestizo* ones, but unlike them, as the Miss Ecuador debate suggests, Afro-Ecuadorians are seen as less Ecuadorian or at least not authentic representatives of the nation. This particular narrative structure can be understood by the fact that all pre-Hispanic excavations are somehow related to the current Ecuadorian (read white and *mestizo*) population even when the excavations are really assessing Indian communities from hundreds, and sometimes thousands, of years before Ecuador even existed. This dual standard in the historical discourse reflects the racial conundrums of the nation and the disparate ways that the pre-Hispanic narrative is incorporated into the current racist structure of the nation-state.

The colonial past of Afro-Ecuadorians becomes a very specific (and absent) marker of archaeological research, while the white and *mestizo* past is picked and chosen from the archaeological elements offered by pre-Hispanic and colonial excavations. It is not surprising that few clearly defined black sites have been the object of archaeological research, with very limited exceptions in the province of Esmeraldas (see DeBoer 1996). This particular lack of interest in the archaeological past of black maroon populations expresses the truer sentiments of most white and *mestizo* Ecuadorians toward Afro-Ecuadorians; it is a particular postcolonial conundrum of Western-influenced racism that is now faced with shifting mores of multiculturalism and the new transnational concerns with embracing global difference.

However, the multicultural present put forward by transnational organizations and the global market of MTVs and show business, contradicts the absence of such a multicultural past not only in the archaeological agenda, but in the imagination of the nation. How does one begin to constitute a past of difference when these particular diasporic black identities only now, in the last decades of modern capital, have been so invested with such high degrees of political signification? How does one translate the cultural resignification of a diasporic black identity that is maligned locally throughout the globe yet constituted as an exoticized precious other within the global definition of democratic ideals?

This particular dynamic immediately questions the uneven assessment of the country's pre-Hispanic heritage as belonging more to some national communities than others, forcing one to extricate the rich cultural legacy in unequal forms. Therefore it is not only, or even mainly, an issue of developing concrete archaeological projects that would address the colonial heritage of Afro-Ecuadorian communities but rather of asking why these archaeological projects must be thought of in this fashion, when those concerning the white and *mestizo* elite are not. Yet it is this same ambiguous reification that makes an Afro-Ecuadorian identity so pregnant with local demarcation that belies at the same time the large global parameters that are being imposed on all the national communities.

The pre-Hispanic archaeological discourses of the country have been, and continue to be, used by differing national groups in a multitude of legitimizing fashions. However, within the hegemonic structure of the state, these archaeological discourses are already limited not only in their productive potential but equally so in their interpretive possibilities, enabling and legitimizing some national communities over others. It is within these inherent structural constraints that a modern Afro-Ecuadorian identity reflects the clear racial fracture in the conflicting order of the nation's imaginary ideal. After all, it is precisely within this striving for the modern that the actual modernity of Afro-Ecuadorians reveals the contradictory origin of the discourse of a multicultural legacy.

The fact that Afro-Ecuadorians are denied an ancient past signals a new sign of the modern that in itself is different from the limited (and safe) one hoped to be achieved by the struggling Ecuadorian nation-state. As is the case with the CONAIE (as discussed above) the Ecuadorian nation-state wants a modernity or a sign of the modern full of a profoundly meaningful, racialized ancient past. However, it is finding an undifferentiated ancient Indian past, without markers of a legacy of exploited Africans that is inherent in the agenda of pre-Hispanic (and colonial) archaeology in the country. This limited multicultural past in many ways is then used to negotiate and support a new multicultural agenda that tries to include all the different races and nationalities that make up the modern Ecuadorian nation-state.

This conflict between a globally infused, racialized, multicultural present and a racist hegemonic past speaks to wider discursive constraints that limit the production of both. The manner in which Afro-Ecuadorians have been erased from the archaeological landscape has less to do, of course, with the archaeological evidence found at sites and throughout the territory than with the racist underpinnings of the nation. The research into a black Ecuadorian past has never been an essential need or desire of the postcolonial structure of the country, and as such the lack of inquiry into these black communities' histories belies the greater discriminatory practices against Afro-Ecuadorians in general.

The problem issues from the fact that in these modern times a generic Indian past and a white and *mestizo* present are no longer viable transnationally. The modern nation-states must be multicultural ones that reincorporate the differentiated pasts of their native and minority communities. And it is at this point that the absence of an Afro-Ecuadorian past mirrors the limited and superficial production of a multicultural present. As in the United States, the archaeological recovery of an African legacy is yet again demanded by the changing politics within the discipline, which must explain the lack of racial diversity among its members and research endeavors. Yet the explicit urgency of recovering the African past in the Americas is only a symptom (not the solution) of the colonial conundrum inherent in the racist structure of the West's historical legacy.

Thus, the concern is not with trying to recover an Afro-Ecuadorian past, but rather with assessing the contemporary motivations that make such an archaeological endeavor valid today throughout the Americas (see also examples from Quilombos in Brazil). Just as the Indian struggle has been permanent for five centuries but only now is being translated in understandable Western terms, the presence of a vibrant Afro-Ecuadorian past is also an element of profound global mechanisms inherent in the production of the local Ecuadorian landscape.

At the same time this racialized archaeological endeavor also always speaks to the vanishing present, questioning the fabric of a recently reformed Ecuadorian constitution that in the 1990s heralded the country as "a multicultural nation." This particular phrasing was one political step shorter than the one advocated by the CONAIE, which demanded the recognition of Ecuador as "a multinational state." Yet again, the modern burden of the global allowed the country to reformulate itself in limited modern ways, assessing the changing nature of its racialized present but still unwilling to thoroughly reexamine the very geno- and ethnocidal origins of all contemporary American nation-states.

As Ernst Renan stated over one hundred years ago, part of being a nation is getting its history wrong, and the lack of a vibrant legacy of Afro-Ecuadorian archaeological research is one more troubling example of the profound truth of this remark. After all it is this very limited facade of racial democracy that has marked Ecuador (and other South American nations) as opposing the supposed racist structure of the United States. Yet it is this actually racist structure supporting the new banner of a multicultural present that speaks most directly to a modern signifier that should allow the country membership into the democratic nations while it is still renegotiating colonial specters of the other that continuously return to repress their contemporary heirs (see Žižek 2004).

"Inconclusion": Translating
Archaeological Modernities in Ecuador

Slavoj Žižek observes in *Organs Without Bodies*: "When G. K. Chesterton describes his conversion to Christianity, he claims that he 'tried to be some ten minutes in advance of the truth. And I found that I was eighteen years behind it.' Does the same not hold even more for those who, today, desperately try to catch up with the New by way of following the latest "post" fashion and are thus condemned to remain forever eighteen years behind the truly New?" The examples of Guayaquilean, Indian, and Afro-Ecuadorian modernities have been used to express the overarching burden of the global upon the contemporary production of identities in Ecuador today. More specifically, these same identities are highly invested in utilizing a pre-Hispanic past to be able to recreate their new local identification in ways that are translatable or legitimized in contemporary terms. All three cases show the subtle, and at times jarring, relationship between the past and the (vanishing) present (see Spivak 1999), as well as between the local and global ideological constructs of our postmodern world. The archaeological enterprise in Ecuador is constrained by local/global discourses that define and structure its parameters yet fail to completely limit its cultural production.

As both Australian examples convey (see the chapters by Lydon and Lilley, this volume) the heritage enterprise highlights the conflict between the construction of a world defined by the local constitution of difference and the supposed global homogeneity of culture. This is what allows native populations to be hailed as central historical figures by a transglobal heritage discourse while these same communities are vilified within their own national realm. This is precisely why all other non-Indian identities are barely the object of archaeological inquiry in the Ecuadorian landscape, since none of them would be translatable in global terms. What constitutes Ecuador as such an example is an Indian past (not present) sustained by an archaeological practice that responds to a Western global ideal of whiteness hidden under the fragile veil of local difference.

However, it is also in this conflicted production that the varying Ecuadorian modernities escape absolute definition (see S. Hall 1997a, 1997b), allowing not only the present but also the pre-Hispanic past to be used in such varying manners by the state, city, Indians, and Afro-Ecuadorians. In this "minimal difference" (see Butler 1997; Žižek

2004) the vanishing and cosmopolitan present is produced. It is not in the glorious reclaiming of authentic Indian identities or in the heralding of an absent black past that the most cosmopolitan sign of the modern is reified in Ecuador, but rather the opposite; that is, it is in these legacies, both historically and culturally speaking, inherent in all of these postcolonial guises of multiculturalism, *mestizo* miscegenation, and political correctness that one must gather the terrifying and productive void of the Real (see Baldwin 1984; Lacan 1995; Žižek 2002).

As postcolonial entities, Ecuador and Ecuadorians have continuously mirrored the outside other to define what it would mean to be truly human and acceptable in global terms. In the colonial process these same otherizing mechanisms created differentiated identities that slowly were internalized no longer as foreign but as national others, creating no longer the dilemma of "not you" but of "like you" (see Trinh T. Minh-ha 1997). And now, under the constraints of a globalizing enterprise of embracing difference, in trying to incorporate the other, the Ecuadorian nation-state must acknowledge the paradox in its historical inconsistencies. Of course there is no turning back to right historical wrongs, but just looking at that past provides shudders of identification that will have structurally transforming implications, precisely because the past has not passed and inhabits our present being in multiple ways. As Baldwin (1990: 480) prefigured: "To overhaul a history, or to attempt to redeem it—which effort may or may not justify it—is not at all the same thing as the descent one must make in order to excavate a history. To be forced to excavate a history is, also to repudiate the concept of history, and the vocabulary in which history is written; for the written history is, and must be, merely the vocabulary of power, and power is history's most seductively attired false witness."

Note

My sincere thanks go to Lynn Meskell for her open support and invitation to participate in this project; to Bernice Kurchin for her editing skills and intellectual camaraderie; and as always to Greg Allen for being a constant source of inspiration, struggle, and love.

✳ BIBLIOGRAPHY

Abdel-Hamid Adil, A. A., and A. Awad. 2000. "Henry Solomon Wellcome and the Sudan. http://www.geocities.com (accessed September 15, 2006).

Abdi, K. 2001. "Nationalism, politics, and the development of archaeology in Iran." *American Journal of Archaeology* 105: 51–76.

Abdussamad, A. 1988. "Hunting in Gojjam: The case of Matakal (1901–1932)." In Tadesse Beyene (ed.), *Proceedings of the Eighth International Conference of Ethiopian Studies*, 237–44. Addis Ababa: University of Addis Ababa.

———. 1999. "Trading in slaves in Bela-Shangul and Gumuz, Ethiopia: Border enclaves in history, 1897–1938." *Journal of African History* 40(3): 433–46.

Abu el-Haj, N. 2001. *Facts on the Ground: Archaeological Practice and Territorial Self-Fashioning in Israeli Society*. Chicago: University of Chicago Press.

Abu-Rabi, I. M. 2006. *The Blackwell Companion to Contemporary Islamic Thought*. Oxford: Blackwell.

Adams, J., and T. McShane. 1996. *The Myth of Wild Africa: Conservation Without Illusion*. Berkeley: University of California Press.

Adams, W. M. 2005. *Against Extinction*. London: Earthscan.

Adams, W. M., and M. Mulligan, eds. 2003a. *Decolonizing Nature: Strategies for Conservation in a Post-colonial Era*. London: Earthscan.

———. 2003b. Introduction. In W. Adams and M. Mulligan (eds.), *Decolonizing Nature: Strategies for Conservation in a Post-colonial Era*, 1–15. London: Earthscan.

Addison, F. 1951. *The Wellcome Excavations in the Sudan*. London: Published for the Trustees of the late Sir Henry Wellcome by Oxford University Press.

Agamben, G. 1998. *Homo Sacer: Sovereign Power and Bare Life*. Trans. D. Heller-Roazen. Stanford, Calif.: Stanford University Press.

Agrawal, A. 2005. *Environmentality: Technologies of Government and the Making of Subjects*. Durham, N.C.: Duke University Press.

Ahmed, A. 2003. *Islam Under Siege*. Cambridge: Polity Press.

Alonso, A. 1988. "The effects of truth: Re-presentation of the past and the imagining of a community." *Journal of Historical Sociology* 1(1): 58–89.

———. 2004. "Conforming discomformity: 'Mestizaje,' hybridity, and the aesthetics of Mexican nationalism." *Cultural Anthropology* 19(4): 459–90.

Anderson, A. 1998. "Cosmopolitanism, universalism, and the divided legacies of modernity." In P. Cheah and B. Robbins (eds.), *Cosmopolitics: Thinking and Feeling Beyond Nation*, 265–89. Minneapolis: Minnesota University Press.

Anderson, B. 1978. "Studies of the Thai state: The state of Thai studies." In E. Ayal (ed.), *The Study of Thailand*, 193–233. Southeast Asia Series 54. Athens: Ohio University Center for International Studies.

——. 1991. *Imagined Communities: Reflections on the Origins and Spread of Nationalism*. London: Verso.

Antoun, R. 2001. *Understanding Fundamentalism: Christian, Islamic, and Jewish Movements*. New York: Rowman and Littlefield.

Anzaldúa, G. 1987. *Borderlands/La Frontera: The New Mestiza*. San Francisco: Aunt Lute Books.

Appadurai, A. 2006. *Fear of Small Numbers: An Essay on the Geography of Anger*. Durham, N.C.: Duke University Press.

Appiah, K. A. 1997a. "Cosmopolitan patriots." *Critical Inquiry* 23(3): 617–39.

——. 1997b. "Is the 'post' in 'postcolonial' the 'post' in postmodern?" In A. McClintock et al. (eds.), *Dangerous Liaisons: Gender, Nation, and Postcolonial Perspectives*, 420–44. Minneapolis: University of Minnesota Press.

——. 2001. "African identities." In G. Castle (ed.), *Postcolonial Discourses: An Anthology*, 222–31. Oxford: Blackwell.

——. 2005. *The Ethics of Identity*. Princeton, N.J.: Princeton University Press.

——. 2006a. *Cosmopolitanism: Ethics in a World of Strangers*. New York: W. W. Norton.

——. 2006b. "The case for contamination." *New York Times, Sunday Magazine*, January 1.

Arce, A., and N. Long, eds. 2000. *Anthropology, Development and Modernities: Exploring Discourses, Counter-tendencies and Violence*. London: Routledge.

Atalay, S. 2006. "Archaeology as decolonizing practice." *American Indian Quarterly* 30: 280–310.

Australia, ICOMOS (International Council on Monuments and Sites). 1981. *The Australia ICOMOS Charter for the Conservation of Places of Cultural Significance (Burra Charter)*. Canberra, Australia.

Australia, Parliament of. 1977. *Ranger Uranium Environmental Inquiry–Second Report, May 1977*. Canberra: Australian Government Publishing Service.

——. Senate, Finance and Public Administration Committee. 2005. *Inquiry into Matters Relating to the Gallipoli Peninsula*. Canberra: Australian Government Publishing Service.

Australia War Memorial. 2007. "Dawn of the legend." *Saluting Their Service*. Minister for Veterans' Affairs Commemorations Program. http://www .awm.gov.au (accessed July 1, 2007).

Avrami, E., M. Demas, R. Mason, G. Palumbo, J. M. Teutonico, and M. de la Torre. 2000. *A Methodological Approach for Conservation Planning*. Los Angeles: Getty Conservation Institute.

Avrami, E., R. Mason, and M. de la Torre. 2000. *Values and Heritage Conservation*. Los Angeles: Getty Conservation Institute.

Bachelard, M. 2003. "Black veto on buried Jabiluka." *The Australian*, September 7.

Bahn, P., ed. 1999. *Archaeology*. Cambridge Illustrated History. Cambridge: Cambridge University Press.

Baldwin, J. 1984. *Notes of a Native Son*. Boston: Beacon Press.

———. 1990. *Just Above My Head*. New York: Laurel.

Barmé, S. 1993. *Luang Wichit Wathakan and the Creation of a Thai Identity*. Singapore: Institute of Southeast Asian Studies.

Barringer, T., and T. Flynn, eds. 1998. *Colonialism and the Object: Empire, Material Culture and the Museum*. London: Routledge.

Bauman, Z. 2004. *Wasted Lives: Modernity and Its Outcasts*. Cambridge, Oxford, and Malden, Mass.: Polity.

Beck, U., and N. Sznaider. 2006. "Unpacking cosmopolitanism for the social sciences: A research agenda." *British Journal of Sociology* 57: 1–23.

Bedford, S. 1996. "Post-contact Maori—The ignored component in Maori prehistory." *Journal of the Polynesian Society* 105: 411–39.

Begay, R. 2001. "Doo dilzin da: Abuse of the natural world." *American Indian Quarterly* 25(1): 21–27.

———. 2003. "Exploring Navajo-Anasazi Relationships Using Traditional (Oral) Histories." Master's thesis, Northern Arizona University.

Behrendt, L. 2002. "Unfinished journey: Indigenous self-determination." *Arena Magazine* 58: 24–27.

———. 2003. *Achieving Social Justice: Indigenous Rights and Australia's Future*. Sydney: Pluto Press.

Beinart, W., and P. Coates. 1995. *Historical Connections: Environment and History*. London: Routledge.

Benavides, O. H. 2002. "The representation of Guayaquil's sexual past: Historicizing the Enchaquirados." *Journal of Latin American Anthropology* 7(1): 68–103.

———. 2004a. *Making Ecuadorian Histories: Four Centuries of Defining Power*. Austin: University of Texas Press.

———. 2004b. "Anthropology's native conundrum: Uneven histories and development." *Critique of Anthropology* 24(2): 159–78.

———. 2006. *The Politics of Sentiment: Imagining and Remembering Guayaquil*. Austin: University of Texas Press.

Bender, B. 1993. *Landscape: Politics and Perspectives*. London: Berg.

———. 2006. "Destabilising how we view the past: Harry Lourandos and the archaeology of Bodmin Moor, south-west England." In B. David, B. Barker, and I. McNiven (eds.), *The Social Archaeology of Australian Indigenous Societies*, 306–18. Canberra: Aboriginal Studies Press.

Benhabib, S. 2002. *The Claims of Culture: Equality and Diversity in a Global Era*. Princeton, N.J.: Princeton University Press.

——. 2004. *The Rights of Others*. Cambridge: Cambridge University Press.

Bernardini, W. 2005a. "Reconsidering spatial and temporal aspects of prehistoric cultural identity: A case study from the American Southwest." *American Antiquity* 70: 31–54.

——. 2005b. *Hopi Oral Tradition and the Archaeology of Identity*. Tucson: University of Arizona Press.

——. 2007. *Hopi Social Memory in Stone: The Tutuveni Petroglyph Site*. Tucson: Arizona State Museum.

Bernbeck, R., H. Fazeli, and S. Pollock. 2005. "Life in a Fifth-Millennium BCE Village." *Near Eastern Archaeology* 68(3): 94–105.

Bhabha, H. 1996. "Unsatisfied: Notes on vernacular cosmopolitanism." In L. Garcia-Morena and P. Pfeifer (eds.), *Text and Nation*, 191–207. London: Camden House.

——. 2001. "Unsatisfied: Notes on vernacular cosmopolitanism." In G. Castle (ed)., *Postcolonial Discourses: An Anthology*, 39–52. Oxford and Malden, Mass.: Blackwell.

Bhabha, H., and J. Comaroff. 2002. "Speaking of postcoloniality in the continuous present: A conversation." In D. T. Goldberg and A. Quayson (eds.), *Relocating Postcolonialism*, 15–46. Oxford: Blackwell.

Binford, L. R. 1983. *In Pursuit of the Past: Decoding the Archaeological Record*. New York: Thames and Hudson.

Blundell, D., ed. 2000. *Austronesian Taiwan: Linguistics, History, Ethnology and Prehistory*. Berkeley: Phoebe A. Hearst Museum of Anthropology with Shung Ye Museum of Formosan Aborigines.

Blundell, G. 1996. "Presenting South Africa's rock art sites." In J. Deacon (ed.), *Monuments and Sites: South Africa*, 71–80. Sri Lanka: International Council on Monuments and Sites.

——. 2002. *The Unseen Landscape: A Journey to Game Pass Shelter (Guide Booklet)*. Johannesburg: Rock Art Research Institute.

——. 2004. *Nquabayo's Nomansland*. Uppsala: Uppsala University.

Bok, S. 2002. "From part to whole." In M. Nussbaum (and respondents), *For Love of Country?* ed. J. Cohen, 38–44. Boston: Beacon Press.

Borrini-Feyerabend, G., A. Kothari, and G. Oviedo. 2004. *Indigenous and Local Communities and Protected Areas: Towards Equity and Enhanced Conservation; Guidance on Policy and Practice for Co-managed Protected Areas and Community Conserved Areas*. Gland, Switzerland and Cambridge: IUCN.

Bourdieu, P. 2001. *Contra-fuegos 2: Por un movimiento social europeo*. Barcelona: Anagrama.

———. 2002. *Interventions, 1961–2001: Science sociale et action politique.* Textes choisis et présentés par Franck Poupeau et Thierry Discepolo. Marseille: Agone; Montréal: Comeau et Nadeau.

———. 2004. *Si le monde social m'est supportable c'est parce que je peux m'indigner: Entretien mené par Antoine Spire assisté de Pascale Casanova et de Miguel Banassayag (1989–1990).* Paris: Aube.

Brading, D. A. 2001. "Monuments and nationalism in modern Mexico." *Nations and Nationalism* 7(4): 521–31.

Bradley, R. 2000. *An Archaeology of Natural Places.* Routledge: London.

———. 2003. "Seeing things: Perception, experience and the constraints of fieldwork." *Journal of Social Archaeology* 3: 151–68.

Breckenridge, C., H. Bhabha, S. Pollock, and D. Chakrabarty, eds. 2002. *Cosmopolitanism.* Durham, N.C.: Duke University Press.

Breglia, L. C. 2005. "Keeping world heritage in the family: A genealogy of Maya labour at Chichén Itzá." *International Journal of Heritage Studies* 11(5): 385–98.

———. 2006. *Monumental Ambivalence: The Politics of Heritage.* Austin: University of Texas Press.

Brockington, D. 2002. *Fortress Conservation: The Preservation of the Mkomazi Game Reserve, Tanzania.* Bloomington: Indiana University Press.

———. 2004. "Community conservation, inequality and injustice: Myths of power in protected area management." *Conservation and Society* 2(2): 411–32.

Brockman, D. and C. van Shaik, eds. 2005. *Seasonality in Primates: Studies of Living and Extinct Human and Non-human Primates.* Cambridge: Cambridge University Press.

Brown, M. F. 2003. *Who Owns Native Culture?* Cambridge, Mass.: Harvard University Press.

Bruce, S. 2002. *God Is Dead: Secularisation in the West.* Oxford: Blackwell.

Brück, J. 2005. "Experiencing the past? The development of a phenomenological archaeology in British prehistory." *Archaeological Dialogues* 12: 45–72.

Bryant, S. 2005. "Slavery and the context of ethnogenesis: African, Afro-Creoles, and the realities of bondage in the Kingdom of Quito, 1660–1800." Ph.D. diss., Ohio State University.

Burton, A. 2003. "On the inadequacy and indispensability of the nation." In A. Burton (ed.), *After the Imperial Turn: Thinking with and through the Nation,* 1–23. Durham, N.C.: Duke University Press.

Butler, J. 1997. *The Psychic Life of Power.* Stanford, Calif.: Stanford University Press.

Butler, J., S. Žižek, and E. Laclau. 2002. *Contingency, Hegemony, Universality: Contemporary Dialogues on the Left.* London: Verso.

Byrne, D. 1991. "Western hegemony in archaeological heritage management." *History and Anthropology* 5: 269–76.

———. 1995. "Buddhist stupa and Thai social practice." *World Archaeology* 27(2): 266–81.

———. 1996. "Deep nation: Australia's acquisition of an indigenous past." *Aboriginal History* 20: 99–100.

———. 1999. "The nation, the elite, and the Southeast Asian antiquities trade with special reference to Thailand." *Conservation and Management of Archaeological Sites* 3: 145–53.

———. 2003. "Nervous landscapes: Race and space in Australia." *Journal of Social Archaeology* 3: 169–93.

———. 2004. "Archaeology in reverse." In N. Merriman (ed.), *Public Archaeology*, 240–54. London: Routledge.

———. 2005. "Messages to Manila." In I. Macfarlane (ed.), *Many Exchanges: Archaeology, History, Community and the Work of Isabel McBryde*, 53–62. Aboriginal History Monograph 11. Canberra: Aboriginal History.

———. 2008. "Heritage conservation as social action." In R. Harrison and J. Jameson (eds.), *The Cultural Heritage Reader*. London: Routledge.

Cachois, H. 2006. "A few words about archaeology in French Polynesia." In I. Lilley (ed.), *Archaeology of Oceania: Australia and the Pacific Islands*, 363–67. Oxford: Blackwell.

Cameron, D., and D. Donlon. 2005. "A preliminary archaeological survey of the ANZAC Gallipoli battlefields of 1915." *Australasian Historical Archaeology* 23: 131–38.

Carneiro, R. 1977. "A theory of the origin of the state." *Science* 169: 733–38.

Carruthers, J. 1995. *The Kruger National Park: A Social and Political History*. Pietermaritzburg: University of Natal Press.

———. 2001. *Wildlife and Warfare: The Life of James Stevenson-Hamilton*. Pietermaritzburg: University of Natal Press.

Castañeda, Q. 1996. *In the Museum of Maya Culture: Touring Chichén Itzá*. Minneapolis: University of Minnesota Press.

———. 2000. "Approaching ruins: A photo-ethnographic essay on the busy intersections of Chichén Itzá." *Visual Anthropology Review* 16(2) (fall-winter): 43–70.

———. 2003. "Stocking's Historiography of Influence: Boas, Gamio and Redfield at the Cross 'Road to Light.'" *Critique of Anthropology* 23(3): 235–262.

Césaire, A. 1956 [1939]. *Cahier d'un retour au pays natal*. Paris: Présence Africaine.

———. 1972 [1955]. *Discourse on Colonialism*. New York: Monthly Review.

Chakrabarty, D. 2002. "Universalism and belonging in the logic of capital." In C. Breckenridge, H. Bhabha, S. Pollock, and D. Chakrabarty (eds.), *Cosmopolitanism*, 1–14. Durham, N.C.: Duke University Press.

Cheah, P. 1998. "Given culture: Rethinking cosmopolitical freedom in transnationalism." In P. Cheah and B. Robbins (eds.), *Cosmopolitics: Thinking and Feeling Beyond Nation*, 290–328. Minneapolis: Minnesota University Press.

———. 2006. "Cosmopolitanism." *Theory, Culture and Society* 23(2–3): 486–96.

Cheah, P., and B. Robbins, eds. 1998. *Cosmopolitics: Thinking and Feeling Beyond Nation*. Minneapolis: Minnesota University Press.

Chew, S. C., and R. A. Denemark. 1996. *The Underdevelopment of Development. Essays in Honor of Andre Gunder Frank*. Thousand Oaks, Calif.: Sage.

Chirapravati, P. 1997. *Votive Tablets in Thailand*. Kuala Lumpur: Oxford University Press.

Clark, N. L. 2002. "The demon-seed: Bioinvasion as the unsettling of environmental cosmopolitanism." *Theory, Culture and Society* 19: 101–25.

Clastres, P. 1989. *Society against the State: Essays in Political Anthropology*. New York: Zone Books.

Cleere, H. F., ed. 1989. *Archaeological Heritage Management in the Modern World*. London: Unwin Hyman.

Clendon, M. 2006. "Reassessing Australia's linguistic prehistory." *Current Anthropology* 47: 39–61.

Clifford, J. 1992. "Traveling cultures." In L. Grossberg, C. Nelson, and P. Treichler (eds.), *Cultural Studies*. London: Routledge.

———. 2004. "Looking several ways: Anthropology and Native heritage in Alaska." *Current Anthropology* 45: 5–30.

Cock, J., and D. Fig. 2002. "From colonial to community-based conservation: Environmental justice and the transformation of national parks." In D. A. McDonald (ed.), *Environmental Justice in South Africa*, 131–55. Athens: Ohio University Press.

Coe, M. D. 2005. *The Maya*. 7th ed. New York: Thames and Hudson.

Coelho, E. M. B. 1987. *Cultura e sobrevivência dos índios no Maranhão*. São Luís, MA: Editora Universitária da UFMA.

Coetzee, J. M. 1996. *Foe*. New York City: Farrar and Strauss.

Cohen, M. 1992. "Rooted cosmopolitanism." *Dissent* (fall): 478–83.

Colchester, M. 2004. *Salvaging Nature: Indigenous Peoples, Protected Areas and Biodiversity Conservation*. Montevideo: World Rainforest Movement and Forest Peoples Program.

Cole, D. 1985. *Captured Heritage: The Scramble for Northwest Coast Artifacts*. Seattle: University of Washington Press.

Cole, J. 1992. *Colonialism and Revolution in the Middle East: Social and Cultural Origins of Egypt's 'Urabi Movement*. Princeton, N.J.: Princeton University Press.

Colwell-Chanthaphonh, C. 2003a. "Signs in place: Native American perspectives of the past in the San Pedro Valley of Southeastern Arizona." *Kiva* 69: 5–29.

———. 2003b. "Dismembering/disremembering the Buddhas: Renderings on the Internet during the Afghan purge of the past." *Journal of Social Archaeology* 3(1): 75–98.

———. 2005. "Footprints of the Hisatsinom: Hopi interpretations of ancient images in the San Pedro Valley of Southern Arizona." in J. K. K. Huang and E. V. Culley (eds.), *Making Marks: Graduate Studies in Rock Art Research in the New Millennium, Occasional Paper No. 5*, 221–28. Tucson: American Rock Art Research Association.

Colwell-Chanthaphonh, C., and T. J. Ferguson. 2004. "Virtue ethics and the practice of history: Native Americans and archaeologists along the San Pedro Valley of Arizona." *Journal of Social Archaeology* 4: 5–27.

———. 2006. "Memory pieces and footprints: Multivocality and the meanings of ancient times and places among the Zuni and Hopi." *American Anthropologist* 108: 148–62.

———, eds. 2007. *The Collaborative Continuum: Archaeological Engagements with Descendent Communities.* Thousand Oaks, Calif.: AltaMira.

CONAIE (Confederación de Nacionalidades Indígenas del Ecuador). 1989. *Las nacionalidades indígenas en el Ecuador: Nuestro proceso organizativo.* Quito: Ed. TINCUI-CONAIE and Abya-Yala.

———. 1997. *Proyecto político de la CONAIE.* Quito: CONAIE.

———. 1998. *Las nacionalidades indígenas y el estado plurinacional.* Quito: CONAIE.

Conkey, M. 2005. "Dwelling at the margins, action at the intersection? Feminist and indigenous archaeologies, 2005." *Archaeologies* 1(1): 9–59.

Conkey, M., with S. Williams. 1991. "Original narratives: The political economy of gender in archaeology." In M. di Leonardo (ed.), *Gender at the Crossroads of Knowledge: Feminist Anthropology in the Postmodern Era*, 102–39. Berkeley: University of California Press.

Connor, T. K. 2003. "Crooks, commuters, and chiefs: Home and belonging in a border zone in Pafuri, Gaza Province, Mozambique." *Journal of Contemporary African Studies* 21: 93–120.

Cormier, L. 2003a. "Decolonizing history: Ritual transformation of the past among the Guajá of Eastern Amazonia." In N. L. Whitehead (ed.), *Histories and Historicities in Amazonia*, 123–39. Lincoln: University of Nebraska Press.

———. 2003b. *Kinship with Monkeys: The Guajá Foragers of the Eastern Amazonia.* New York: Columbia University Press.

Cort, M. L. 1886. *Siam: Or the Heart of Farther India.* New York: Anson D. F. Randolph.

Cowan, J., M. Dembour, and R. Wilson, eds. 2001. *Culture and Rights: Anthropological Perspectives.* Cambridge: Cambridge University Press.

Crain, M. 1990. "The Social construction of national identity in highland Ecuador." *Anthropological Quarterly* 63(1): 43–59.

Cronin, C., and P. De Greiff. 1998. *Jürgen Habermas*. Cambridge, Mass.: MIT Press.

Curthoys, A., and M. Lake. 2005. *Connected Worlds: History in Transnational Perspective*. Canberra: Australian National University Press.

Daes, E.-I. A. 1999. *Human Rights of Indigenous Peoples: Indigenous People and Their Relationship to Land*. Geneva: United Nations.

David, B. 2006. "Archaeology and the dreaming: Toward an archaeology of ontology." In I. Lilley (ed.), *Archaeology of Oceania: Australia and the Pacific Islands*, 48–68. Oxford: Blackwell.

David, B., J. Crouch, and U. Zoppi. 2005. "Historicizing the spiritual: Bu shell arrangements on the island of Badu, Torres Strait." *Cambridge Archaeological Journal* 15: 71–91.

David, B., and I. McNiven. 2004. "Western Torres Strait Cultural History Project: Research design and initial results." In I. McNiven and M. Quinnell (eds.), *Torres Strait Archaeology and Material Culture*, 199–208. Memoirs of the Queensland Museum Cultural Heritage Series 3(1). Brisbane: Queensland Museum.

David, B., I. McNiven, W. Bowie, M. Nomoa, P. Ahmat, J. Crouch, L. Brady, M. Quinnell, and A. Herle. 2004. "Archaeology of Torres Strait turtle-shell masks: The Badu cache." *Australian Aboriginal Studies* 2004(1): 18–25.

Dawisha, A. 2003. *Arab Nationalism in the Twentieth Century: From Triumph to Despair*. Princeton, N.J.: Princeton University Press.

DeBoer, W. 1996. *Traces Behind the Esmeraldas Shore: Prehistory of the Santiago-Cayapas Region, Ecuador*. Tuscaloosa: University of Alabama Press.

De la Cadena, M. 2000. *Indigenous Mestizos: The Politics of Race and Culture in Cuzco, Peru, 1919–1991*. Durham, N.C.: Duke University Press.

De la Pena, G. 2005. "Social and cultural policies toward indigenous peoples: Perspectives from Latin America." *Annual Review of Anthropology* 34: 717–39.

De la Torre, M., ed. 1997. *The Conservation of Archaeological Sites in the Mediterranean Region*. Los Angeles: Getty Conservation Institute.

Deloria, V., Jr. 1979. *Custer Died for Your Sins*. New York: Avon.

Department of the Environment and Heritage, Australia. 2007a. "Australian heritage." http://www.deh.gov.au/heritage (accessed June 29, 2007).

———. 2007b. "Environmental research and supervision of uranium mining: Jabiluka." http://www.deh.gov.au/ssd/uranium-mining (accessed June 29, 2007).

Derrida, J. 1997. *On Cosmopolitanism and Forgiveness*. London: Routledge.

Dever, W. 1997. "Archaeology and the emergence of early Israel." In J. Bartlett (ed.), *Archaeology and Biblical Interpretation*, 20–50. London: Routledge.

Diaz-Andreu, M., and T. C. Champion, eds. 1996. *Nationalism and Archaeology*. London: UCL Press.

Dikeç, M. 2002. "Pera Peras Poros: Longings for Spaces of Hospitality." *Theory, Culture and Society* 19: 227–47.

Dobres, M. 2000. *Technology and Social Agency*. Oxford: Blackwell.

Dobres, M., and J. Robb, eds. 2000. *Agency in Archaeology*. New York: Routledge.

Dominguez, V. 1986. "The marketing of heritage." *American Ethnologist* 13(3): 546–55.

Dongoske, K. E., L. Jenkins, and T. J. Ferguson. 1993. "Understanding the past through Hopi oral history." *Native Peoples* 6(2): 24–31.

Doyel, D. E. 1982. "Medicine men, ethnic significance, and cultural resource management." *American Antiquity* 47(3): 634–42.

Drower, M. 1996. *Flinders Petrie: A Life in Archaeology*. 2nd ed. Madison: University of Wisconsin Press.

Duffy, R. 2002. *A Trip Too Far: Ecotourism, Politics and Exploitation*. London: Earthscan.

Dugay-Grist, M. 2006. "Shaking the pillars." In I. Lilley (ed.), *Archaeology of Oceania: Australia and the Pacific Islands*, 357–79. Oxford: Blackwell.

Dural, S. 2006. *Protecting Çatalhöyük*. Walnut Creek: Left Coast Press.

Duwe, Sam. 2006. "Public archaeology in an Andean community." *SAA Archaeological Record* 6(2): 6–11.

Eade, J. 1991. "Order and power at Lourdes." In J. Eade and M. Sallnow (eds.), *Contesting the Sacred*, 51–76. London: Routledge.

Echo-Hawk, R. 2000. "Ancient history in the new world: Integrating oral traditions and the archaeological record in deep time." *American Antiquity* 65(2): 267–90.

Eck, D. W., and P. Gerstenblith. 2003. "International cultural property." *International Lawyer* 37: 565–73.

Edelman, M., and A. Haugerud. 2003. "Development." In D. Nugent and J. Vicent (eds.), *A Companion to the Anthropology of Politics*, 86–106. Malden, Mass.: Blackwell.

Eggan, F. 1994. "The Hopi Indians, with special reference to their cosmology or world view." In P. Schaafsma (ed.), *Kachinas in the Pueblo World*, 7–16. Albuquerque: University of New Mexico Press.

Eire, C. M. 1986. *War Against the Idols*. Cambridge: Cambridge University Press.

Eiss, P. 2004. "Deconstructing Indians, reconstructing patria." *Journal of Latin American Anthropology* 9(1): 119–50.

Elden, S. 2001. *Mapping the Present: Heidegger, Foucault and the Project of a Spatial History*. London: Continuum.

Engmann, R. Ama-Asaa. 2008. "Cosmopolitan theory, heritage, museum practice and development in Ghana." Paper presented at the World Archaeology Congress, Dublin, June 30, 2008.

Eriksen, T. H. 2001. "Between universalism and relativism: A critique of the UNESCO concept of culture." In J. Cowan, M. Dembour, and R. Wilson (eds.), *Culture and Rights: Anthropological Perspectives*. Cambridge: Cambridge University Press.

Escobar, A. 1994. *Encountering Development: The Making and Unmaking of the Third World*. Princeton, N.J.: Princeton University Press.

———. 1998. "Whose knowledge, whose nature? Biodiversity, conservation, and the political ecology of social movements." *Journal of Political Ecology* 5: 53–82.

Fabian, J. 1983. *Time and the Other: How Anthropology Constructs Its Object*. New York: Columbia University Press.

Fagan, B. 2005. *Peoples of the Earth: An Introduction to World Prehistory*. New York: Prentice-Hall.

Fairhead, J., and M. Leach. 1996. *Misreading the African Landscape: Society and Ecology in a Forest-Savanna Mosaic*. Cambridge: Cambridge University Press.

———. 2003. *Science, Society and Power: Environmental Knowledge and Policy in West Africa and the Caribbean*. Cambridge: Cambridge University Press.

Farred, G. 2004. "The not-yet counterpartisan: A new politics of oppositionality." Special issue, *After the Thrill Is Gone: A Decade of Post-Apartheid South Africa. South Atlantic Quarterly* 103: 589–605.

Featherstone, M. 1990. *Global Culture: Nationalism, Globalization, and Modernity*. Special issue of *Theory, Culture and Society*. London: Sage.

Feiler, B. 2001. *Walking the Bible: A Journey by Land Through the Five Books of Moses*. New York: HarperCollins.

Fein, H. 1984. "Scenarios of genocide: models of genocide and critical responses." In I. Charney (ed.), *Toward the Understanding and Prevention of Genocide: Proceedings on the International Conference on the Holocaust and Genocide*, 3-31. Boulder, Colo.: Westview.

Ferguson, J. 1990. *The Anti-Politics Machine: Development, Depoliticization, and Bureaucratic Power in Lesotho*. Cambridge: Cambridge University Press.

Ferguson, T. J. 1990. "The repatriation of Ahayu:da Zuni war gods: An interview with the Zuni Tribal Council on April 25, 1990." *Museum Anthropology* 14(2): 7–14.

———. 2004. "Academic, legal, and political contexts of social identity and cultural affiliation research in the Southwest." In B. J. Mills (ed.), *Identity, Feasting, and the Archaeology of the Greater Southwest*, 27–41. Boulder: University Press of Colorado.

Ferguson, T. J., R. Anyon, and E. J. Ladd. 1996. "Repatriation at the Pueblo of Zuni: Diverse solutions to complex problems." *American Indian Quarterly* 20(2): 251–73.

Ferguson, T. J., and C. Colwell-Chanthaphonh. 2006. *History Is in the Land: Multivocal Tribal Traditions in Arizona's San Pedro Valley.* Tucson: University of Arizona Press.

Ferguson, T. J., K. E. Dongoske, and L. Kuwanwisiwma. 2001. "Hopi perspectives on southwestern mortuary studies." In D. R. Mitchell and J. L. Brunson-Hadley (eds.), *Ancient Burial Practices in the American Southwest: Archaeology, Physical Anthropology, and Native American Perspectives*, 9–26. Albuquerque: University of New Mexico Press.

Ferguson, T. J., and R. E. Hart. 1985. *A Zuni Atlas.* Norman: University of Oklahoma Press.

Ferreira, L. M. 2005. "Solo civilizado, chão antropofágico: A arqueologia imperial e os sambaquis." In P. P. A. Funari, C. E. Orser, and S. N. O. Schiavetto (eds.), *Identidades, discurso e poder: Estudos da arqueologia contemporânea*, 135–46. São Paulo: FAPESP/Anna Blume.

Fewkes, J. W. 1892. "A few Tusayan pictographs." *American Anthropologist* 5(1): 9–25.

———. 1906. "Hopi Shrines near the East Mesa, Arizona." *American Anthropologist* 8(2): 346–75.

Finn, C. 1997. "'Leaving more than footprints': Modern votive offerings at Chaco Canyon prehistoric site." *Antiquity* 71: 169–78.

Fleming, A. 2006. "Post-processual landscape archaeology: A critique." *Cambridge Archaeological Journal* 16: 267–80.

Fontein, J. 2005. *The Silence of Great Zimbabwe: Contested Landscapes and the Power of Heritage.* London: University College London Press.

Forline, C. 1997. "The persistence and cultural transformation of the Guajá Indians: Foragers of Maranhão State, Brazil." Ph.D. diss., University of Florida.

Fortmann, L. 2005. "What we need is a community Bambi: The perils and possibilities of powerful symbols." In J. P. Brosius, A. L. Tsing, and C. Zerner (eds.), *Communities and Conservation: Histories and Politics of Community-Based Natural Resource Management*, 195–205. Walnut Creek, Calif.: AltaMira.

Foucault, M. 1967. *Madness and Civilization.* Trans. R. Howard. London: Tavistock.

———. 1973. *The Order of Things.* Trans. A. S. Smith. New York: Vintage.

Fox, R., ed. 1990. *Nationalist Ideologies and the Production of National Cultures.* American Ethnology Monograph Series 2. Washington: American Anthropological Association.

Frank, A. G. 1996. "The underdevelopment of development." In S. C. Chew and R. A. Denemark (eds.), *The Underdevelopment of Development: Essays in Honour of Andre Gunder Frank*, 17–55. Thousand Oaks, Calif.: Sage.

Funari, P. P. A. 2004. "The archaeological study of the African diaspora in Brazil." In T. Falola and A. Ogundiran (eds.), *The Archaeology of Atlantic Africa and the African Diaspora*. Studies in African History and the Diaspora. Rochester, N.Y.: University of Rochester Press.

Galison, P. 1996. "Computer simulation and the trading zone." In P. Galison and D. Stump (eds.), *The Disunity of Science: Boundaries, Contexts and Power*. Stanford, Calif.: Stanford University Press.

García-Canclini, N. 1992. "Cultural reconversion." In G. Yúdice, J. Flores, and J. Franco (eds.), *On Edge: The Crisis of Contemporary Latin American Culture*, 29–43. Minneapolis: University of Minnesota Press.

Gatewood, J. B., and C. M. Cameron. 2004. "Battlefield pilgrims at Gettysburg National Park." *Ethnology* 43(3): 193–216.

Geary, P. 1986. "Sacred commodities: The circulation of medieval relics." In A. Appadurai (ed.), *The Social Life of Things*, 169–91. Cambridge: Cambridge University Press.

Gebre, A. 2004. "The effects of development projects on the Karrayu in Metahara area." In A. Pankhurst and F. Piget (eds.), *People, Space and the State: Migration, Resettlement and Displacement in Ethiopia*, 243–63. Addis Ababa: Addis Ababa University.

Geertz, C. 1983. *Local Knowledge: Further Essays in Interpretive Anthropology*. New York: Basic Books.

Gell, A. 1998. *Art and Agency: An Anthropological Theory*. Oxford: Oxford University Press.

Gerini, G. E. 1904. "To contributors." *Journal of the Siam Society* 1: 228–32.

Gesick, L. M. 1995. *In the Land of Lady White Blood*. Ithaca, N.Y.: Southeast Asia Program, Cornell University.

Girma, K. 1992. *The State and Development in Ethiopia*. Atlantic Highlands, N.J.: Humanities Press.

Göçek, F. M. 1999. "To veil or not to veil. The contested location of gender in contemporary Turkey." *Interventions* 1(4): 521–35.

Godwin, L., and J. Weiner. 2006. "Footprints of the ancestors: The convergence of anthropological and archaeological perspectives in contemporary Aboriginal heritage studies." In B. David, B. Barker, and I. McNiven (eds.), *The Social Archaeology of Australian Indigenous Societies*, 124–38. Canberra: Aboriginal Studies Press.

González-Ruibal, A. 2005. "The need for a decaying past: An archaeology of oblivion in Galicia (NW Spain)." *Home Cultures* 2(2): 129–52.

———. 2006a. "The past is tomorrow: Towards an archaeology of the vanishing present." *Norwegian Archaeological Review* 39(2): 110–25.

———. 2006b. "The dream of reason: An archaeology of the failures of modernity in Ethiopia." *Journal of Social Archaeology* 6(2): 175–201.

Goodman, J. 2006. "Leave it in the ground! Eco-social alliances for sustainability." In J. Johnston, M. Gismondi, and J. Goodman (eds.), *Nature's Revenge: Reclaiming Sustainability in an Age of Corporate Globalization*, 155–82. Toronto: Broadview and Garamond Press.

Graeber, D. 2002. "The anthropology of globalization (with notes on neomedievalism and the end of the Chinese model of the nation-state)." *American Anthropologist* 104: 1222–27.

Graham, W. A. 1924. *Siam*. 2 vols. London: Alexander Moring.

Greenenough, P., and A. Tsing, eds. 2003. *Nature in the Global South: Environmental Projects in South and Southeast Asia*. Durham, N.C.: Duke University Press.

Griffiths, E. 2005. "No heritage listing for Gallipoli." AM, Australian Broadcasting Commission, April 27. Transcript. http://www.abc.net.au.

Grigorova, B., W. Smith, K. Stülpner, J. A. Tumilty, and D. Miller. 1998. "Fingerprinting of gold artefacts from Mapungubwe, Bosutswe and Thulamela." *Gold Bulletin* 31: 99–102.

Groarke, L., and G. Warrick. 2006. "Stewardship gone astray? Ethics and the SAA." In C. Scarre and G. F. Scarre (eds.), *The Ethics of Archaeology: Philosophical Perspectives on Archaeological Practice*, 163–77. Cambridge: Cambridge University Press.

Gundjehmi Aboriginal Corporation. 1998. "The Facts of Jabiluka." *Journal of Australian Indigenous Issues* 1(1): 34–37.

Habermas, J. 2000. *The Inclusion of the Other*. Cambridge: MIT Press.

———. 2003a. "Intolerance and discrimination." *International Journal of Constitutional Law* 1(1): 2–12.

———. 2003b. "Equal treatment of cultures and the limits of postmodern liberalism." *Journal of Political Philosophy* 13: 1–28.

Hall, D. G. E. 1981. *A History of South-east Asia*. New York: St. Martin's Press.

Hall, M. 2000. *Archaeology and the Modern World: Colonial Transcripts in South Africa and the Chesapeake*. London: Routledge.

———. 2005. "Situational ethics and engaged practice: The case of archaeology in Africa." In L. M. Meskell and P. Pels (eds.), *Embedding Ethics: Shifting the Boundaries of the Anthropological Profession*, 169–94. Oxford: Berg.

Hall, S. 1997a. "The local and the global: Globalization and ethnicity." In A. King (ed.), *Culture, Globalization and the World-System: Contemporary Conditions for the Representation of Identity*, 19–39. Minneapolis: University of Minnesota Press.

———. 1997b. "Old and new identities, old and new ethnicities." In A. King (ed.), *Culture, Globalization and the World-System: Contemporary Conditions for the Representation of Identity*, 41–68. Minneapolis: University of Minnesota Press.

Halliday, F. 2000. *Nation and Religion in the Middle East*. Boulder, Colo.: Lynne Rienner.

Handler, R. 2003. "Cultural property and culture theory." *Journal of Social Archaeology* 3: 353–65.

Handler, R., and E. Gable. 1997. *The New History in an Old Museum: Creating the Past at Colonial Williamsburg*. Durham, N.C.: Duke University Press.

Hannerz, U. 1992. *Cultural Complexity: Studies in the Social Organization of Meaning*. New York: Columbia University Press.

———. 1996. *Transnational Connections: Culture, People, Places*. London: Routledge.

———. 2006. "Cosmopolitanism." In J. Vincent and D. Nugent (eds.), *A Companion to the Anthropology of Politics*, 69–85. Oxford: Blackwell.

Hansen, D. T. 2007. *Ethical Visions of Education: Philosophy in Practice*. New York: Teachers College Press.

Harding, L. 2001. "How the Buddha got his wounds." *The Guardian*, March 3.

Harmon, D., and A. D. Putney, eds. 2003. *The Full Value of Parks: From Economics to the Intangible*. Lanham, Md.: Rowan and Littlefield.

Harvey, D. 2000. "Cosmopolitanism and the banality of geographical evils." *Public Culture* 12: 529–64.

Hawkes, J. 1982. *Adventurer in Archaeology: The Biography of Sir Mortimer Wheeler*. New York: St. Martin's Press.

Hawkes, K., J. F. O'Connell, and L. Rogers. 1997. "The behavioral ecology of modern hunter-gatherers and human evolution." *Trends in Ecology and Evolution* 12: 29–32.

Hayashida, F. M. 2005. "Archaeology, ecological history, and conservation." *Annual Review of Anthropology* 34: 43–65.

Hayden, C. 2003. *When Nature Goes Public: The Making and Unmaking of Bioprospecting in Mexico*. Princeton, N.J.: Princeton University Press.

Heathcote, A. 2003. "Nuclear paradox." *Business Review Weekly*, July 10.

Held, D. 2003. "Culture and political community: National, global, and cosmopolitan." In S. Vertovec and R. Cohen (eds.), *Conceiving Cosmopolitanism*, 48–58. New York: Oxford University Press.

Hernando Gonzalo, A. 2006. "Arqueología y globalización: El problema de la definición del 'otro' en la posmodernidad." *Complutum* 17: 221–34.

Hill, E. 2002. *New Frontiers in the Social History of the Middle East*. Cairo Papers in Social Science. Cairo: Cairo University Press.

Himmelfarb, G. 2002. "The illusions of cosmopolitanism." In M. Nussbaum (and respondents), *For Love of Country?* ed. J. Cohen, 72–77. Boston: Beacon Press.

Hinsley, C. M. 1992. "Collecting cultures and cultures of collecting: The lure of the American Southwest, 1880–1915." *Museum Anthropology* 16(1): 12–20.

Hodder, I. 1998. "The past and passion and play: Çatalhöyük as a site of conflict in the construction of multiple pasts." In L. M. Meskell (ed.), *Archaeology Under Fire: Nationalism, Politics and Heritage in the Eastern Mediterranean and Middle East*, 124–39. London: Routledge.

———. 2003. "Archaeological reflexivity and the 'local' voice." *Anthropological Quarterly* 76(1): 55–69.

———, ed. 2000. *Towards a Reflexive Method in Archaeology: The Example of Çatalhöyük*. Monograph 28. Ankara: McDonald Institute for Archaeological Research/British Institute of Archaeology.

Holt, H. B. 1983. "A cultural resource management dilemma: Anasazi ruins and the Navajos." *American Antiquity* 48(3): 594–99.

Holt, J. C. 2003. "Minister of defense: The Visnu controversy in contemporary Sri Lanka." In J. Holt, J. Kinnard, and J. Walters (eds.), *Constituting Communities: Theravāda Buddhism and the Religious Cultures of South and Southeast Asia*, 107–30. Albany: State University of New York.

Honey, M. 1999. *Ecotourism and Sustainable Development: Who Owns Paradise?* Washington, D.C.: Island Press.

Howard, J. 2005. "Address at Anzac Day Dawn Service, Gallipoli, April 25, 2005." Transcript of the prime minister, the Hon. John Howard, M.P. http://www.pm.gov.au (accessed July 27, 2006).

———. 2006. "Address to the National Press Club, Great Hall, Parliament House, January 25, 2006." http://www.pm.gov.au.

Hughes, D. M. 2005. "Third nature: Making space and time in the Great Limpopo Conservation Area." *Cultural Anthropology* 20(2): 157–84.

Huntington, S. 1998. *The Clash of Civilizations and the Making of the New World Order.* New York: Simon and Schuster.

ICOMOS (International Council on Museums and Sites). 2003. *Advisory Board Evaluation, Bamiyan Valley (Afghanistan)*. No. 208 rev. Paris: UNESCO, International Council on Museums and Sites.

Igoe, J. 2006. Measuring the costs and benefits of conservation to local communities. *Journal of Ecological Anthropology* 10: 72–77.

Inda, J. X. 2000. "A flexible world: Capitalism, citizenship, and postnational zones." *POLAR* 23(1): 86–102.

Inda, J. X., and R. Rosaldo, eds. 2002. *The Anthropology of Globalization: A Reader*. Malden, Mass.: Blackwell.

Ireland, T. 2002. "Giving value to the Australian historic past: Archaeology, heritage and nationalism." *Australasian Historical Archaeology* 20: 15–25.

Ireland, T., and J. Lydon. 2005. "Introduction: Touchstones." In J. Lydon and T. Ireland (eds.), *Object Lessons: Archaeology and Heritage in Australia*, 1–30. Melbourne: Australian Scholarly Publishing.

Ishii, Y. 1986. *Sangha, State, and Society: Thai Buddhism in History*. Trans. Peter Hawkes. Honolulu: University of Hawaii Press.

Ivison, D. 2002. *Postcolonial Liberalism*. Cambridge: Cambridge University Press.

———. 2006a. "Emergent cosmopolitanism: Indigenous peoples and international law." In R. Tinnevelt and G. Verschraegen (eds.), *Between Cosmopolitan Ideals and State Sovereignty*. New York: Palgrave.

———. 2006b. "Historical injustice." In J. Dryzek, B. Honnig, and A. Philipps (eds.), *Oxford Handbook to Political Theory*. Oxford: Oxford University Press.

Ivy, M. 1995. *Discourses of the Vanishing: Modernity, Phantasm, Japan*. Chicago: University of Chicago Press.

Jackson, P. 1999a. "Royal spirits, Chinese gods, and magic monks: Thailand's boom-time religions of prosperity." *South East Asian Research* 7(3): 245–320.

———. 1999b. "The enchanting spirit of Thai capitalism: The cult of Luang Phor Khoon and the post-modernization of Thai Buddhism." *Southeast Asian Research* 7(1): 5–60.

Jan, A. U. 2003. *The End of Democracy*. Toronto: Pragmatic Publishing.

JanMohamed, A. 1985. "The economy of Manichean allegory: The function of racial difference in colonialist literature." *Critical Inquiry* 12(1): 57–87.

Jaspers, K. 1953. *The Origin and Goal of History*. Trans. Michael Bullock. New Haven, Conn.: Yale University Press.

Johanson, D. C., and M. E. 1981. *Lucy, the Beginnings of Humankind*. New York: Simon and Schuster.

Jones, L. 1995. *Twin City Tales: A Hermeneutical Reassessment of Tula and Chichén Itzá*. Niwot: University of Colorado Press.

———. 1997. "Conquests of the imagination: Maya-Mexican polarity and the story of Chichén Itzá." *American Anthropologist* 99(2): 275–90.

Jones, R., ed. 1985. *Archaeological Research in Kakadu National Park*. Special Publication 13. Canberra: Australian National Parks and Wildlife Service.

Jones, S. 1997. *The Archaeology of Ethnicity: Constructing Identities in the Past and Present*. London: Routledge.

———. 2003. *Early Medieval Sculpture and the Production of Meaning, Value and Place: The Case of Hilton of Cadboll*. Research Report, Conservation Research and Education Division. Edinburgh: Historic Scotland.

Jordan, P. 1996. "Thulamela excavation proves black heritage." Speech delivered in Kruger National Park, September 24.

Joseph, G. 1988. *Revolution from Without: Yucatán, Mexico, and the United States, 1880–1924*. Durham, N.C.: Duke University Press.

Joyce, R. A. 2005. "Solid histories for fragile nations: Archaeology as cultural patrimony." In L. M. Meskell and P. Pels (eds.), *Embedding Ethics*, 253–73. Oxford: Berg.

Kahn, J. S. 2003. "Anthropology as cosmopolitan practice?" *Anthropological Theory* 3: 403–15.

Kalb, J. 2001. *Adventures in the Bone Trade: The Race to Discover Human Ancestors in Ethiopia's Afar Depression*. New York: Copernicus.

Kaltal, M., Y. Nojima, and S. Bedford. 2004. *Wokbaot Bakagen Wetem Olgeta Blong VCHSS: Sait Sevei mo Arkeoloji*. Port Vila: Vanuatu National Cultural Council.

Kane, S., ed. 2003. *The Politics of Archaeology and Identity in a Global Context*. Boston: AIA Monographs.

Kassa, G. 2004. "Settlement among the Afar pastoralists of the Awash valley." In A. Pankhurst and F. Piget (eds.), *People, Space and the State: Migration, Ressetlement and Displacement in Ethiopia*, 222–42. Addis Ababa: Addis Ababa University.

Katona, J. 1998. "'If native title is us, it's inside us': Jabiluka and the politics of intercultural negotiation." *Australian Feminist Law Journal* 10: 1–12.

———. 1999. "Conservationists claim Kakadu decision risks world heritage." *7.30 Report*, Australian Broadcasting Commission, March 7. Interview transcript.

———. 2001. "Mining uranium and indigenous Australians: The fight for Jabiluka." In G. Evans, J. Goodman, and N. Lansbury (eds.), *Moving Mountains: Communities Confront Mining and Globalisation*, 195–206. London: Zed Books.

———. 2002. "Cultural protection in frontier Australia." *Flinders Journal of Law Reform* 6(1): 29–39.

Keller, R., and M. Turek. 1998. *American Indians and National Parks*. Tucson: University of Arizona Press.

Kelley, K., and H. Francis. 1993. "Places important to Navajo people." *American Indian Quarterly* 17(2): 151–69.

———. 1994. *Navajo Sacred Places*. Bloomington: Indiana University Press.

Keyes, C. F., L. Kendall, and H. Hardacre, eds. 1994. *Asian Visions of Authority*. Honolulu: University of Hawaii Press.

Kilicbay, B., and M. Binark. 2002. "Consumer culture, Islam and the politics of lifestyle: Fashion for veiling in contemporary Turkey." *European Journal of Communication* 17(4): 495–511.

Kincaid, J. 1997. *A Small Place*. New York City: Farrar, Straus, and Giroux.

Kirch, P. 2000. *On the Road of the Winds: An Archaeological History of the Pacific Islands before European Contact*. Berkeley: University of California Press.

Kirk, A. 2000. "John Howard to visit Gallipoli." *AM*, Australian Broadcasting Commission, April 22. Transcript. http://www.abc.net.au (accessed July 1, 2007).

Kirshenblatt-Gimblett, B. 2006. "World heritage and cultural economics." In I. Karp, C. Kratz, L. Szwaja, and T. Ybarra-Frausto (eds.), *Museum Frictions: Public Cultures/Global Transformations*, 161–202. Durham, N.C.: Duke University Press.

Kitiarsa, P. 1999. "You may not believe, but never offend the spirits: Spirit-medium cult discourses and the postmodernization of Thai religion." Ph.D. diss., University of Washington.

Kloppers, J. J., and H. Bornman. 2005. *A Dictionary of Kruger National Park Place Names*. Barberton, South Africa: SA Country Life.

Kohl, P., and C. Fawcett, eds. 1995. *Nationalism, Politics and the Practice of Archaeology*. Cambridge: Cambridge University Press.

Knepper, C. 2002. *Natural do Maranhão/The Natural World of Maranhão*. São Luís do Maranhão: Governo Estadual do Maranhão.

Kristeva, J. 1997. "Strangers to ourselves." In K. Oliver (ed.), *The portable Kristeva*, 264–94. New York: Columbia University Press.

Küsel, U. S. 1992. "A preliminary report on settlement layout and gold smelting at Thulamela, a Late Iron Age site in the Kruger National Park." *Koedoe* 35: 55–64.

Kuwanwisiwma, L. J., and T. J. Ferguson. 2004. "Ang Kuktota: Hopi ancestral sites and cultural landscapes." *Expedition* 46(2): 25–29.

Labadi, S. 2005. "A review of the global strategy for a balanced, representative and credible World Heritage List 1994–2004." *Conservation and Management of Archaeological Sites* 7(2).

——. 2006. "From exclusive to inclusive representations of the nation and cultural identity and diversity within discourses on world heritage." Paper presented at "Cultures of Contact: Archaeology, Ethics, and Globalization," Stanford University, February 18–19. http://metamedia.stanford.edu/3455/CulturesofContact (accessed July 1, 2007).

Lacan, J. 1975. *Ecrits: A Selection*. New York: W. W. Norton.

Latour, B. 1993. *We Have Never Been Modern*. Trans. C. Porter. Cambridge, Mass.: Harvard University Press.

——. 1999. *Politiques de la nature, comment faire entrer les sciences en démocratie*. Paris: La Découverte.

——. 2004. "Whose cosmos, which cosmopolitics?" *Common Knowledge* 10: 450–62.

Le Goff, J. 1988 [1985]. *The Medieval Imagination*. Trans. A. Goldhammer. Chicago: University of Chicago Press.

Leone, M. P. 2005. *The Archaeology of Liberty in an American Capital: Excavations in Annapolis*. Berkeley: University of California Press.

Lewis, B. 2001. *What Went Wrong? Western Impact and Middle Eastern Response*. New York: Oxford University Press.

———. 2004. *From Babel to Dragomans: Interpreting the Middle East*. New York: Oxford University Press.

Lilley, I., ed. 2000a. *Native Title and the Transformation of Archaeology in the Postcolonial World*. Sydney: Oceania Monographs.

———. 2000b. "Professional attitudes to indigenous interests in the native title era." In I. Lilley (ed.), *Native Title and the Transformation of Archaeology in the Postcolonial World*, 99–119. Sydney: Oceania Monographs.

———. 2004. "Diaspora and identity in archaeology: Moving beyond the black Atlantic." In L. Meskell and R. Preucel (eds.), *A Companion to Social Archaeology*, 287–312. Oxford: Blackwell.

———. 2006a. 2004. "After Captain Cook: The archaeology of the recent indigenous past in Australia." Review of R. Harrison and C. Williamson, eds. *Asian Perspectives* 45: 112–15.

———. 2006b. "Archaeology and Aboriginal and Torres Strait Islander studies at the University of Queensland." In S. Ulm and I. Lilley (eds.), *An Archaeological Life: Papers in Honour of Jay Hall*. Research Report Series 7. Brisbane: Aboriginal and Torres Strait Islander Studies Unit, University of Queensland.

———. 2008. "Archaeology, human rights and postcolonial politics." In U. Rizvi and M. Leibmann (eds.), *Postcolonialism and Archaeology*, 141–64. Walnut Creek, Calif.: AltaMira.

Lilley, I., and M. Williams. 2005. "Archaeological and indigenous significance: A view from Australia." In C. Mathers, T. Darvill, and B. Little (ed.), *Heritage of Value, Archaeology of Renown: Reshaping Archaeological Assessment and Significance*, 227–47. Gainesville: University of Florida Press.

Lindholm, C. 2002. *The Islamic Middle East: Tradition and Change*. Oxford: Blackwell.

Little, D. 2004. *American Orientalism: The United States and the Middle East Since 1945*. Chapel Hill: University of North Carolina Press.

Litzinger, R. A. 2006. "Contested sovereignties and the Critical Ecosystem Partnership Fund." *Political and Legal Anthropology Review* 29: 66–87.

Lockman, Z. 2004. *Contending Visions of the Middle East: The History and Politics of Orientalism*. Cambridge: Cambridge University Press.

Logan, W. 2002. "Globalizing heritage: World heritage as a manifestation of modernism and challenges from the periphery." In D. Jones (ed.), *20th Century Heritage: Our Recent Cultural Legacy; Proceedings of the Australia ICOMOS National Conference 2001*. Adelaide: University of Adelaide and Australia ICOMOS Secretariat.

———. 2008. "Closing Pandora's Box: Human rights conundrums in cultural heritage protection." In H. Silverman and D. R. Fairchild (eds.), *Cultural Heritage and Human Rights*. New York: Springer.

Long, B. 1996. *Scenery of Eternity: William Foxwell Albright and Notions of "Holy Land."* GAIR Constructions of Ancient Space Seminar Members' Papers. Cleveland: Case Western Reserve University.

Lubbock, J. 1865. *Pre-historic Times, as Illustrated by Ancient Remains, and the Manners and Customs of Modern Savages*. London: Williams and Norgate.

Lydon, J., and T. Ireland, eds. 2005. *Object Lessons: Archaeology and Heritage in Australia*. Melbourne: Australian Scholarly Publishing.

Lynott, M. J., and A. Wylie, eds. 2000. *Ethics in American Archaeology*. Washington, D.C.: Society for American Archaeology.

Maalouf, A. 1984. *The Crusades Through Arab Eyes*. Trans. by Jon Rothschild. New York: Schocken Books.

Macintyre, S., and A. Clark. 2003. *The History Wars*. Melbourne: Melbourne University Press.

Magome, H., and J. Murombedzi. 2003. "Sharing South African national parks: Community land and conservation in a democratic South Africa." In W. Adams and M. Mulligan (eds.), *Decolonizing Nature: Strategies for Conservation in a Post-colonial Era*, 108–34. London: Earthscan.

Malkki, L. 1995. *Purity and Exile: Violence, Memory, and National Cosmology Among Hutu Refugees in Tanzania*. Chicago: University of Chicago Press.

Mallon, F. 1996. "Constructing *mestizaje* in Latin America: Authenticity, marginality, and gender in the claiming of ethnic identities." *Journal of Latin American Anthropology* 2(1): 170–81.

Marcos, J. 1986. "La situación actual y las perspectivas de las investigaciones arqueológicas en el Ecuador." In J. Marcos (ed.), *Arqueología de la Costa Ecuatoriana: Nuevos Enfoques*. Quito: ESPOL and Corporación Editora Nacional.

———. 1988. *Real Alto: La Historia de un Centro Ceremonial Valdivia*. 2 vols. Quito: ESPOL and Corporación Editora Nacional.

Marshall, R. 2005. "Bush's flight from reality." *Washington Report on Middle East Affairs* 24(8): 7–10.

Marshall, Y. 2002. "What is community archaeology?" *World Archaeology* 34(2): 211–19.

Martin, E. J. 1978. *A History of the Iconoclastic Controversy*. New York: Macmillan.

Massad, J. 2001. *Colonial Effects: The Making of National Identity in Jordan*. New York: Columbia University Press.

Maybury-Lewis, D. 2002. "Genocide against indigenous peoples." In A. L. Hinton (eds.), *Annihilating Difference: The Anthropology of Genocide*, 120–37. Berkeley and Los Angeles: University of California Press.

Mazar, A. 2000. *Archaeology of the Land of the Bible*. New York: Doubleday.

McDonald, D. A., ed. 2002. *Environmental Justice in South Africa*. Athens: Ohio University Press.

McEwan, C. 1990. *El Sitio Arqueológico de Agua Blanca, Manabí, Ecuador*. Guayaquil: Report on file at the Instituto Nacional de Patrimonio Cultural.

McEwan, C., and C. Hudson. 2006. "Using the past to forge the future: The genesis of the Community Site Museum at Agua Blanca, Ecuador." In H. Silverman (ed.), *Archaeological Site Museums in Latin America*. Gainesville: University Press of Florida.

McGuire, R. 2004. "Contested pasts: Archaeology and Native Americans." In L. Meskell and R. Preucel (eds.), *A Companion to Social Archaeology*, 374–95. Oxford: Blackwell.

McKinsey Report. 2002. SANPARKS *and McKinsey Final Meeting*. Pretoria: South Africa National Parks.

McNiven, I. 2003. "Saltwater people: Spiritscapes, maritime rituals and the archaeology of Australian indigenous seascapes." *World Archaeology* 35: 329–49.

McNiven, I., and R. Feldman. 2003. "Ritually orchestrated seascapes: Hunting magic and dugong bone mounds in Torres Strait, NE Australia." *Cambridge Archaeological Journal* 13: 169–94.

McPherson, R. S. 1992. *Sacred Land, Sacred View*. Provo, Utah: Brigham Young University.

Meijer, R. 1999. "Introduction." In R. Meijer (ed.), *Cosmopolitanism, Identity and Authenticity in the Middle East*, 1–14. London: Routledge.

Mellaart, J. 1967. *Çatal Hüyük: A Neolithic Town in Anatolia*. London: Thames and Hudson.

Merrill, W. L., E. J. Ladd, and T. J. Ferguson. 1993. "The Return of the Ahayu: da: Lessons for repatriation from Zuni Pueblo and the Smithsonian Institution." *Current Anthropology* 34(5): 523–67.

Merry, S. E. 2003. "Human rights law and the demonization of culture (and anthropology along the way)." *PoLAR: Political and Legal Anthropology Review* 26(1): 55–77.

———. 2006. "Transnational human rights and local activism: Mapping the middle." *American Anthropologist* 108: 38–51.

Merryman, J. H. 1986. "Two ways of thinking about cultural property." *American Journal of International Law* 80: 831–53.

———. 2005. "Cultural property internationalism." *International Journal of Cultural Property* 12: 11–39.

Meskell, L. 2002. "Negative heritage and past mastering in archaeology." *Anthropological Quarterly* 75(3): 557–74.

———. 2004. *Object Worlds in Ancient Egypt*. Oxford: Berg.

———. 2005a. "Archaeological ethnography: Conversations around Kruger National Park." *Archaeologies: Journal of the World Archaeology Congress* 1: 83–102.

———. 2005b. "Recognition, restitution and the potentials of postcolonial liberalism for South African heritage." *South African Archaeological Bulletin* 60: 72–78.

———. 2005c. "Object orientations." In L. M. Meskell (ed.), *Archaeologies of Materiality*, 1–17. Oxford: Blackwell.

———. 2005d. "Sites of violence: Terrorism, tourism and heritage in the archaeological present." In L. Meskell and P. Pels (eds.), *Embedding Ethics*, 123–46. Oxford: Berg.

———. 2006a. "Deep past, divided present: South Africa's heritage at the frontier." *Western Humanities Review*: 110–16.

———. 2006b. "Trauma culture: Remembering and forgetting in the new South Africa." In D. Bell (ed.), *Memory, Trauma, and World Politics*, 157–74. New York: Palgrave Macmillan.

———. 2007a. "Falling walls and mending fences: Archaeological ethnography in the Limpopo." *Journal of Southern African Studies* 33: 383–400.

———. 2007b. "Heritage ethics for a present imperfect." *Archaeologies: Journal of the World Archaeology Congress* 3: 441–45.

Meskell, L. M., and P. Pels, eds. 2005. *Embedding Ethics*. Oxford: Berg.

Meskell, L. M., and L. Weiss. 2006. "Coetzee on South Africa's past: Remembering in the time of forgetting." *American Anthropologist* 108(1): 88–99.

Messenger, P. M., ed. 1999. *The Ethics of Collecting Cultural Property*. Albuquerque: University of New Mexico Press.

Michaelis, H. 1981. "Willowsprings: A Hopi petroglyph site." *Journal of New World Archaeology* 4(2): 1–23.

Mignolo, W. 2002. "The many faces of Cosmo-polis." In C. Breckenridge, H. Bhabha, S. Pollock, and D. Chakrabarty (eds.), *Cosmopolitanism*, 721–48. Durham, N.C.: Duke University Press.

Mill, J. S. 1985. *On Liberty*. London: Penguin.

Milne, G. 1998. "Howard's in the red over Brown and Greens." *The Australian*, December 7, 1998.

Mirarr. 2007. "The fight against the Ranger Uranium Mine." http://www.mirarr .net/history (accessed November 11, 2006).

Mitchell, P. 2002. *The Archaeology of Southern Africa*. Cambridge: Cambridge University Press.

Mizoguchi, K. 2004. "Identity, modernity and archaeology: The case of Japan." In L. Meskell and R. Preucel (eds.), *A Companion to Social Archaeology*, 396–414. Oxford: Blackwell.

Moore, D. S. 1998. "Clear waters and muddied histories: Environmental history and the politics of community in Zimbabwe's Eastern Highlands." *Journal of Southern African Studies* 24: 377–403.

———. 2005. *Suffering for Territory: Race, Place, and Power in Zimbabwe*. Durham, N.C.: Duke University Press.

Moore, D. S., J. Kosek, and A. Pandian, eds. 2003. *Race, Nature, and the Politics of Difference*. Durham, N.C.: Duke University Press.

Moorehead, A. 2000 [1961]. *The Blue Nile*. New York: Perennial.

Moscrop, J. 2000. *Measuring Jerusalem: The Palestine Exploration Fund and British Interests in the Holy Land*. New York: Continuum.

Moseley, E. H., and E. D. Terry, eds. 1980. *Yucatan: A World Apart*. Tuscaloosa: University of Alabama Press.

Munro-Hay, S. C. 1991. *Aksum: An African Civilisation of Late Antiquity*. Edinburgh: Edinburgh University Press.

Naipaul, V. 1964. *A House for Mr. Biswas*. London: Deutsch.

Narli, N. 1999. "The rise of the Islamist movement in Turkey." *Middle East Review of International Affairs Journal* 3(3): 38–48.

Ndoro, W. 2001. *Your Monument Our Shrine: The Preservation of Great Zimbabwe*. Studies in African Archaeology 19. Uppsala: Uppsala University.

Neumann, R. P. 1998. *Imposing Wilderness: Struggles Over Livelihood and Nature Preservation in Africa*. Berkeley and Los Angeles: California University Press.

Nicholas, G., and T. Andrews, eds. 1997. *At a Crossroads: Archaeology and First Peoples in Canada*. Burnaby, British Columbia: Archaeology Press, Simon Fraser University.

Niezen, R. 2004. *A World Beyond Difference: Cultural Identity in the Age of Globalization*. Oxford: Blackwell.

Nimuendajú, K. 1949. "The Guajá." In J. Steward (ed.), *Handbook of South American Indians*, 3: 135–36. Washington: U.S. Government Printing Office.

Noble, D. G., ed. 2004. *In Search of Chaco: New Approaches to an Archaeological Enigma*. Santa Fe: School of American Research Press.

Norton, P. 1986. "El Señorío de Salangone y la Liga de Mercaderes." In A. Franch and S. Moreno Yanez (comps.), *Miscelánea Antropológica Ecuatoriana, Arqueología y Etnohistoria del Sur de Colombia y Norte del Ecuador, Boletín 6 del Museo del Banco Central*. Quito: Banco Central and Abya-Yala.

N.S.W. (New South Wales), Legislative Assembly. 2003. "Anzac Cove World Heritage Listing." Hansard Papers, July 1, 2003 (item 22 of 41: 2454). Sydney: Parliament of New South Wales. http://www.parliament.nsw.gov.au (accessed July 1, 2007).

Nussbaum, M. 1994. "Patriotism and cosmopolitanism." *Boston Review*, October–November, 3–6.

———. 1996. "Patriotism and cosmopolitanism." In M. Nussbaum (and respondents), *For Love of Country?* ed. J. Cohen, 3–17. Boston: Beacon Press.

———. 2002a. "Patriotism and cosmopolitanism." In M. Nussbaum (and respondents), *For Love of Country?* ed. J. Cohen, 3–17. Boston: Beacon Press.

———. 2002b. "Reply." In M. Nussbaum (and respondents), *For Love of Country?* ed. J. Cohen, 131–44. Boston: Beacon Press.

———. 2006. *Frontiers of Justice: Disability, Nationality, Species Frontiers of Justice: Disability, Nationality, Species Membership.* Cambridge: Belknap Press of Harvard University Press.

O'Brien, J. O. 2003. "Canberra yellowcake: The politics of uranium and how Aboriginal land rights failed the Mirrar people." *Journal of Northern Territory History* 14: 79–91.

O'Dwyer, E. C. 2000. "Laudo antropológico: Área Indígena Awá." 5ª Vara Federal da Seção Judiciária do Maranhão. Processo n° 95.0000353-8. Unpublished report. São Luís do Maranhão.

O'Keefe, P. 2000. "Archaeology and human rights." *Public Archaeology* 1: 181–94.

Oliveira, R. C. de. 1960. "The role of Indian posts in the process of assimilation." *América Indígena* 20: 89–95.

Olivé Negrete, J. C. 1991. "Para la historia de la arqueología Mexicana: El Caso Thompson." *Arqueología* 5(2): 119–27.

Orlove, B., and S. B. Brush. 1996. "Anthropology and the conservation of biodiversity." *Annual Review of Anthropology* 25: 329–52.

Osborne, T. 2004. "On mediators: Intellectuals and the ideas trade in the knowledge society." *Economy and Society* 33: 430–47.

Ostigard, T. 2001. "The Bible and believers: The power of the past and antiquated archaeology in the Middle East." In J. Bergstol (ed.), *Scandinavian Archaeological Practice in Theory*, 302–14. Proceedings from the Sixth Nordic TAG. Oslo: Oslo Archaeological Series.

Pankhurst, R. 1977. "The history of the Bareya, Shanqella, and other Ethiopian slaves from the borderlands of the Sudan." *Sudan Notes and Records* 59: 1–43.

———. 2001. *The Ethiopian Borderlands: Essays in Regional History from Ancient Times to the End of the 18th Century.* Lawrenceville, N.J.: Red Sea Press.

Parezo, N. J. 1985. "Cushing as part of the team: The collecting activities of the Smithsonian Institution." *American Ethnologist* 12(4): 763–74.

———. 1987. "The formation of ethnographic collections: The Smithsonian Institution in the American Southwest." *Advances in Archaeological Method and Theory* 10: 1–47.

Patterson, T., and P. Schmidt, eds. 1995. "Introduction: From constructing to making alternative histories." In *Making Alternative Histories: The Practice of*

Archaeology and History in Non-Western Settings. Santa Fe: School of American Research Press.

Pauketat, T. 2001. *The Archaeology of Traditions: Agency and History Before and After Columbus*. Florida Museum of Natural History, Ripley P. Bullen Series. Gainesville: University Press of Florida.

Peleggi, M. 1996. "National heritage and global tourism in Thailand." *Annals of Tourism Research* 23: 432–48.

Perkins, C. S. 1884. "Laos land and life." In M. Backus (ed.), *Siam and Laos as Seen by Our American Missionaries*, 419–59. Philadelphia: Presbyterian Board of Publication.

Peterson, G., 2000. "Indigenous island empires: Yap and Tonga considered." *Journal of Pacific History* 35: 5–27.

Phillips, A. 2003. "Turning ideas on their head: The new paradigm for protected areas." *George Wright Forum* 20(2): 8–32.

Plumwood, V. 2003. "Decolonizing relationships with nature." In W. Adams and M. Mulligan (ed.), *Decolonizing Nature: Strategies for Conservation in a Post-colonial Era*, 51–78. London: Earthscan.

Politis, G. 2001. "On archaeological praxis, gender bias and indigenous peoples in South America." *Journal of Social Archaeology* 1: 90–107.

Pollock, S. 2000. "Cosmopolitan and vernacular in history." *Public Culture* 12(3): 591–625.

Pollock, S., and R. Bernbeck. 2005. "Introduction." In S. Pollock and R. Bernbeck (eds.), *Archaeologies of the Middle East*, 1–10. Oxford: Blackwell.

Pollock, S., H. Bhabha, C. Breckenridge, and D. Chakrabarty. 2002. "Cosmopolitanisms." In C. Breckenridge, H. Bhabha, S. Pollock, and D. Chakrabarty, *Cosmopolitanism*, 1–14. Durham, N.C.: Duke University Press.

Poston, L. 1973. "Browning's political skepticism: Sordello and the Plays." *PMLA* 88(2): 260–70.

Pratt, M. L. 1992. *Imperial Eyes*. London: Routledge.

Price, T. D., and G. Feinman. 2001. *Images of the Past*. Mountain View: Mayfield Publishing.

Prott, L. 2002. "Individual or collective rights for cultural heritage in the information society." *Museum International* 54: 7–12.

Punt, W. H. J. 1975. *The First Europeans in Kruger National Park 1725*. Pretoria: National Parks Board of Trustees.

Ramos, M. J., and I. Boavida, eds. 2004. *The Indigenous and the Foreign in Christian Ethiopian Art: On Portuguese-Ethiopian Contacts in the 16th–17th Centuries*. London: Ashgate.

Rapport, N., and R. Stade. 2007. "A cosmopolitan turn—or return?" *Social Anthropology* 15: 223–35.

Rawls, J. 1993. *Political Liberalism*. New York: Columbia University Press.

Reinerman, A. 1971. "Metternich Italy and the Congress of Verona, 1821–1822."
  The Historical Journal 14(2): 263–87.
Restall, M. 2004. "Maya ethnogenesis." *Journal of Latin American Anthropology*
  9(1): 64–89.
Reynolds, C. 1976. "Buddhist cosmography in Thai history, with special refer-
  ence to nineteenth-century culture change." *Journal of Asian Studies* 35(2):
  203–20.
———, ed. 1991. *National Identity and Its Defenders: Thailand, 1939–1989*. Monash
  Papers on Southeast Asia 25. Melbourne: Centre for Southeast Asian Stud-
  ies, Monash University.
Ritvo, H. 1987. *The Animal Estate*. Cambridge, Mass.: Harvard University
  Press.
Robbins, B. 1998. "Introduction: Part 1." In P. Cheah and B. Robbins (eds.),
  Cosmopolitics: Thinking and Feeling Beyond Nation, 1–19. Minneapolis: Min-
  nesota University Press.
Roberts, R. G., R. Jones, and M. Smith. 1990. "Thermoluminescence dating
  of a 50,000 year old human occupation site in northern Australia." *Nature*
  345: 62–71.
Rosenblum, A. 1996. "Prisoners of conscience: Public policy and contempo-
  rary repatriation discourse." *Museum Anthropology* 20(3): 58–71.
Ruiters, G. 2002. "Race, place, and environmental rights: A radical critique of
  environmental justice discourse." In D. A. McDonald (ed.), *Environmental
  Justice in South Africa*, 112–26. Athens: Ohio University Press.
Rundell, J. 2004. "Strangers, citizens and outsiders: Otherness, multicultural-
  ism and the cosmopolitan imaginary in mobile societies." *Thesis Eleven* 78:
  85–101.
Rushdie, S. 1989. *Satanic Verses*. New York: Viking.
Russell, B. 1979. *A History of Western Philosophy*. London: Unwin Hyman.
Russo, J. 1994. "Imitating the Italians: Wyatt, Spenser, Synge, Pound, Joyce."
  Modern Philology 92(1): 117–22.
Russouw, S. 2006. "Africa has a wealth of fragile heritage sites." *The Star* (Jo-
  hannesburg), June 24, 15.
Ryals, C. de L. 1996. *The Life of Robert Browning: A Critical Biography*. Cambridge: Blackwell.
Sahlins, M. 1994. "Cosmologies of Capitalism: The Trans-Pacific Sector
  of 'The World System.'" In N. Dirks, G. Eley, and S. Ortner (eds.), *Cul-
  ture/Power/History: A Reader in Contemporary Social Theory*, 412–56. Princeton, N.J.: Princeton University Press.
Said, E. 1978. *Orientalism*. New York: Pantheon Books.
———. 1994. *Culture and Imperialism*. New York: Vintage Books.
———. 1996. *Cultura e imperialismo*. Barcelona: Anagrama.

———. 2003. *Orientalism*. 25th anniversary ed. New York: Penguin.

Sand, C. 1998. "Recent archaeological research in the Loyalty Islands of New Caledonia." *Asian Perspectives* 37: 194–223.

———. 2000a. "Archaeology as a way to a shared future in New Caledonia?" In I. Lilley (ed.), *Native Title and the Transformation of Archaeology in the Postcolonial World*, 164–80. Sydney: Oceania Monographs.

———. 2000b. "The specificities of the 'Southern Lapita Province': The New Caledonian case." *Archaeology in Oceania* 35: 20–33.

Sand, C., J. Bole, and A. Ouetcho. 2006. "What is archaeology for in the Pacific? History and politics in New Caledonia." In I. Lilley (ed.), *Archaeology of Oceania: Australia and the Pacific Islands*, 321–45. Oxford: Blackwell.

Sassen, S. 1996. *Losing Control? Sovereignty in the Age of Globalization*. New York: Columbia University Press.

Scates, B. 2002. "In Gallipoli's shadow: Pilgrimage, memory, mourning and the Great War." *Australian Historical Studies* 119: 1–21.

———. 2003. "Walking with history: Children, pilgrimage and war's 'restless memory.'" *Australian Cultural History* 23: 83–104.

———. 2006. *Return to Gallipoli: Walking the Battlefields of the Great War*. Cambridge: Cambridge University Press.

Scham, S. 2001. "A fight over sacred turf—Who controls Jerusalem's holiest shrine?" *Archaeology* 54(6): 62–67, 72–74.

———. 2002. "Legacy of the Crusades." *Archaeology* 55(5): 24–31.

———. 2003a. "From the river unto the land of the Philistines: The 'memory' of Iron Age landscapes in modern visions of Palestine." In M. Dorrian and G. Rose (eds.), *Deterritorializations—Revisioning Landscapes and Politics*, 73–79. London: Black Dog Publishing.

———. 2003b. "High place: Symbolism and monumentality on Mount Moriah, Jerusalem." *Antiquity* 78(301): 647–60.

Scham, S., and A. Yahya. 2003. "Heritage and reconciliation." *Journal of Social Archaeology* 3: 399–416.

Schneider, G. W., and M. J. DeHaven. 2003. "Revisiting the Navajo way: Lessons for contemporary healing." *Perspectives in Biology and Medicine* 46(3): 413–27.

Sen, A. 2002. "Humanity and citizenship." In M. Nusbaum (and respondents), *For Love of Country?* ed. J. Cohen, 111–18. Boston: Beacon Press.

Service, E. 1964. *Primitive Social Organization: An Evolutionary Perspective*. New York: Random House.

Shankland, D. 1996. "The anthropology of an archaeological presence." In I. Hodder (ed.), *On the Surface: Çatalhöyük 1993–95*, 218–26. Cambridge: McDonald Institute for Archaeological Research/British Institute of Archaeology at Ankara Monograph.

Sheehan, N., and I. Lilley. 2008. "Things are not always what they seem: Indigenous knowledge and pattern recognition in archaeological analysis." In C. Colwell-Chanthaphonh and T. J. Ferguson (eds.), *Collaboration in Archaeological Practice: Engaging Descendent Communities*, 87–116. Walnut Creek, Calif.: AltaMira.

Shepherd, N. 2002. "The politics of archaeology in Africa." *Annual Review of Anthropology* 31: 189–209.

Silberman, N. A. 1995. "Promised lands and chosen people: The politics and poetics of archaeological narrative." In P. Kohl and C. Fawcett (eds.), *Nationalism, Politics, and the Practice of Archaeology*, 246–67. Cambridge: Cambridge University Press.

———. 1998. "Whose game is it anyway? The political and social transformations of American biblical archaeology." In L. M. Meskell (ed.), *Archaeology Under Fire: Nationalism, Politics and Heritage in the Eastern Mediterranean and Middle East*, 175–88. London: Routledge.

Silliman, S. 2005. "Culture contact or colonialism? Challenges in the archaeology of native North America." *American Antiquity* 70: 55–74.

Sillitoe, P. 1998a. "The development of indigenous knowledge: A new applied anthropology." *Current Anthropology* 39: 223–52.

———. 1998b. "What know natives? Local knowledge in development." *Social Anthropology* 6: 203–20.

Silverstein, P., and U. Makdisi, eds. 2006. *Memory and Violence in the Middle East and North Africa*. Bloomington: Indiana University Press.

Smith, B., J. D. Lewis-Williams, G. Blundell, and C. Chippendale. 2000. "Archaeology and symbolism in the new South African coat of arms." *Antiquity* 74: 467–68.

Smith, C. 2004. *Country, Kin and Culture: Survival of an Australian Aboriginal Community*. Adelaide: Wakefield Press.

Smith, C., and G. Jackson. 2006. "Decolonizing indigenous archaeology developments from down under." *American Indian Quarterly* 30: 311–49.

Smith, C. E. and G. K. Ward, eds. 2000. *Indigenous Cultures in an Interconnected World*. Sydney: Allen and Unwin; Vancouver: University of British Columbia.

Smith, C., L. Willika, P. Manabaru, and G. Jackson. 1995. "Looking after the land: The Barunga rock art management programme." In I. Davidson, C. Lovell-Jones, and R. Bancroft (eds.), *Archaeologists and Aborigines*, 36–37. Armidale, N.S.W.: University of New England Press.

Smith, C., and H. M. Wobst. 2005. "The next step: An archaeology for social justice." In C. Smith and H. M. Wobst (eds.), *Indigenous Archaeologies: Decolonizing Theory and Practice*, 392–94. One World Archaeology 47. London: Routledge.

Smith, L. 2000. "A history of Aboriginal heritage legislation in south-eastern Australia." *Australian Archaeology* 50: 109–18.

Smith, L. T. 1999. *Decolonizing Methodologies: Research and Indigenous Peoples.* Dunedin, New Zealand: University of Otago Press.

Soper, K. 2000. *What Is Nature?* Oxford: Blackwell.

Sorensen, P. 1988. *Archaeological Excavations in Thailand.* Scandinavian Institute of Asian Studies, Occasional Papers No. 1. London: Curzon Press.

South African National Parks. 2005. SANPARKS' *Biodiversity Custodianship and Management Plan Framework.* Pretoria: South African National Parks.

Spain, J. N. 1982. "Navajo culture and Anasazi archaeology: A case study in cultural resource management." *The Kiva* 47(4): 273–78.

Spivak, G. 1999. *A Critique of Postcolonial Reason: A History of the Vanishing Present.* London: Routledge.

Stahl, A. B. 2004. "Ancient political economies of West Africa." In G. Feinman and L. M. Nichols (eds.), *Archaeological Perspectives on Political Economies,* 253–70. Salt Lake City: University of Utah Press.

Steele, C. 2005. "Who has not eaten cherries with the devil?" In S. Pollock and R. Bernbeck (eds.), *Archaeologies of the Middle East: Critical Perspectives,* 45–65. Oxford: Blackwell.

Stein, R., and T. Swedenburg. 2005. *Palestine, Israel, and the Politics of Popular Culture.* Durham, N.C.: Duke University Press.

Stevenson, M. C. 1898. "Zuni ancestral gods and masks." *American Anthropologist* 11(2): 33–40.

Steyn, M., S. Miller, W. C. Neinaber, and M. Loots. 1998. "Late Iron Age gold burials from Thulamela (Parfuri region, Kruger National Park)." *South African Archaeological Bulletin* 53: 73–85.

Stoffle, R. W., M. N. Zedeno, and D. B. Halmo, eds. 2001. *American Indians and the Nevada Test Site: A Model of Research and Consultation.* Washington: U.S. Government Printing Office.

Strang, V. 2004. *The Meaning of Water.* Berg: Oxford.

Strathern, M. 2006. "A community of critics? Thoughts on new knowledge." *Journal of the Royal Anthropological Institute* (n.s.) 12: 191–209.

Sullivan, S. 2005. "Loving the ancient in Australia and China." In J. Lydon and T. Ireland (eds.), *Object Lessons: Archaeology and Heritage in Australia,* 265–85. Melbourne: Australian Scholarly Publishing.

Swidler, N., K. Dongoske, R. Anyon, and A. Downer, eds. 1997. *Native Americans and Archaeologists: Stepping Stones to Common Ground.* Walnut Creek, Calif.: AltaMira.

Szerszynski, B., and J. Urry. 2006. "Visuality, mobility and the cosmopolitan: Inhabiting the world from afar." *British Journal of Sociology* 57: 113–31.

Tambiah, S. J. 1970. *Buddhism and the Spirit Cults in North-east Thailand*. Cambridge: Cambridge University Press.

———. 1984. *Buddhist Saints of the Forest and the Cult of Amulets*. Cambridge: Cambridge University Press.

Taylor, C. 1994. "The politics of recognition." In A. Gutmann (ed.), *Multiculturalism: Examining the Politics of Recognition*, 25–73. Princeton, N.J.: Princeton University Press.

Taylor, J. L. 1993. "Embodiment, nation, and religio-politics in Thailand." *South East Asia Research* 9(2): 129–47.

Thomas, J. 2001. "Archaeologies of place and landscape." In Ian Hodder (ed.), *Archaeological Theory Today*, 165–86. Cambridge: Polity Press.

Thomas, K. 1971. *Religion and the Decline of Magic*. London: Weidenfeld and Nicholson.

Thongchai, W. 1994. *Siam Mapped*. Honolulu: University of Hawaii Press.

———. 1995. "The changing landscape of the past: New histories in Thailand since 1973." *Journal of Southeast Asian Studies* 26(1): 99–120.

———. 2000. "The quest for 'Siwilai': A geographical discourse of civilizational thinking in the late nineteenth and early twentieth century Siam." *Journal of Asian Studies* 59(3): 528–49.

Thorley, P. 1996. "Self-representation and Aboriginal communities in the Northern Territory: Implications for archaeological research." *Australian Archaeology* 43: 7–12.

———. 2002. "Current realities, idealised pasts: Archaeology, values and indigenous heritage management in Central Australia." *Oceania* 73: 110–25.

Tilley, C. 1994. *A Phenomenology of Landscape: Places, Paths and Monuments*. Oxford: Berg.

Tiyavanich, K. 1993. "The wandering forest monks in Thailand, 1900–1992: Ajan Mun's lineage." Ph.D. diss., Cornell University.

Towner, R. H., and J. S. Dean. 1996. "Questions and problems in pre-Fort Sumner Navajo archaeology." In R. H. Towner (ed.), *The Archaeology of Navajo Origins*, 3–18. Salt Lake City: University of Utah Press.

Treece, D. 1987. *Bound in Misery and Iron: The Impact of the Grande Carajás Programme on the Indians of Brazil*. London: Survival International.

Trigger, B. 1989. *A History of Archaeological Thought*. Cambridge: Cambridge University Press.

Trinh T. Minh-ha. 1997. "Not you/like you: Postcolonial women and the interlocking questions of identity and difference." In A. McClintock et al. (eds.), *Dangerous Liaisons: Gender, Nation, and Postcolonial Perspectives*. Minneapolis: University of Minnesota Press.

Trouillot, M.-R. 1995. *Silencing the Past: Power and the Production of History*. Boston: Beacon Press.

Tsing, A. L. 2000. "Inside the economy of appearances." *Public Culture* 12(1): 115–44.

Turton, A. 1978. "Architectural and political space in Thailand." In G. Milner (ed.), *Natural Symbols in South East Asia*, 113–32. London: School of Oriental and African Studies, University of London.

———. 1991. "Invulnerability and local knowledge." In M. Chitakasem and A. Turton (eds.), *Thai Constructions of Knowledge*, 155–82. London: School of Oriental and African Studies, University of London.

UNESCO (United Nations Educational, Scientific and Cultural Organization). 1972. *Convention Concerning the Protection of the World Cultural and Natural Heritage*. Paris: UNESCO.

———. 1998. "Information document: Report on the mission to Kakadu National Park, Australia, 26 October to 1 November 1998." World Heritage Committee, Twenty-second session, Kyoto, Japan, 30 November–5 December 1998. Paris: UNESCO.

———. 1999. "In Depth Debate on Kakadu National Park in Extraordinary Session of UNESCO's World Heritage Committee." December 7. http://whc .unesco.org (accessed July 1, 2007).

———. 2001. *Universal Declaration of Cultural Diversity 2001*. Paris: UNESCO.

Valkenburgh, R. V. 1999. *Navajo Country (Diné Bikéyah): A Geographic Dictionary of Navajo Lands in the 1930s by Richard van Valkenburgh, Navajo Agency, Window Rock, Arizona (Reprint)*. Mancos, Colo.: Time Traveler Maps.

Vaughn, A., and C. Rollston. 2005. "The antiquities market, sensationalized textual data and modern forgeries." *Near Eastern Archaeology* 68(1–2): 61–68.

Vella, W. F. 1978. *Chaiyo!: King Vajiravudh and the Development of Thai Nationalism*. Honolulu: University of Hawaii Press.

Vitelli, K. D., and C. Colwell-Chanthaphonh, eds. 2006. *Archaeological Ethics*. Walnut Creek, Calif.: AltaMira.

Viveiros de Castro, E., and L. M. M. de Andrade. 1990. "Xingu hydroelectrics: The state versus indigenous societies." In L. A. de O. Santos and L. M. M. de Andrade (eds.), *Hydroelectric Dams on Brazil's Xingu River and Indigenous Peoples*, 1–18. Cambridge, Mass.: Cultural Survival.

Vos, H. 1999. *How the People of the Bible Really Lived*. Nashville: Thomas Nelson.

Waldron, J. 1995. "Minority cultures and the cosmopolitan alternative." In W. Kymlicka (ed.), *Rights of Minority Cultures*, 93–122. Oxford: Oxford University Press.

———. 1996. "Multiculturalism and melange." In Robert K. Fullinwider (ed.), *Public Education in a Multicultural Society: Policy, Theory, Critique*, 90–119. Cambridge: Cambridge University Press.

Walker, C. 2006. "Delivery and disarray: The multiple meanings of land restitution." In S. Buhlungu, J. Daniel, R. Southall, and J. Lutchman (eds.),

State of the Nation: South Africa 2005–2006, 67–92. Pretoria: Human Sciences Research Council.

Wallerstein, I. 1996. "Neither patriotism nor cosmopolitanism." In M. Nussbaum (and respondents), *For Love of Country?* ed. J. Cohen, 122–24. Boston: Beacon Press.

Warren, M. 1998. "Comment on Sillitoe." *Current Anthropology* 39: 244–45.

Watkins, J. 2000. *Indigenous Archaeology: American Indian Values and Scientific Practice*. Walnut Creek, Calif.: AltaMira.

———. 2004. "Becoming American or becoming Indian?: NAGPRA, Kennewick, and cultural affiliation." *Journal of Social Archaeology* 4: 60–80.

———. 2005. "Cultural nationalists, internationalists, and 'intra-nationalists': Who's right and whose right?" *International Journal of Cultural Property* 12(1): 78–94.

———. 2006. "Communicating Archaeology." *Journal of Social Archaeology* 6: 100–18.

Weber, M. 1946. *Essays in Sociology*. Ed. and trans. H. Gerth and C. Mills. New York: Oxford University Press.

Weismantel, M. 2001. *Cholas and Pishtacos: Stories of Race and Sex in the Andes*. Chicago: University of Chicago Press.

Wenke, R. 1999. *Patterns in Prehistory*. Oxford: Oxford University Press.

Werbner, P. 2006. "Understanding vernacular cosmopolitanism." *Anthropology News*, May, 7, 11.

———, ed. 2008. *Anthropology and the New Cosmopolitanism*. Oxford: Berg.

West, P. 2006. *Conservation Is Our Government Now: The Politics of Ecology in Papua New Guinea*. Durham, N.C.: Duke University Press.

Whiteley, P. 2002. "Archaeology and oral tradition: The scientific importance of dialogue." *American Antiquity* 67: 405–15.

Wijeyewardene, G. 1986. *Place and Emotion*. Bangkok: Pandora.

William, Prince of Sweden. 1926. *Among Pygmies and Gorillas with the Swedish Zoological Expedition to Central Africa 1921*. New York: E. P. Dutton.

Williams, B. 1990. "Nationalism, traditionalism, and the problem of cultural inauthenticity." In R. Fox (ed.), *Nationalist Ideologies and the Production of National Cultures*. American Ethnology Monograph Series 2. Washington: American Anthropological Association.

———. 1991. *Stains on My Name, War in My Veins: Guyana and the Politics of Cultural Struggle*. Durham, N.C.: Duke University Press.

Wilson, R. A., ed. 1997. *Human Rights, Culture and Context: Anthropological Perspectives*. London: Pluto Press.

Winter, J. 1995. *Sites of Memory, Sites of Mourning*. Cambridge: Cambridge University Press.

Wittfogel, K. 1967. *Oriental Despotism*. New Haven, Conn.: Yale University Press.

Wobst, H. M. 2005. "Power to the (indigenous) past and present! Or: the theory and method behind archaeological theory and method." In C. Smith and H. M. Wobst (eds.), *Indigenous Archaeologies: Decolonizing Theory and Practice*, 17–32. One World Archaeology 47. London: Routledge.

Wolde-Selassie, A. 2004a. *Gumuz and Highland Resettlers: Differing Strategies of Livelihood and Ethnic Relations in Metekel, Northwestern Ethiopia.* Göttingen: Göttinger Studien zur Ethnologie.

———. 2004b. "Impact of resettlement in Beles valley, Metekel." In A. Pankhurst and F. Piget (eds.), *People, Space and the State: Migration, Resettlement and Displacement in Ethiopia*, 76–91. Addis Ababa: Addis Ababa University.

Wolf, S. 1992. "Morality and partiality." *Philosophical Perspectives* 6: 243–59.

Wren, L., and P. Schmidt. 1991. "Elite interaction during the Terminal Classic Period: New evidence from Chichen Itza." In T. Patrick Culbert (ed.), *Classic Maya Political History: Hieroglyphic and Archaeological Evidence*, 199–225. Cambridge: Cambridge University Press.

Wyatt, D. K. 1976. "Chronicle traditions in Thai historiography." In C. D. Cowan and O. W. Wolters (eds.), *Southeast Asian History and Historiography*, 107–22. Ithaca, N.Y.: Cornell University Press.

Wylie, A. 1992. "The interplay of evidential constraints and political interests: Recent archaeological research on gender." *American Antiquity* 57: 15–35.

Yahya, A. 2005. "Archaeology and nationalism in the Holy Land." In S. Pollock and R. Bernbeck (eds.), *Archaeologies of the Middle East: Critical Perspectives*, 66–77. Oxford: Blackwell.

Yntiso, G. 2004. "The Metekel resettlement in Ethiopia. Why did it fail?" In A. Pankhurst and F. Piget (eds.), *People, Space and the State: Migration, Resettlement and Displacement in Ethiopia*, 92–111. Addis Ababa: Addis Ababa University.

Young, L. 1999. "Globalisation, culture and museums: A review of theory." *International Journal of Heritage Studies* 5(1): 6–15.

Yusuf, A. 2005. "Towards a convention on cultural diversity: Background and evolution." Presentation to the Third Forum on Human Development, Paris, January 17, 2005. Paris: United Nations Development Programme.

Zedeno, M. 2000. "On what people make of places: A behavioral cartography." In M. Schiffer (ed.), *Social Theory in Archaeology*, 97–111. Salt Lake City: University of Utah Press.

Zermeño, G. 2002. "Between anthropology and history: Manuel Gamio and Mexican anthropological modernity, 1916–1935." *Nepantla: Views from the South* 3(2): 315–31.

Zimmerman, L. J. 1989. "Made radical by my own: An archaeologist learns to accept reburial." In R. Layton (ed.), *Conflict in the Archaeology of Living Traditions*, 60–67. London: Unwin Hyman.

Zimmerman, L. J., K. D. Vitelli, J. Hollowell-Zimmer, and R. D. Maurer, eds. 2003. *Ethical Issues in Archaeology*. Walnut Creek, Calif.: AltaMira.

Žižek, S. 2002. *Welcome to the Desert of the Real*. London: Verso.

——— 2004. *Organs without Bodies: Deleuze and Consequences*. New York: Routledge.

———. 2005. "Neighbors and other monsters: A plea for ethical violence." In S. Žižek, E. L. Santner, and K. Reinhard (eds.), *The Neighbor: Three Inquiries in Political Theology*. Chicago: University of Chicago Press.

Žižek, S., and G. Daly. 2004. *Conversations with Žižek*. Cambridge: Polity.

Zubaida, S. 1996. "Turkish Islam and national identity." *Middle East Report* 199: 10–15.

———. 1999. "Cosmopolitanism and the Middle East." In R. Meijer (ed.), *Cosmopolitanism, Identity and Authenticity in the Middle East*, 1–14. London: Routledge.

✳ CONTRIBUTORS

O. HUGO BENAVIDES is an associate professor of anthropology and is currently the director of the M.A. program in humanities and sciences at Fordham University. His books include *Making Ecuadorian Histories: Four Centuries of Defining the Past* (2004), *The Politics of Sentiment: Imagining and Remembering Guayaquil* (2006), and, *Drugs, Thugs and Divas: Telenovelas and Narco-Dramas in Latin America* (2008).

LISA BREGLIA is a cultural anthropologist who teaches at George Mason University, where she also serves as the assistant director of the global affairs program. She is the author of *Monumental Ambivalence: The Politics of Heritage* (2006), a comparative ethnographic study of Maya archaeological sites in Yucatán, Mexico. Her current research ranges from the cultural meanings of resources to an examination of the oil industry on Mexico's Gulf Coast.

DENIS BYRNE leads the research program in cultural heritage at the Department of Environment and Climate Change N.S.W. in Sydney, Australia. He has a long-term interest in the spiritual and social construction of archaeological heritage objects and places in Australia and Southeast Asia. His current research includes a study of how urban parklands in Sydney are inscribed with meaning by Arabic-speaking and Vietnamese-migrant Australians. His book *Surface Collection: Archaeological Travels in Southeast Asia* (2007) relates a series of personal encounters with that region's material past.

CHIP COLWELL-CHANTHAPHONH is the curator of anthropology at the Denver Museum of Nature and Science and the author and editor of five books, most recently *Massacre at Camp Grant: Forgetting and Remembering Apache History* (2007). He serves on the Book Award Committee and Native American Scholarships Committee of the Society for American Archaeology and on the Committee on Practicing, Applied, and Public Interest Anthropology of the American Anthropological Association. He is also a member of the editorial board of *American Anthropologist*.

ALFREDO GONZÁLEZ-RUIBAL is an assistant professor of prehistory at the Complutense University of Madrid. He has carried out archaeological and ethnoarchaeological research in Spain, Ethiopia, and Brazil. His current research focuses on the archaeological record produced by the destructive forces of late modernity (globalization, social engineering, migration, war). His work on the contemporary past has been published in major archaeological journals.

IAN HODDER taught for twenty-one years at Cambridge University. Since 1999 he has been at Stanford University, where he is now the Dunlevie Family Professor in the Department of Anthropology and the director of the Archaeology Center. He is a fellow of the British Academy and has been a Guggenheim fellow. Since 1993 he has been the director of the Çatalhöyük Research Project. He has written several books, including *The Leopard's Tale* (2006).

IAN LILLEY is a professor of Aboriginal and Torres Strait Islander studies at the University of Queensland. He has worked throughout Australia and in Papua New Guinea and currently does research in northern Australia and New Caledonia. He is a past secretary of the World Archaeological Congress and a past president of the Australian Archaeological Association. He serves on the Executive Committee of the Indo-Pacific Prehistory Association and is a member of Australia ICOMOS. He has recently edited *Archaeology of Oceania* (2006).

JANE LYDON is a research fellow at the Centre for Australian Indigenous Studies at Monash University. Her most recent books include *Eye Contact: Photographing Indigenous Australians* (2005) and, co-edited with Tracy Ireland, *Object Lessons: Archaeology and Heritage in Australia* (2005). She is currently working in collaboration with the Aboriginal community at Ebenezer Mission, northwestern Victoria, in reconstructing the visual regimes and embodied experiences that structured encounters between whites and indigenous peoples in southeastern Australia. This research forms the basis for a forthcoming book about spatial politics, material culture, and missionization in Australia.

LYNN MESKELL is a professor of anthropology at Stanford University. Her most recent books include *Object Worlds in Ancient Egypt: Material Biographies Past and Present* (2004), *Embedding Ethics*, co-edited with Peter Pels (2005), and the edited volume *Archaeologies of Materiality* (2005). She is the founding editor of the *Journal of Social Archaeology* (Sage) and of the Material Worlds series for Duke University Press. Her current research examines the constructs of natural and cultural heritage and the related discourses of empowerment around the Kruger National Park, ten years after democracy developed in South Africa. This forms the basis of a forthcoming book entitled *The Nature of Culture in the New South Africa*.

SANDRA ARNOLD SCHAM has worked in Middle East archaeology for some seventeen years and has lived in both Jordan and Israel. She has done fieldwork in Peru, North America, Israel, Jordan, and Turkey. She was an initiator and leader on a recent three-year project that brought Israeli and Palestinian archaeologists together to discuss issues relating to how archaeology is practiced and taught in the region. She has written both academic and popular articles about archaeology, serving as the editor of the journal *Near Eastern Archaeology* and as a contributing editor to *Archaeology Magazine*. For the past four years she has taught in the Anthropology Department of the Catholic University of America in Washington.

communities, 4–5, 89, 99, 102, 115, 131, 142, 151, 154–155, 158; archaeological evidence disputed by local, 63, 150; archaeology, effects on local, 95, 121; border, 124, 127, 130; cosmopolitan networks and, 25, 90, 94, 120, 151, 157; development and, 137; heritage projects and, 26, 32, 42, 87, 94, 143, 152; identity building and recognition of, 19–20, 23, 113, 161; marginalization of local, 100, 103, 119–120, 129, 132; obligations of archaeologists and anthropologists to living, 1, 8–9, 12, 15–16, 25, 49, 52, 55–56, 65, 138, 144, 150–151, 160–161, 165; objects and, 162; petitions for reparations by, 108. *See also* Aboriginal peoples; Awá; forced relocation; Gumuz; Kanak; Native American communities

community involvement, in archaeology and heritage, 49, 56–57, 186. *See also* communities

consent, 12, 19, 42–43, 92, 115–116

conservation, 2, 25–26, 68, 86–87, 105, 109; biodiversity and, 97, 102; as cosmopolitan value and legacy, 18–20, 90, 109; of cultural heritage, 69, 87, 136; of environment, 1, 18, 68, 95, 109; at expense of local communities, 97–99; "fortress conservation," 19, 68, 92; ideologies of, 103; indigenous land rights and, 46; local communities and interactions with, 25; protectionism and, 90, 110; SANPARKS and, 89, 96–99, 111, 112 n. 1; sustainability and, 95, 109

Conservation Corporation Africa, 98

conservation refugees, 68, 88 n.2

Convention on International Trade in Endangered Species of Wild Flora (CITES), 90

cosmopolitan heritage: ethics of, 1–26, 142; rights of, 191, 203

cosmopolitanism, 1–7, 10, 16, 17–26, 51, 68–69, 71, 86, 104, 121, 167, 184–185, 191–193, 201, 204; biodiversity and, 89–90, 94–96, 98–99, 109; counter-cosmopolitanism, 131, 137, 168; education and, 164; emergent, 14, 29, 40; heritage as, 45, 47, 152, 195; Kantian conceptions of, 29–30, 48; local, 77, 197–199 202, 208; nationalism and, 174–175, 227 n. 5; new knowledge and, 48–49. 63; as prescriptive, 143; preservation paradox and, 143; principle of stewardship and, 155; quotidian, 205–206, 217–219, 224–225; rooted, 156–159, 174; vernacular, 12, 15, 51, 56, 113–114, 117–120, 138; Victorian, 168, 183. *See also* Appiah, K. Anthony; Bhabha, Homi; Nussbaum, Martha

cosmopolitan nations, 121–123

cosmopolitan patriotism, 174–175. *See also* cosmopolitanism: rooted

cultural diversity, 7, 13, 29, 31, 94, 96, 190, 211

cultural heritage, 3, 21, 109, 153, 184, 193, 201, 214; discourses, 18, 20; intangible, 32, 34; in Kruger National Park, 99, 101–102, 111; local identity and, 194–195, 239; management of, 51–53, 87, 98; multicultural heritage, 190; vs. natural heritage (biodiversity) in South Africa, 94, 96, 99; preservation of, 142–143, 155; as property of nation-state, 191, 218; rights to, 6, 17, 24, 32, 161, 185,

cultural heritage (*cont.*)
202–203; transnational influence on, 90, 193
Cynics, 3

Daes Report, 15–16
Derrida, Jacques, 21, 167, 169
development: agencies, 92, 95, 128, 136–137, 220; discourses of, 95; displacement of local communities and, 125–128; globalization and, 230–231; heritage and, 1–2, 9, 11–12, 43, 91, 109, 116–117; local rights and, 45, 108; nature conservation (biodiversity) and, 93, 95–96, 98–99; promises and real effects of neoliberal, 22–24, 26, 113, 114–115; sustainable, 23, 26, 96; tourism and, 101–102, 106, 115, 221–222. *See also* forced relocation; *terra nullius*
Dreamtime, 60

ecology, 18, 103; human, 136
eco-tourism, 23, 26, 99, 231
Ecuador, 23–24, 213, 228–248
emotion, 152, 174, 178–179, 181–182
Enlightenment, 2, 69, 124; post-Enlightenment, 177
ethics, 8, 29, 51, 109; archaeological, 151, 199, 202–203; cosmopolitan, 118–119, 143, 156–159, 184; Kantian, 114; of museum, 144, 146, 151; radical, 121; of stewardship, 152, 160–164; tourism and, 190; universalist, 31, 152; of World Archaeological Congress, 185, 191
Ethiopia, 11–12, 120–129, 132
European Union (EU), 12, 120, 188, 194, 200

forced relocation, 11, 68, 88 n. 1, 93, 105, 126, 132, 175

Gallipoli, Turkey, 35–39, 45
Gallipoli Peninsula Peace Park, 14
genocide, 3, 131–132, 201, 232
Getty Conservation Institute, 191
Gettysburg National Park, 153
Ghana, 3, 157
Gilroy, Paul, 3
global patrimony, 5, 22; vs. local community control, 3
globalization: capitalist, 30; cosmopolitanism and, 3, 12, 25, 155, 184, 229; destructive effects of, 113, 118–120; effects on identity and culture, 31–32, 39, 201, 230, 237, 240; heritage and, 28–29, 37, 207, 225; of political power, 44
governance, 95; archaeology and, 214; modes of, 95; transnational, 18
government, 226 n. 4; actions against Aboriginal claims and identities, 41–45, 239; heritage management and, 14, 36, 36, 38, 51, 81–83, 136, 142, 151, 191–192; policy, 167, 189–190; subsidies, 194
governmentality, 11, 96
green movement, 103
Guayaquil (Ecuador): postcolonial structure of, 237; pre-Hispanic origins of, 233–235
Gumuz, 11, 124–128, 131–132, 137
Gundjehmi Aboriginal Corporation, 41, 43

Habermas, Jürgen, 3, 11, 13, 21, 88, 169, 202
head scarf, 189–190, 200, 204
heritage: ethics of, 1–26, 142; management of, 19, 33, 48, 51–53, 80, 87, 191, 193; natural, 7, 18, 21, 44, 91, 99; rights to, 6, 17–18, 185, 191–193, 201, 203, 218; transnational, 10, 13,

28, 33, 47; workers, 13, 22, 24. *See also* biodiversity; cultural heritage

Homo habilis, 136

homo sacer, 125, 134

Hopi, 148–151, 162

Howard, John (Australian prime minister), 12, 36

human rights, 6, 18, 55, 67, 190, 202, 221, 243; culture and, 13, 17, 203, 240; universal vs. individual, 29–32, 40, 48, 185

humanitarianism, 11, 140; heritage and, 12

identity, 50, 118, 120, 164, 177, 241; African, 228; Afro-Ecuadorian, 242–247; archaeology and, 193; Australian national, 28, 35–39; cultural heritage and, 95, 190, 194; Ecuadorian, 233, 248; global, 40, 161; Hopi, 149; Indian-Ecuadorian, 235–242; indigenous use of transnational processes in, 19, 47; of Kruger National Park, 91; Mayan, 218–220; Mexican, 211–213; national, 23, 80, 95, 100, 142, 178, 210, 224; postcolonial, 235; rights and, 152; territory and, 213–214, 218–219

identity politics, 7–8, 23, 57, 100, 109, 154, 206, 217, 221, 225. *See also* identity: Indian-Ecuadorian, Mayan, Mexican

"Indianness": construction of, 238–241

indigenous communities, 90, 103, 113, 131–132, 151; archaeology and, 56, 59, 63, 65; human history as natural history applied to, 136–137; rights to culture of, 10, 16, 23. *See also* Aboriginal peoples; identity politics; *terra nullius*

internationalism, 8, 22, 95, 155, 206

Iraq, 11, 21, 51

Jabiluka, 14, 19, 40–47

Kanak, 15, 61–64, 67

Kant, Immanuel, 3, 29, 48–50, 66, 114

knowledge: archaeological, 136; ancestral, 15, 59; authorized bodies of, 79–80; conservation and, 105; cosmopolitan new, 48, 51, 63–64; dissemination of, 167, 179, 200, 204; indigenous, 78, 103; local, 60, 116; lost, 131; popular, 79–80; shared, 16; traditional, 149

Konya, Turkey, 187–189, 197, 200, 204

Kruger National Park (South Africa), 19–21, 89–111, 171

landscape: archaeology and, 58, 65–66; cultural, 64, 146, 162, 191; erasure of anthropogenic, 20 90, 105–106; sacred, 83, 147; values for Aboriginal peoples, 15–16, 34, 41, 58–60

language, 24, 55–58, 66; lingua franca, 15, 54, 64, 71

liberalism, 30, 131, 157; postcolonial, 7, 16, 108

lifestyles, traditional, 13, 31–32, 42–43

lingua franca, 15, 54, 64, 71. *See also* language

living tradition, 42–46

local communities. *See* communities

materiality, 9, 19, 75, 79, 105; of archaeological evidence, 63

Maya, 210–212, 221–222, 224, 226 n. 2; identity, 218–220; workers, 205–209, 214–216

mestizos, 232, 234–235, 237, 239, 243–245

Mexico, 205–226, 234

Middle East, 3, 8, 21–22, 166–168, 171–183

Mill, John Stuart, 3–4

minority groups, 4, 7, 20, 30, 39, 120, 245; interests of, 192, 196; rights of, 32, 202–203. See also *mestizos*

missionaries, 74–75, 85

multiculturalism, 94, 127, 244–246; in archaeology, 243; pitfalls of, 12, 20, 118

multivocality, 12

nationalism, 3, 8, 18, 173, 175; Afrikaner, 93; archaeology and, 83, 205, 208; Mexican, 22, 213; methodological, 225, 227 n. 5; patriarchical, 193; religious, 177. See also cosmopolitanism: nationalism and

nation building, 82, 84, 209, 212

nation-state, 94, 208, 217; American, 246; archaeology, heritage practices and, 17–19, 22, 69, 191–192, 223; construction of Thai, 80, 84; decline of, 207, 225, 227 n. 5, 231; Ecuadorian, 236, 239, 244–245, 248; Mexican, 209; minority rights to heritage and, 23, 202

Native American communities, 142, 220, 232, 238. See also Guayaquil; Hopi; Maya; Navajo; Zuni

natural heritage, 7, 18, 21, 44, 91, 99. See also biodiversity

nature conservation. See conservation: of environment

Navajo, 16, 143, 146–151, 162–163

negotiation: conflict, 162; for heritage, 16–18, 64, 100, 185, 193, 202; of intellectual property, 59; of land claims, 42, 45; of land use, 108

neoliberalism, 11, 93, 95; critiques of, 117–118, 138; decline of nation-state

and, 207–208, 223; development and, 22–23, 113

neoliberal market economies, 18, 195–196, 224

New Caledonia, 15, 52, 57, 64, 67

non-governmental organizations (NGOs), 9, 20, 24–25, 46, 94, 114, 116, 120, 121, 192, 240, 242; funding by, 56, 90, 110, 196

Nussbaum, Martha C., 114, 118, 121, 143, 154–156, 159, 164, 167, 174–175, 182

Open Declaration on Cultural Heritage at Risk, 21

Orientalism, 22, 168, 171, 178, 180, 183

People and Conservation Unit, 98, 101, 108, 111

postcolonial critique, 34

pre-Hispanic past, 23–24; of Chichén Itzá, 210–213, 215–216, 226 n. 1; of Ecuador, 231, 234–247

preservation: of archaeological sites, 102; archaeology and, 4; complex stewardship and, 159–163; cultural, 5, 13, 31, 142, 182, 184; as cultural construct, 16, 152; of heritage, 26; human cost of, 98; of nature, 94, 130; politics of proximity in, 153, 155–156

preservation paradox, 53, 142–146, 150, 160, 162

protected areas, 19, 68, 90, 97

protectionism, 10, 16; heritage and, 11, 36, 44, 151; natural and cultural, 19, 68, 94, 110; UNESCO and, 31, 182

public archaeology, critique of, 114–117

recognition, 6–7, 20, 36, 92, 103, 107–108, 160, 185, 201, 246; global,

LYNN MESKELL IS A PROFESSOR OF
ANTHROPOLOGY AT STANFORD UNIVERSITY.

Library of Congress Cataloging-in-Publication Data

Cosmopolitan archaeologies / Lynn Meskell, editor.
p. cm. — (Material worlds)
Includes bibliographical references and index.
ISBN 978-0-8223-4432-2 (cloth : alk. paper)
ISBN 978-0-8223-4444-5 (pbk. : alk. paper)
1. Archaeology—Moral and ethical aspects.
2. Archaeology—Political aspects. 3. Cultural property—Moral
and ethical aspects. 4. Archaeologists—Professional ethics.
I. Meskell, Lynn. II. Series: Material worlds (Duke University Press)
CC175.C676 2009
930.1—dc22   2008051103